Struggling in Good Faith

LGBTQI Inclusion from 13 American Religious Perspectives

Edited by Mychal Copeland, MTS, and D'vorah Rose, BCC
Foreword by Bishop Gene Robinson
Afterword by Ani Zonneveld,
founder and president, Muslims for Progressive Values

Walking Together, Finding the Way®
SKYLIGHT PATHS®
PUBLISHING
Woodstock, Vermont

Struggling in Good Faith:
LGBTQI Inclusion from 13 American Religious Perspectives

2016 Quality Paperback Edition, First Printing
© 2016 by Mychal Copeland and D'vorah Rose

For information regarding permission to reprint material from this book, please mail or
fax your request in writing to SkyLight Paths Publishing, Permissions Department, at the
address / fax number listed below, or email your request to permissions@skylightpaths.com.

Unless otherwise noted, all biblical quotations in Christian chapters are from the *New
Revised Standard Version* (Anglicized Edition), © 1989, 1995 by the Division of Christian
Education of the National Council of the Churches of Christ in the United States of
America. Used by permission. All rights reserved. Biblical quotations in the introduction
are from *The Holy Scriptures According to the Masoretic Text* (Philadelphia: Jewish Publication
Society, 1917). In Jane Rachel Litman's chapter on Judaism, all biblical and Talmudic
translations are the author's.

Library of Congress Cataloging-in-Publication Data
Struggling in good faith : LGBTQI inclusion from 13 American religious perspectives /
edited by Mychal Copeland and D'vorah Rose ; foreword by Bishop Gene Robinson; afterword by Ani Zonneveld.
    pages cm. — (Walking together, finding the way)
  Includes bibliographical references.
  ISBN 978-1-59473-602-5 (quality pbk)—ISBN 978-1-59473-609-4 (ebook) 1. Gender identity—Religious aspects. 2. Sex role—Religious aspects. 3. Sexual minorities—Religious life.
4. United States—Religion. I. Copeland, Mychal, 1970– editor.
  BL65.S4S77 2016
  200.86'60973—dc23
                              2015035799
10   9   8   7   6   5   4   3   2   1
Manufactured in the United States of America

Cover design: Michael J. Myers
Cover art: © Lana Smirnova/Shutterstock, modified by Michael J. Myers
Interior design: Tim Holtz

SkyLight Paths Publishing is creating a place where people of different spiritual traditions come together for challenge and inspiration, a place where we can help each other
understand the mystery that lies at the heart of our existence.

SkyLight Paths sees both believers and seekers as a community that increasingly transcends traditional boundaries of religion and denomination—people wanting to learn
from each other, *walking together, finding the way.*

SkyLight Paths, "Walking Together, Finding the Way" and colophon are trademarks of
LongHill Partners, Inc., registered in the U.S. Patent and Trademark Office.

Walking Together, Finding the Way®
Published by SkyLight Paths Publishing
A Division of LongHill Partners, Inc.
Sunset Farm Offices, Route 4, P.O. Box 237
Woodstock, VT 05091
Tel: (802) 457-4000 Fax: (802) 457-4004
www.skylightpaths.com

Contents

A Brief Overview
of LGBTQI Terms

ally: A term used to describe someone who does not identify as LGBTQI but is supportive of LGBTQI individuals and the community, either personally or as an advocate.[1]

androgynous: A person with both male and female characteristics or qualities.

cisgender: Feeling internally that one's gender is aligned with one's assigned sex. For example, a cisgender man is someone who was assigned male at birth and who lives and identifies as a man.

eunuch: The eunuchs of the Bible were castrated males or those incapable of reproduction.

gender: A set of cultural identities, expressions, and roles—codified as feminine or masculine—that are assigned to people based on the interpretation of their bodies and, more specifically, their sexual and reproductive anatomy. Since gender is a social construction, it is possible to reject or modify the assignment made.

gender binary: The concept that there are only two genders, male and female, and that everyone must be one or the other. This also implies the assumption that gender is biologically determined.[2]

gender expression: The outward signs a person uses—such as clothing, behaviors, language, and attitude choices—to project a desired gender identity to others.

gender identity: A person's inner understanding of their gender(s). This is each person's unique knowing or feeling and is separate from a person's physical body or appearance (although they are often related).

gender nonconforming: Used to describe those who feel constricted by the majority culture's artificially constructed gender categories of male and female. Other terminology includes "third gender," "gender expansive," "gender fluid," and "genderqueer."

homosexual: A less frequently used term for people who are romantically or sexually attracted to members of the same sex, sometimes considered to be outdated or even offensive. Preferred terms include "gay" and "lesbian."

intersex: An umbrella term used to describe a variety of circumstances in which a person is born with reproductive and/or sexual anatomy that does not fit the medical definitions of female or male.

LGBTQI: Lesbian, gay, bisexual, transgender, queer or questioning, intersex.

lifestyle: An antiquated term often pejoratively used to describe the lives of people who are LGBTQI.

queer: A term encompassing a broad range of gender identities or sexual orientations that challenge dominant societal norms. While many contemporary LGBTQI people reclaim it as neutral or even positive, "queer" was used derogatorily toward those who were attracted to members of the same sex from the late nineteenth century until the 1980s.

reparative or conversion therapy: Any treatment that aims to change sexual orientation from homosexual to heterosexual based on the view that homosexuality is a mental disorder and/or a "sin."

sex: Refers to anatomical, physiological, genetic, or physical attributes that define a person as male, female, or intersex. Sex is often confused or interchanged with "gender," which is thought of as more social and less biological, though there is a strong relationship between sex and gender identity.[3]

sexual orientation: How one identifies in terms of sexual or romantic interest and behavior; for example: lesbian, gay, bisexual, pansexual, heterosexual.

transgender: A person whose gender identity and/or expression are not aligned with the gender they were assigned at birth.[4] "Transgender" is often used as an umbrella term encompassing a large number of identities related to gender nonconformity.[5]

Foreword

Bishop Gene Robinson

M ost people would tell you that religions are the keepers and pre-servers of unchanging, eternal truths. They would be wrong.

Although, of course, every religion is based upon principles, understandings, and revelations that remain fairly constant over time. Even the methodologies with which a particular religion sorts out truth from untruth remain similar and distinctive to that "brand" of religion or its specific manifestation in a denomination or subgrouping.

But on the other hand, religion is constantly changing. While the underpinnings for a religion remain fairly constant, the *application* of those principles to modern situations is a day-to-day task for a religion's leaders and followers. A religion is a living, breathing organism. Most religions are based on beliefs, practices, stories, or texts from long ago when many of today's circumstances did not yet exist. Encountering modern-day situations, religious people turn to their faith for guidance and understanding, but that is not always an easy or clear task. That is a very dynamic process.

Change happens. People have certain worldviews, created in part by our religious beliefs (or lack of them). That worldview interprets our personal experiences and relationships as well as our encounters with the wider community and the world. It gives us a way of understanding what is happening around us. It categorizes and simplifies reality, allowing us to take in and cope with an overwhelming amount of input. But then, something (or someone) happens to us for which our current worldview is insufficient to decipher or explain. That inability to satisfactorily absorb a newly presented reality into our settled understanding of the world is a painful and disturbing experience. In an attempt to make sense of this, the individual wrestles with the old worldview until that understanding is reshaped and refashioned into a *revised* worldview, which now incorporates this new reality.

Nowhere is such a process more visible than in our American culture's wrestling with the issue of sexuality, especially in understanding gay, lesbian, bisexual, transgender, queer, and intersex people. For instance, it was not very long ago that there was a prevailing understanding that sexual intimacy between people of the same gender was morally unacceptable to God and therefore to society. That worldview was in place for countless generations. And then a new reality appeared and demanded our attention: gay and lesbian people who did not seem either mentally ill or spiritually corrupt, who wanted to contribute to society, who wanted the responsibilities and rewards of marriage and family, and who were no more objectionable in their behavior than most other people. In particular, some of these maintained that they were also religious people, loved by the Creator, and precious in the eyes of God (however understood). Ancient texts were not discarded, but rather declared misunderstood, and those texts that had long been thought to be obvious in their meaning were questioned. Because many of these people were our sons and daughters, mothers and fathers, classmates and coworkers, we could dismiss neither them nor the claims they were making. And often, it felt like chaos. And then, over time, after much wrestling, a new worldview and a new religious understanding emerged that included this new reality.

This book is a collection of stories about how this process of change has occurred in this country's religions around the issue of sexuality. These stories show how painful the wrestling can be, how divisive the battles, and how difficult it is to let go of older understandings and embrace new ones. Some of the contributors portray the change as "almost done," while others tell of a process barely begun. No matter what stage in the process of change, religious belief is unveiled in all its dynamism, with real-life consequences for believer and nonbeliever alike.

Ultimately, these are stories of hope. Wrestling with issues and struggling for better understanding of one's fellow human beings is at the center of every religion, no matter how old or new, narrow or expansive, Western or Eastern, that religion is. The struggle itself is a sign of life in these religious endeavors, and with life there is hope.

One last invitation to the reader, from whatever tradition: As you read the chapters that follow, look for God's action in and among God's people. Look for the eternal breaking into the temporal. As one of the Jewish patriarchs, Jacob, found when he wrestled with the angel, one never emerges from an encounter with God without being transformed in some way. Look for God in the transformations taking place in virtually every religion or denomination described here. My guess is that in keeping an eye out for God in these chapters, you will find your own faith strengthened.

Introduction

Mychal Copeland, MTS, and D'vorah Rose, BCC

> Jacob was left alone. And a man wrestled with him until
> the break of dawn.... Said the other, "What is your name?"
> He replied, "Jacob." Said he, "Your name shall no longer
> be Jacob, but Israel, for you have striven with beings divine
> and human, and have prevailed."
>
> —Genesis 32:25, 28-29

From the outside, religions often look dogmatic, inflexible, unchanging, and closed-minded. But from the inside, their adherents wrestle: they debate theology; they grapple with how to maintain tradition in a constantly shifting landscape; they struggle with boundaries of inclusion and exclusion. In our era, religious institutions struggle with the place of lesbian, gay, bisexual, transgender, queer, and intersex (LGBTQI[1]) people in religious life. The biblical story of Jacob wrestling with an angel of God throughout a long night tells of a sacred struggle that can serve as a metaphor for the way religious institutions approach LGBTQI inclusion. Jacob's wrestling match was an inner battle that led to a profound spiritual transformation. So, too, religious institutions will not be left unchanged by the divine wrestling of LGBTQI individuals and their allies.

This book seeks to bring depth and nuance to our overly polarized national conversation. We hope to strengthen the movement toward LGBTQI integration by examining faith communities within their own religious and cultural contexts while bringing them into conversation with one another. *Struggling in Good Faith* ushers the reader across the American religious landscape, highlighting the gains and setbacks of LGBTQI advocates within different traditions and demonstrating the ways in which each religion evolves and ultimately changes in response to the faithful struggle of its adherents.

The integration of LGBTQI people into institutional religious life has reached a point unparalleled in history. LGBTQI people are filling the pews, creating theology and liturgy, providing pastoral care, and leading religious organizations and congregations. Yet the image of two opposing and separate entities persists, diminishing both our religious institutions and our quest for LGBTQI equality. Jay Michaelson, author of *God vs. Gay? The Religious Case for Equality*, writes, "'God versus Gay' is a myth. It is untrue, unsupported by Scripture, and contradicted every day by the lives of religious gay people. Yet it is also among the most pervasive and hurtful untruths in American religion today, and people all across the ideological spectrum believe it."[2] American religion is far from monolithic. Some religious factions have put their hearts, souls, and pocketbooks into maintaining a traditional heterosexual family model, whereas other groups have been on the forefront of the fight for LGBTQI equality. The stance many conservative churches have taken on the same-sex marriage debate, noted in our chapters on Protestant evangelical traditions and the black church, has dominated the conversation about the intersection of LGBTQI issues and American religion. However, other religious denominations, such as the Buddhist Churches of America, the Metropolitan Community Church, Reform Judaism, and Unitarian Universalism, were sanctifying same-sex relationships long before it was on the national agenda. Illustrations of religions in support of LGBTQI equality abound throughout this book, breaking down the myth that religion speaks with one voice that opposes inclusion.

Although all of the religious entities in this book have engaged in a sacred struggle in one way or another, they are not uniform in the way LGBTQI issues have emerged in their communities. For many traditions, the challenge arises from scripture. But the Roman Catholic Church, as contributor Sister Jeannine Gramick, SL, points out, "does not use the Bible as the basis for opposing same-sex acts"; instead, it is "the church's tradition about natural law and the purpose of sexuality" that brings the challenge for LGBTQI inclusion. For the Mormon Church, a core belief is that sexuality in this world affects one's life after death. Not all religions contain early teachings prohibiting a variety of sexual and gender expressions. Some communities originated in a more expansive place and became more restrictive over time because of outside influences. As Alex Wilson, EdD, writes in her chapter, First Nations (Native American) ideologies tend toward expansive definitions and roles for people who do not conform to a gender binary or heterosexual orientation. But colonialism in America methodically assimilated native traditions, practices, and ideas, replacing them with the Bible-based homophobia of that period. Likewise, Ruth Vanita, PhD, explains in her chapter that "Hinduism has no history of persecuting gender-variant people or same-sex relations, but in the last two centuries, as a result of internalizing the attitudes of Victorian British colonizers, many Hindus have become embarrassed about sexuality in general and same-sex sexuality in particular." These communities are undergoing a different process of reconciling their complex histories than are other traditions presented in this book, further disproving notions of uniformity across the American religious spectrum.

Another fallacy that deepens the LGBTQI versus religion divide is the perception that religions are, or should be, unchanging and timeless, unaffected by their surroundings. If a religion has stood the test of time, it is because its adherents have struggled with new ideas and found ways to incorporate them. In fact, confronting and incorporating change is built into many religions. Contributor Annette S. Marquis highlights how Ralph Waldo Emerson's belief that, as Marquis states, "revelation is continuously unfolding and that God is alive in human souls" deeply influenced the principles of Unitarian Universalism. Likewise, Shehnaz Haqqani, Laury Silvers, El-Farouk Khaki, and Troy Jackson comment in their chapter that "for all Muslims, no matter their sect, law and even theology are constantly shifting to account for changing times and circumstances." The contributions in this collection challenge the notion that religious institutions are inflexible and static.

Throughout history, every faith community has grappled with internal and external pressures to respond to current social issues. Our contributors offer models for religious change by addressing a variety of historical challenges within their traditions. We can extrapolate lessons from these profound moments of conflict and transformation that are relevant for our quest for LGBTQI integration. For instance, the Church of Jesus Christ of Latter-day Saints struggled in the 1970s over their policy banning black men from the priesthood. Demonstrating the principle that revelation is ongoing, the ban was overturned, as contributor John Gustav-Wrathall writes, despite a deep-seated belief by many Mormons that segregation was divinely ordained. If that degree of doctrinal resistance could make way for such a significant reversal, a change in policy around LGBTQI issues no longer seems so implausible.

Most of our authors address how their traditions evolved over time regarding the issue of gender equality as a model for what is possible for LGBTQI people. For example, in many liberal Jewish and Christian denominations, the admission of women to the clergy paved the way for LGBTQI people to be ordained as well. The chapter on Islam goes further by demonstrating how struggles for gender and LGBTQI equality are inextricably linked. The authors point out that women as well as gay men have both been traditionally barred from leading Muslim prayer, since neither could serve as adequate stand-ins for the straight male Muslims in the prayer community. Deeply embedded in the texts and traditions of many religions are mandates that men behave like men and women behave like women according to a rigid societal power dynamic. On the surface, many people believe that a verse such as the oft-quoted Leviticus 18:22 ("Do not lie with a male as one lies with a woman") is mainly concerned with same-sex sexual behavior. However, an arguably more significant undercurrent is that one male sexual partner is behaving like a woman by taking on the role as receiver, thus upsetting the gender hierarchy that underlies every societal institution. Rev. Dr. Cameron Partridge in his chapter on the Episcopal Church points out that when 1 Corinthians 6:9–10 calls out judgment concerning the "effeminate man," it challenges the performance of gender roles rather than the same-sex sexual behavior the verse is usually thought to address. Since most of the traditions presented in this book were born out of patriarchal frameworks, maintaining the subjugated role of women was, and remains, paramount. When a man assumes the role of a woman, the underlying societal power structure is overturned as he takes on a "passive" position, both literally and figuratively. Many religious denominations have made great strides with respect to gender equality, but this transformation will not be fully realized until they acknowledge the interrelated issue of LGBTQI discrimination.

While all religions evolve, some religious institutions claim to be unchanging, positioning themselves as intentionally and authentically countercultural. In an age of rapid change, religious institutions, especially those on the more conservative end of the spectrum, may resist coercion from external forces and movements. When communities feel pressured, unable to process contentious issues on their own terms and on their own timelines, backlash can ensue. Change is most successful and transformative when a new circumstance or approach is recognized as consistent with a community's foundational principles. Regardless of rhetoric, all religious organizations evolve, but crucial to this societal transformation will be listening to how they do so, understanding their internal processes, and hearing how they discuss that development among themselves.

Some advocates of LGBTQI transformation may be exasperated by the slow progress in religious institutions illustrated in these chapters. What may seem to one reader like a minor step or even "too little too late" is to another a life-changing development. Rabbi Jane Rachel Litman observes in her chapter on Judaism that over one hundred North American Modern Orthodox rabbis and lay leaders signed on to a statement rejecting reparative therapy, a treatment thought to change a person's sexual orientation from homosexual to heterosexual. While the proclamation was an enormous step for a traditional community, it was criticized by many as a mark of sluggish progress. Likewise, Ryan Bell, DMin, points out that within many evangelical churches, "as long as same-sex attracted individuals remain celibate they can be accepted by God and the church ... sometimes referred to as a 'third way,' between the supposed extremes of outright rejection of gays and lesbians, on the one hand, and full acceptance of their sexuality on the other."

Even where religious institutions have adopted a more positive embrace of gays and lesbians on the grounds that they are "just born that way," such an approach is also a mark of too-slow progress. Many proclaim that they are forward thinking when they preach that same-sex attraction is inborn and immutable (compared to preaching that this was a changeable trait and sending people to be electrically shocked out of it), when in fact their thinking has not evolved past the notion that same-sex attraction, or at least same-sex acts, are wrong, unnatural, and perverted. This is how we arrive at the deeply harmful "hate the sin, love the sinner" paradigm that mirrors the "third way" mentioned above. Rather than truly celebrating sexual diversity or understanding the complex nature of sexual fluidity, this argument assumes that people would choose to be heterosexual if they could. Legal scholar Kenji Yoshino asserts in his book *Covering: The Hidden Assault on Our Civil Rights*, "The [immutability] defense is flawed because it is an implied apology ... by saying, 'I cannot change' rather than by saying 'I will not change.'"[3] He continues, "If an identity is valid, people are much less likely to ask whether it is immutable."[4] In most religious communities, even where much progress has been made, this full affirmation of the myriad of identities has not yet arrived.[5]

These advances may feel unsatisfactory because religions characteristically move more slowly than other cultural institutions. We hope that *Struggling in Good Faith* will provide the necessary context to inform that forward movement. As our political institutions advance, other pillars of our community must progress as well. In order to become truly celebratory of LGBTQI people, religious institutions must not be left behind. We must acknowledge even the seemingly small or partial victories, because they were hard won and represent the promise that, even if they trail behind, these establishments will change.

While working toward this transformation, it is not too much to expect that religious institutions abide by one principle. Inherent in every religious tradition is the notion that each human being possesses inherent worth and dignity. Even in those instances in which a religious community, its leaders, or family members are staunchly anti-LGBTQI, they must acknowledge that every individual is deserving of respect, love, safety, and compassion. Even where doctrine, scripture, or policy seems to be unmoving, an individual still must be treated as a reflection of divinity rather than as an abomination. Not requiring this simple acknowledgment would be exempting religious organizations from their very spiritual mandate. Religions do and will evolve as they engage in sacred struggle, but at every step of that journey, human dignity must be preserved.

THE ONGOING STRUGGLE

Since setting out to write this book, we have heard countless times, "But isn't that struggle over?" The implication is that with all of the recent wins, especially the legalization of same-sex marriage, LGBTQI people have achieved full acceptance. When that remark comes from LGBTQI people, there may be a tinge of concern that talking too much about the subject right now could rock the boat. Now that we have gained some acceptance, pushing for more may be construed as asking for too much and could backfire. For some straight supporters, the sentiment may speak to a fatigue about the issue, much like other historical struggles for equality. Writing from within one of the most welcoming religious traditions, Annette S. Marquis notes the comment of a heterosexual Unitarian Universalist congregant: "I don't mind having gays, lesbians, and bisexuals in my congregation, if only they would stop discussing it all the time." Some Unitarian Universalists so fear being called "the gay church" that LGBTQI ministers still face obstacles getting hired.

Such attitudes, however, could be symptomatic of a larger phenomenon that Michelangelo Signorile, author of *It's Not Over: Getting Beyond Tolerance, Defeating Homophobia, and Winning True Equality*, names "victory blindness": "We're overcome by the heady whirl of a narrative of victory, a kind of bedtime story that tells us we've reached the promised land."[6] We still face rampant homophobia, sometimes in spite of recent wins for LGBTQI equality and in other instances as a reaction to it. Even if we could claim victory in the secular realm, failing to recognize the political power that particular religious institutions hold could undo the strides we have made.

Despite astounding progress, our work is certainly not done. Hate crimes against LGBTQI people have risen dramatically in recent years, and the LGBTQI murder rate is at its highest point in recorded history, with LGBTQI people of color targeted disproportionately.[7] In more than twenty states, people can be fired from their jobs simply for being LGBTQI, and businesses can deny service to anyone as long as they deem their religious beliefs to be compromised.[8] While the suicide rate among the heterosexual American population is 4.6 percent, in the lesbian, gay, and bisexual population it ranges from 10 to 20 percent, and rises to 41 percent among the transgender population.[9]

Perhaps the most troubling sign that we are still struggling with LGBTQI issues is that our youth are suffering. Studies have demonstrated consistently that people of all ages who identify as LGBTQI or gender nonconforming experience significantly higher rates of interpersonal violence.[10] For instance, the National Transgender Discrimination Survey found that among transgender and gender-nonconforming students, 50 to 54 percent "had been harassed or bullied at any level of school" and 63 to 78 percent had been subject to "physical or sexual violence at any level of school."[11] Another study found that lesbian, gay, or bisexual youth "questioning their sexual orientation reported more bullying, homophobic victimization, unexcused absences from school, drug use, feelings of depression, and suicidal behaviors than either heterosexual or LGB students."[12] Especially pertinent for our book is the correlation between anti-LGBTQI religious practice and negative impact on health. LGBTQI people who either grow up in households practicing religions that are not affirming of these identities or affiliate with them as adults are at increased risk for negative health behaviors, such as excessive alcohol use, smoking, drugs, and other high-risk behaviors, and mental health issues, frequently culminating in suicidal behavior.[13] While marriage equality has become a tangible marker of progress for gays and lesbians, the struggle for full integration for LGBTQI people is far from over.

Underlying LGBTQI persecution is the desperate need to push our religious and other cultural ideologies along the spectrum from abomination to tolerance to celebration. In her chapter on the Lutheran Church, Beth Ann Doerring presents a continuum of attitudes toward same-sex attraction that is mirrored in many religious systems, ranging from "perversion" on one end to celebrating "diversity" on the other. As long as LGBTQI people are still viewed by so many as possessing an inborn defect to be tolerated or pitied, it is no wonder that they are treated as second-class citizens at best and as unnatural aberrations at worst. Since religious institutions are a primary place people receive messages about LGBTQI people, this book will examine the language and ideologies various traditions call on when they talk about the place of LGBTQI people in their communities. Lasting change will occur when more religious institutions are preaching "diversity" and the full range of LGBTQI voices are heard.

The most powerful transformation will occur when people are able to bring their entire, authentic, spiritual selves to their communities. Rather than expanding the table to "include" a diversity of individuals within American religious life, we must look to see who is already there, eager to be profoundly transformed by their presence. In fact, the word "inclusion" in this book expands further than merely welcoming people and expecting them to melt into an elusive "mainstream." As Marvin M. Ellison, PhD, and Sylvia Thorson-Smith, MS, write in their chapter on the Presbyterian Church:

> Non-heterosexual and transgender persons reside in every faith community, so the change agenda is not how to include "outsiders" and bring them inside, but rather how to create together the communal conditions of hospitality, safety, and respect so that people of diverse sexual orientations and gender identities alike can acknowledge and share what they have come to know, often at great risk, about resisting injustice, enhancing human dignity, and revitalizing community.

In the early days of women in the clergy, similar discussions took place in which many felt they were "accepted" or "included" as long as they played by existing rules, leading like their male counterparts. The reality in subsequent years is that women clergy have transformed contemporary religion. They have brought new language for the divine, innovative life-cycle rituals marking previously ignored milestones, awareness of particular local and global issues, and challenges to religious institutional hierarchies. Likewise, when LGBTQI people are able to bring themselves fully and authentically to the project of religious and spiritual life, they create theologies and ideologies that challenge traditional notions of gender and relationship, institute new approaches to pastoral care, and bring an awareness of particular political struggles and paradigms of power and oppression. Such transformation does not merely affect the particular group in question. Rev. Dr. Cameron Partridge illustrates this as he describes the Task Force on Marriage of the Episcopal Church, whose mandate is not only to make sure LGBTQI congregants are recognized and included in religious ceremonies, but also to explore "constructions of family and sexual ethics, particularly for those who are not married and do not necessarily discern a call to marriage." Being open to change from within means that we hear the diverse perspectives of everyone at the table more clearly, including our own, and the interaction of that expanded and varied group results in new perspectives that will deepen and grow everyone's spiritual experience.

STRUGGLING FROM WITHIN

Our contributors are dedicated to expanding boundaries and definitions. They have been present at the table as LGBTQI people and allies, clergy, activists, and scholars. They do not represent everyone in their religious traditions but speak to us with their unique voices as individuals passionate and knowledgeable about the intersection of religious and LGBTQI issues. They demonstrate how their traditions remain true to their own doctrines while acknowledging the wide range of human sexual and gender identities. They have committed themselves to doing the work necessary to see their institutions grow, often at great personal risk, in the ways they feel are closest to its core ideals. Of course, change does not *only* occur from within. But those who work for transformation from the inside of religious institutions play a crucial role, and this book acknowledges their contributions as agents of change and models for those seeking to transform their own communities.

After centuries of oppression at the hands of religious institutions, many LGBTQI people have understandably written off faith communities. So many have been robbed of their spiritual homes, either because they were rejected by them or because they made a courageous, self-preserving decision to "come out of the closet and out of the church." The very place we go for spiritual guidance and sustenance should never diminish our personhood. But there is an incredibly wide range of attitudes preached across the religious spectrum. When LGBTQI people are able to find meaning and community within welcoming religious institutions, they powerfully refuse to cede religion to others who are working to define them out of it. From the inside of religious life, they are poised to effect great change while holding institutions accountable. As modern historian Beth Kraig writes, "Whether for reasons of personal spiritual belief or pragmatic political policy, LGBT people and their ... allies need to understand the language and nature of faith organizations. LGBT people need to engage in, rather than spurn, opportunities to situate their identities and human rights within the larger frameworks of religion and theology in the United States."[14] As a powerful corrective to the devastating statistics discussed earlier, when LGBTQI people affiliate with *affirming* religious communities, based on what we know of other populations, there will be a positive effect on both their physical and their mental health status.[15] Researchers posit that some combination of increased social networks and connection to beliefs or activities that create a sense of meaning leads to healthier LGBTQI lives. LGBTQI people need places to turn for meaningful religious or spiritual support. One of the many successes of congregations specifically serving this population has been that after having experienced a lifetime of overt and latent homophobia within their families, communities, schools, and workplaces, as well as the devastating effects of the AIDS crisis and the homophobia that ensued, LGBTQI people desperately need spiritual community.[16]

That kind of spiritual support can aid people in the complicated and often nonlinear process of coming out. Being out for one person can mean revealing an LGBTQI identity to everyone, while for another it can mean being out only in certain arenas. LGBTQI people may preference a racial, ethnic, or religious affiliation and may make personally consistent decisions based on that hierarchy of identities.[17] Many LGBTQI people feel the weight of what Minister Rob Newells describes in his chapter on the black church as a "double consciousness," or even a triple or quadruple consciousness, depending on the number of identities an individual may hold. Developing a sense of self amid this juggling act can look radically different for each individual. From tradition to tradition, notions of personhood and identity differ dramatically. Acharya Rita M. Gross, PhD, in her chapter on Buddhism, for example, speaks to the idea that "clinging to any belief in a permanent or unchanging identity" keeps the individual "imprisoned in cyclic existence," while Alex Wilson, EdD, in the First Nations chapter, mentions the term "coming in" to community rather than "coming out" as a purely individual process. The myriad ideologies presented in different religious traditions can profoundly influence a given individual's process toward self-expression and fulfillment.

As individuals wend their way toward coming out, perhaps, too, religious institutions "come out," or come to terms with changing attitudes, in a nonlinear way. As an individual undergoes a process of wrestling with layers of identity, religions also undergo a process of sacred struggling with definitions and identities, framing and reframing, eventually (hopefully) synthesizing and integrating this piece of its institutional story. Recognizing the wide diversity of religious narratives, we hold the same paradox for communities struggling with LGBTQI inclusion as we do for individuals processing and integrating their seemingly disparate identities. As we struggle in good faith, we acknowledge the complexity of this process for American religious traditions while striving for the day when all people can live lives of spiritual wholeness in the institutions they call home.

The Black Church

Minister Rob Newells

I want it to be very clear that I regard myself as an evangelical pastor who believes in the authority of Scripture. As such, my unapologetic support for gay and lesbian Christians is not despite my view of Scripture, but because of it.[1]

—Rev. Delman Coates, PhD, Senior Pastor,
Mt. Ennon Baptist Church (Clinton, MD)

LAYING THE GROUNDWORK

A burden of American history is that the black church begins in slavery. "Between 1619, when the initial group of Africans stolen from their homeland arrived in the New World, and 1865, the conclusion of the Civil War, black chattel mixed the remnants of their African traditional religions with biblical Christianity," writes theologian Dwight N. Hopkins.[2] Southern churches were integrated until the end of the Civil War because white Southerners were afraid black preachers would encourage revolt. Slaves were not allowed to have their own congregations, so they would steal away into the woods to worship. "White power structures created a racist Jesus," says professor Reggie L. Williams,[3] but black people told their own stories. "The black church" was born.

Minister Rob Newells spent three decades in active membership at the St. Paul AME Church in Berkeley, California, before moving to the Imani Community Church (ABCUSA) in Oakland, where he received his license to preach and trains under the mentorship of Rev. George C. L. Cummings, PhD. Minister Rob served as the Umoja California chair for the Coalition of Welcoming Congregations of the Bay Area and piloted the Umoja: Unity in the Community Bible study series. He serves as president of the board of directors for AIDS Project of the East Bay.

1

There is no singular entity that can be called the black church, and there is no leader of the black church. Today, the commonly used terms "the black church" and "black churches" refer to congregations of black people of faith, whether they are affiliated with the seven historically black denominations (African Methodist Episcopal, AME Zion, Christian Methodist Episcopal, Church of God in Christ, three National Baptist conventions, and the Church of God in Christ) or they worship in predominately black congregations within white denominations.[4] It is virtually impossible to make generalizations about the black church without being able to cite significant exceptions, but there is still a sense that all black congregations and denominations respond to the same external circumstances and share common internal strengths, pressures, and tensions.[5]

FOUNDATIONAL NARRATIVES

The black church is a place where black people praise, organize, and socialize. It's also a place where LGBTQI people are often ostracized. Many Christian denominations teach that the Bible is "the inspired, inerrant, infallible Word of God." As a result of Christian conversion during slavery, most black churches in the United States today are Baptist, Methodist, or Pentecostal. And as a result of the indoctrination of rigid gender and sexual attitudes through the church, black churches generally support traditional views of homosexuality as sinful and LGBTQI people as morally depraved.[6]

The handful of passages in the Bible used to support those views are often referred to as "clobber scriptures" because preachers use them to clobber LGBTQI people with biblical texts. Even younger generations of black people who don't have direct ties to the traditional black church have been raised with these beliefs, which have been passed down through parents and grandparents and are reinforced in many modern-day pulpits. In this chapter, I include the words of some of these young people, as recorded in interviews by the Kujichagulia Project.

> I think that a lot of people are scared to talk about the subject because God has wrote it in the Bible that says you should not be homosexual. You don't lay with another man. You lay with a woman. A lot of people

are scared of that scripture right there. That's why. Fear brings a lot of issues.[7]

—Charles Hill, twenty-three years old

You shall not lie with a male as with a woman; it is an abomination.

—Leviticus 18:22

If a man lies with a male as with a woman, both of them have committed an abomination; they shall be put to death; their blood is upon them.

—Leviticus 20:13

These scriptures seem to be interpreted in the same way from generation to generation, yet when it comes to things like shellfish, eating and touching pigs, cutting our sideburns and beards, and stoning children who mouth off to their parents,[8] Christian communities, including black churches, have been able to keep Leviticus in its appropriate historical context. Even as public policy continues to evolve and biblical scholarship on the clobber scriptures over the last fifty years has helped many progressive Christian communities to welcome LGBTQI people,[9] the black church has remained a staunch supporter of conservative policies and attitudes like "Don't ask, don't tell"—a U.S. Department of Defense policy ended in 2011 that barred openly gay members from military service while at the same time prohibiting the harassment of closeted gays. African Americans have spent the years since emancipation from slavery seeking to gain mainstream respectability as sexually moral beings and to overcome the historical labeling as a sexually perverse people. In an effort to receive acceptance from a homophobic society, black communities and churches have strongly condemned homosexuality.[10] Still, the black church passively accepts the faithful service of LGBTQI members as long as they remain in the closet.

ENCOUNTERING LGBTQI ISSUES

The presence of gays and lesbians in black churches is common, and the fact that they often hold leadership positions in their congregations is the worst-kept secret in black America. While many black pastors condemn gays and lesbians from the pulpit, the choir lofts behind them often are filled with gay singers and musicians. Some male pastors themselves have been entangled in scandals involving alleged affairs with men. The San Francisco Bay Area in the 1970s had arguably the most visible presence of LGBTQI members in black churches, just as the broader gay rights movement had gained momentum in the region. The Love Center Church in Oakland, founded by the late gospel music star Bishop Walter Hawkins, made waves for welcoming black gays and lesbians. Following the 1991 death of Rev. James Cleveland, the gospel music legend still regarded as the "king" of the genre, a male member of Cleveland's choir sued his estate, claiming that he contracted HIV due to his five-year sexual relationship with the singing icon. The lawsuit was settled out of court.[11] The black church was silent.

Black liberation theology—a theology that seeks to liberate people of color from multiple forms of political, social, economic, and religious subjugation by contextualizing Christianity through the lens of the black experience in America—is silent on issues of black sexuality, but black theologians like Dr. Dwight N. Hopkins have helped black liberation theology to evolve by expanding its scope. In his article "Toward a Positive Black Male Heterosexuality," Hopkins suggests that "one of the greatest points of unity that black heterosexuals have is their agreement to oppress and discriminate against black lesbians and gays in the church, family and larger society."[12] The black church with its heterosexism serves to continue a system of oppression using some of the same arguments that white people have used against black people and that men have used against women throughout history.

Womanist theology deals directly with issues of sexism, and *queer theology* deals directly with issues of homophobia, and both counter the absence of gender and sexuality in *black liberation theology*. None of these theologies on its own encompasses the fullness of black LGBTQI people's lived experiences. W. E. B. DuBois's theory of "double consciousness" is a multifaceted conception of self that is experienced by African Americans trying to reconcile the two cultures that compose their identity. A triple or quadruple consciousness may be experienced by African American LGBTQI people, making it even more difficult to develop a sense of self.

> I think that gay white men have this interesting social
> construction where they're really care-free. They don't
> have to worry about their race and then their sexual-
> ity at the same time. They don't have to think about
> it…. Our music is different and the culture is different
> and the language is different and I think that, day to
> day, black men that are othered—gay black men, queer
> black men—are constantly having to reinforce their
> identity every day.[13]
>
> —Andrew Wilson, twenty-five years old

Sexuality and homophobia were at the center of national debates
about marriage equality in 2008 when opponents of same-sex marriage championed California ballot Proposition 8. While the black
community is no more unified on issues of sexuality than other
American ethnic groups, all black church denominations hold the
view that homosexuality is immoral, save for some liberal urban congregations.[14] The passage of Prop 8 in California spurred the rise
of LGBTQI advocacy targeted specifically toward black churches.
The Center for Lesbian and Gay Studies in Religion and Ministry
in Berkeley, California, developed the Umoja Project to facilitate
dialogue within African American faith communities through Bible
studies and clergy training. Filmmaker Yoruba Richen's documentary film *The New Black* examined homophobia in the black church in
the context of the marriage equality debate.

For many black people, marriage equality has not been a civil
rights issue since *Loving v. Virginia*, the landmark civil rights decision
of the United States Supreme Court that invalidated laws prohibiting interracial marriage in 1963. Black Christians' understanding
of homosexuality as immoral often makes it hard for them to see
the discrimination against gays as unjust, even when the victims
are their own people.[15] LGBTQI equality is not a civil rights issue
in the black church. Disparities in how black people are treated by
police, the courts, public schools, and other key community institutions are allowed to be classified as civil rights issues, as demonstrated
by the national response to the Black Lives Matter movement. The
black church responds to *racial* disparities, but even as communities

protest the deaths of black men and boys to community and police violence, violence committed against the lives of black women and LGBTQI people is largely ignored. When discussing the twelve trans women of color who were murdered in 2014 with no response from the black community, Lourdes Ashley Hunter, who serves as executive director of the Trans Women of Color Collective, observed that "when folks scream, 'Black Lives Matter,' they're not talking about black trans women. Most of the time, they're not even talking about black women."[16]

There are, however, conversations about sex and sexuality beginning to take place in increasing numbers of black churches, motivated by alarming HIV infection rates among young black men. Research confirms that sexual stigma as experienced in black churches and families contributes to the racial disparities in HIV infection rates.[17]

> Religion plays a barrier in my life. Whenever I go to church, I can't do anything that's homosexual. I can't do anything that's gay. I have self-stigma. I doubt myself. I'm like, "Why am I this way?" I am very conscious of how I dress. I'm very conscious of what I say to certain people and who I invite in my trusting circle, and I'm very private when it comes to church. I keep to myself. I'm very observant of who's watching me. Who's looking at me. It's just a whole internal thing with me. It's a really traumatic thing that I'm working on.[18]
>
> —Charles Hill, twenty-three years old

The Church of God in Christ 2014 Holy Convocation in St. Louis, Missouri, gained national attention because of a viral video of twenty-two-year-old churchgoer Andrew Caldwell, who claimed that he was no longer gay after being delivered from homosexuality through the power of prayer. That same night, Missouri pastor Earl Carter had preached that gay men were "sissies" whom he hoped would "bleed from their butts." While distancing himself and the church from the language used by Pastor Carter, Bishop Charles Blake, presiding bishop of the Church of God in Christ, reaffirmed the church's biblical position against same-sex unions and its support for biblical teachings on matters of sexual conduct.

The National Black Church Initiative, a faith-based coalition made up of thirty-four thousand churches, with 15.7 million African American members, broke its fellowship with Presbyterian Church (U.S.A.) following that body's 2015 vote to approve same-sex marriage. In the same year, the National Baptist Fellowship of Concerned Pastors collected about 390 online signatures in a petition to try to halt the appearance of Bishop Yvette Flunder during the 2015 Garnett-Nabrit Lecture Series at American Baptist College in Nashville, Tennessee. They didn't want a legally married lesbian woman preaching during a worship service. (National Baptists are predominately African American Christian congregations; American Baptists are not.)

In contrast to the National Baptist Fellowship of Concerned Pastors, the Association of Welcoming and Affirming Baptists, a group that grew out of the American Baptist Churches and is committed to advocating and encouraging the full inclusion of LGBTQI individuals, collected more than two thousand signatures on an online petition in support of Bishop Flunder's appearance. She spoke at American Baptist College, and at the end of her sermon she forgave the black preachers who had called for her to be disinvited: "I'm not using my energy for useless fights. I'm using my energy to find peace. Let there be peace on earth."[19]

TRADITION AND TRANSFORMATION

Historically, faith leaders have been a very strong voice for justice and compassion in African American political and social life. Faith leaders, time and again, have taken the lead and have been a voice of conscience on issues ranging from poverty and homelessness to peace and civil rights, but religious diversity can be the enemy of political unity. During the civil rights era, "some churches and their organizations were completely opposed to any involvement in the political struggle for civil rights. Others chose to participate and did so passionately, organizing rallies, protests, and marches, while teaching Christianity and community involvement."[20] Today, some black churches are completely opposed to any involvement in the political struggle for LGBTQI equality. Others choose to participate and do so passionately.

On October 3, 2000, Tommie Watkins made history as the first black gay person to seek ordination in the oldest of the historically black denominations—the African Methodist Episcopal Church. He was rejected by the denomination in the same year that Bishop Vashti McKenzie became the first woman bishop in the denomination.[21] In the words of Dr. Martin Luther King Jr., "The arc of the moral universe is long, but it bends towards justice."[22]

In 2012, researchers in Duke University's National Congregations Study interviewed the leaders of 1,331 American churches, mosques, temples, synagogues, and other houses of worship. The data from that study found the following:

> Acceptance of homosexual members in black Protestant churches has surged of late. The percentage of churches accepting gay and lesbian members has risen from 44 percent in 2006 to 62 percent in 2012. Further, 22 percent of black churches reported being accepting of gays in volunteer leadership roles, up from 6.5 percent six years prior.[23]

Barack Obama became the first sitting president to endorse marriage equality in 2012, and less than two weeks after President Obama's endorsement of marriage equality, the NAACP's board of directors followed suit. Bishop Timothy Clarke of the First Church of God in Columbus, Ohio, summed up his congregation's mixed feelings on the issue, which mirror the varied positions taken by black churches and church leaders around the nation: "No church or group is monolithic. Some were powerfully agitated and disappointed. Others were curious—why now? To what end? Others were hurt. And others, to be honest, told me it's not an issue and they don't have a problem with it."[24]

LOOKING FORWARD

Bishop Flunder leads the Fellowship of Affirming Ministries, which has some sixty predominantly African American member churches mostly led by LGBTQI or LGBTQI-affirming clergy. The overriding purpose of the Fellowship of Affirming Ministries is to support religious leaders and laity in moving toward "a theology of radical inclusivity which, by its very nature, requires an equally radical social ministry reaching to the furthest margins of society to serve all in need without prejudice or discrimination."[25]

Bishop Flunder calls her own City of Refuge United Church of Christ in Oakland "a community of openness and inclusivity, where other people from the edge gather."[26] The nation's first all-transgender gospel choir, Transcendence Gospel Choir, born at City of Refuge, challenges the misogyny, homophobia, transphobia, and intolerance still common at many traditional black churches by using music to gain acceptance and visibility, express pride, and offer hope to the hopeless.

As time passes, there will continue to be fewer black church members and church leaders who are powerfully agitated, disappointed, or hurt by progress made toward LGBTQI equality, and there will be increasing numbers of those who don't have a problem with it. Sometimes progress is made quickly. Sometimes not. Our time is not God's time.

> For my thoughts are not your thoughts, nor are your
> ways my ways, says the Lord.
>
> —Isaiah 55:8

In *Sounding the Trumpet: How Churches Can Answer God's Call to Social Justice*, Dr. J. Alfred Smith Sr. reminds us of the parable that Jesus taught about the sower who went out to sow the seed. He says that "we sow in fields with known and unknown variables determining our success. Ultimately, we sow with limited control over what happens. And yet, we sow in faith and in prayer with patience knowing that God works in mystery and miracle."[27]

Dr. Smith goes on to say that "many people would do better if they knew better."[28]

SUGGESTED RESOURCES

Center for Lesbian and Gay Studies in Religion and Ministry, http://clgs.org; clgs.org/our-work/roundtable-projects/african-american-roundtable. A program of Pacific School of Religion, including the African American LGBT Roundtable, Souls A'Fire conferences, and the Umoja Project, promoting unity in the African American faith community.

The Fellowship of Affirming Ministries, www.radicallyinclusive.com. A network of Christian ministries committed to working together for inclusivity, founded by Rev. Yvette Flunder.

Flunder, Yvette A. *Where the Edge Gathers: Building a Community of Radical Inclusion.* Cleveland: Pilgrim Press, 2005.

Griffin, Horace L. *Their Own Receive Them Not: African American Lesbians and Gays in Black Churches.* Eugene, OR: Wipf & Stock, 2010.

The Kujichagulia Project, www.imanicc.org/n/stigma.html. Addressing homophobia and the stigmatization of HIV/AIDS, based out of Imani Community Church in Oakland.

Buddhism

Acharya Rita M. Gross, PhD

If we are to use the Buddha's words from the Dhamma-pada to judge homosexuality or in this instance homosexual marriage: "The deed which causes remorse afterwards and results in weeping and tears is ill-done. The deed which causes no remorse afterwards and results in joy and happiness is well done." What do you believe to be the result? I have only observed tears of joy from those couples that were finally recognized as a couple. Why would you deny them that because of your own personal prejudice or discrimination?[1]

—Rev. Jerry Hirano, Salt Lake Buddhist Temple

LAYING THE GROUNDWORK

Buddhists in the United States have a reputation for being "liberal" on most social and political issues, including issues stemming from sexual orientation and gender identity. This reputation is probably largely deserved, though there are exceptions, of course. How does this reputation and the behaviors associated with it accord with

---

Acharya Rita M. Gross, PhD, is a Buddhist scholar-practitioner, university professor, and Buddhist teacher who has been authorized as a senior dharma teacher by Her Eminence Jetsun Khandro Rinpoche. She teaches at Mindrolling Lotus Garden Meditation Center and throughout North America at Buddhist centers and at universities. She received her doctorate from the University of Chicago in 1975 for the first dissertation on women's studies or feminist methodology in religious studies and is the author of ten books, including *Buddhism after Patriarchy: A Feminist History, Analysis, and Reconstruction of Buddhism* and *Feminism and Religion;* her forthcoming book is *How Clinging to Gender Identity Subverts Enlightenment.*

traditional Buddhist teachings and with how Buddhists throughout history have dealt with LGBTQI issues and people?

Because Buddhism is an old and diverse religion with no central authority figure or text that all Buddhists recognize as authoritative and to which they owe allegiance, most generalizations one could make about Buddhism will have exceptions. Although sexuality receives attention in religious texts and from religious communities, until recently most Buddhists have not widely discussed or even recognized alternative sexual orientations and identities. Scholars who have thus far researched Buddhist ideas and practices regarding alternative sexual orientations and identities report that such research is minimal, tentative, and preliminary. The word "alternative" in the previous sentence recognizes that, insofar as we can make generalizations, heterosexuality has been the presumed norm and most widespread sexual orientation for Buddhists. This heterosexuality was grounded in male-dominant institutions. But male dominance has always been questioned by some thinkers in all varieties of Buddhism, which means that these thinkers have questioned the reality of the "male/female" sexual dichotomy, and they have entertained notions of the possibility of differences in sexual orientation and gender identity.

Older than Christianity or Islam, Buddhism is one of the world's oldest and most internally diverse religions. Buddhism traces itself to a single historical founder, an Indian named Siddhartha Gautama, often called by his title "the Buddha" (meaning "Awakened One"). In textbooks his dates are often given as 563–481 BCE, but most scholars have recently concluded that these dates are probably too early by about a century. At first this new religion was a small community of monks and nuns, along with their lay supporters and followers. Some centuries later, the religion grew more popular and became the dominant religion in India for several centuries. During the reign of Emperor Ashoka (269–232 BCE), Buddhism spread to Sri Lanka, and by the early centuries of the Common Era, it was rapidly spreading into East Asia, despite vast cultural differences between East Asian and Indian cultures. By the seventh century CE, it was dominant in much of Asia. However, its importance gradually declined in India as Hinduism grew more popular, while in many other parts of Asia the newly emergent Muslim religion gained dominance in many areas.

In the West, widespread knowledge of Buddhism did not occur until the late nineteenth century, and only in the latter half of the twentieth century did a significant minority of Westerners begin to study and practice Buddhism seriously.

SIGNIFICANT BRANCHES

Due to its long history and culturally diverse homes, Buddhism today is split into many subgroups or denominations. What is now called "Buddhism" is so internally diverse that some scholars claim it is actually three closely related but different religions having much the same relationship to each other as do Judaism, Christianity, and Islam. They can conveniently be grouped culturally or geographically and are sometimes called Southern, Northern, and Eastern (meaning East Asian) Buddhisms. In India, Buddhism split into two major divisions and many subgroups, many of which survived outside India. Descendants of the earliest Buddhist groups, now usually called Theravada Buddhism, dominate in Southeast Asia. Another major Indian group called itself Mahayana and spread most successfully into East Asia and north to Tibet and Mongolia. There are many subdivisions within Mahayana Buddhism, especially within the East Asian cultural orbit. Northern Buddhisms are significantly different from East Asian forms of Buddhism.

All these forms of Buddhism claim to follow the teachings of the Buddha, but Mahayana Buddhists revere completely different texts from those followed by Theravada Buddhists. Sectarian relationships between these forms of Buddhism are often tense, with each version of Buddhism claiming to be more authentic, to have truly preserved "what the Buddha taught" or, more precisely, what the Buddha intended to become the religion named after him.

Though Buddhism is a major world religion, often reckoned as one of five major world religions, its presence in the United States is both recent and minor. Buddhism in the United States is especially rich and diverse, because all the forms of Buddhism found worldwide are practiced in North America, often in the same city, which never happened in Asia. All varieties of Buddhism worldwide are represented in the West and are practiced by both immigrants from Asia and their descendants, sometimes called "cradle Buddhists," and by non-Asians, most of them converts without any significant family history of Buddhist identity, though they are now producing a small second generation of non-Asian cradle Buddhists. As a result, especially because Buddhism is a minor religion in the West, each group is quite small. Any consideration of LGBTQI issues and identities among North American Buddhists must take into account how small and diverse the North American Buddhist community is. This small "community" also has no ideological unity or centrally recognized authoritative leader or text. Even the authority of Asian teachers has diminished in most North American Buddhist groups as Western students become much more experienced, both in Buddhist practice and in the intricacies of Buddhist views of how things work.

Because Buddhism in the West is so diverse, it is difficult to generalize how Buddhists practice on a daily, weekly, or yearly basis. For starters, though historically Buddhism has been highly monastic, Western Buddhism is largely lay rather than monastic. Additionally, the way Buddhism is practiced by immigrants and their descendants from traditionally Buddhist cultures is considerably different from how many converts practice Buddhism. For Asian American Buddhists, Buddhist practice is often community based and a way of maintaining ties with their indigenous cultures. For converted Buddhists, the practice of meditation and Buddhist ideas are often paramount, even though many scholars love to point out that throughout history most Buddhists have not emphasized meditation as much as Western Buddhist converts do. Many Buddhist groups either rent or own a physical space where weekly meetings can be held. The content of these meetings varies greatly depending on the teachings and practice of each specific Buddhist denomination. Many Buddhists maintain a shrine room or practice space in their homes and engage in daily practices of meditation or chanting. Many groups also own or rent residential retreat centers, usually in rural settings, where people gather for weekend or longer programs under the guidance of an authorized Buddhist teacher.

FOUNDATIONAL NARRATIVES

Perhaps one of the most reliable generalizations one can make about Buddhism is that for most forms of Buddhism, the lay/monastic distinction takes precedence over the heterosexual/homosexual divide. Thus, the primary question for each individual is whether to be a celibate monk/nun or a householder able to engage in sexual activity, as long as it is not "sexual misconduct." What is now called "sexual orientation" was much less debated historically, and most scholars doubt that an equivalent to the modern term "homosexual" can be found in Buddhist traditions and teachings. The benefits of celibacy received far more attention than the "evils" of homosexuality. Therefore, if all heteronormative sexual activity, including masturbation, was deemed to be off-limits by Buddhist communities, homosexual activity would have also been out of the question.

Because monastic celibacy has been so highly valued in most forms of Buddhism for so long, Buddhism is often accused of being sex averse. However, that is not quite accurate, just as it is not accurate to claim that Buddhism is pleasure averse. It would be much more accurate to say that Buddhism is suffering averse, and it claims that celibacy can help one avoid suffering, counterintuitive as that statement may sound to some. To understand the high value placed on celibacy, one must understand the links between craving and suffering in Buddhism, as well as the links between abandoning craving and finding freedom and happiness, which, according to Buddhism, represent the first three Noble Truths. Buddhists often claim that all beings prefer happiness to suffering and habitually pursue happiness, but the ways in which they go about trying to secure happiness eventually result in suffering. Contentment is regarded as a state of happiness. Instead of being content with what is, with things as they are, people want things to be different or hope for something that is not currently present. Though many people do not realize it, the very experience of craving, of desire, of wanting something desperately, is itself a painful condition. Thus, craving and happiness are incompatible, and we need to clarify which is more valuable to us. The fault lies not with what we want but with the mind that craves insatiably or obsessively. The remedy lies not so much in banishing the things we crave but in training the mind not to crave, not to be obsessed, compulsive, or addicted to what it wants. What does this have to do with celibacy? For untrained minds, sexual pleasure is addictive. Since most people's minds are untrained, part of finding freedom and happiness would lie in craving sexual pleasure less or not at all—the operative word being "craving," not "sex." Hence the discipline of celibacy. Being practical, the historical Buddha realized that such discipline was counterproductive for many people, hence the lay/ monastic division that has loomed so large in most, but not all, forms of Buddhism. Monastics were to avoid all forms of sexual experience, while lay people were to avoid all forms of sexual misconduct, usually defined as sexual activities harmful to oneself or one's partner. Most of the time, Buddhists defined what would constitute sexual experience for a monastic much more closely than they defined sexual misconduct for laity.

For someone with a thoroughly trained mind, it might be possible to engage in sexual activity without the suffering brought about by compulsive clinging and craving. Thus, there are forms of Buddhism, especially Vajrayana Buddhism, a form of Mahayana Buddhism prevalent in Tibet and popular in the West, in which sexual symbolism and the practice of "sexual yoga" is common. When these innovations occurred in Buddhism, they occurred for both monastic and lay practitioners.

Non-Buddhists often marvel at the seemingly erotic nature of much Indian and Tibetan Buddhist art, which they find odd in a context in which celibacy is so valued. Naked voluptuous females and naked muscular males with erect phalluses are fairly common, and in specifically Vajrayana symbolism and art, the message is even clearer. Heterosexual—or heterosexist, as some would call it—imagery is widespread. Actually, behind the visual imagery is a nonsexual message. Wisdom and compassion are the two primary achievements pursued by Buddhists; their perfect balance and inseparability are all-important and bring realization and release. From fairly early times, wisdom was gendered feminine and called "the Mother of All Buddhas." That left an opening, as compassion and/or skillful methods came to be paired with wisdom, for compassion to be gendered male. This association, which mystifies some North Americans when they first hear it, also demonstrates how culturally specific and inaccurate most gender stereotypes really are. Visually, the heterosexual union of wisdom and compassion became one of the most frequent symbols in Vajrayana Buddhism. Two cloth paintings representing this inseparability of female wisdom and male compassion adorn two of the walls of my work area. As a feminist Buddhist, I have often commented on the androcentric quality of this imagery, in which the male dominates the female visually. Gay and lesbian Buddhists understandably sometimes object or wonder why homosexual sex is never so represented. However, I would claim that their aim is not to validate or elevate any kind of sex but to express the non-dual inseparability of wisdom and compassion. What should be questioned and analyzed is whether it is appropriate to genderize wisdom and compassion.

In these same forms of Buddhism, "sexual yoga," using physiological sex as a meditative technique, is sometimes taught. Sexual yoga is not well understood or frequently taught in the West. Because so many North Americans find tantric sex (sexual yoga) titillating, finding a qualified, authorized teacher and mistrusting anything one might find on the Internet about this topic are recommended. Nevertheless, it seems that such heterosexual practices were once important and reasonably common in Vajrayana Buddhism. They could emerge only in a form of Buddhism that was able to imagine that thorough mind training could obviate the usual compulsive desire accompanying sexual activity. I know of no instances traditionally or in Asian Buddhism in which this logic has been applied to homosexual sex, though some North American Buddhists are beginning to do so.

For monastics, rules about what constituted sexual activity were clearly defined. Deliberate violation of the most serious rules resulted in immediate expulsion from the monastic community, with no possibility of eventual reinstatement, for both women and men. Most of the rules define sexual activity as penetration of an orifice, especially penile penetration of any orifice. Deliberate emission of semen is less serious but still requires confession and expiation. Rules for nuns can include not swimming, not traveling alone, and not sleeping under a single blanket with another nun. In somewhat later compilations of rules about sexual conduct it is even forbidden for the laity to penetrate any orifice with an "inappropriate" organ. Penile to vaginal contact was the only appropriate sexual contact. Exceptions to these rules and generalizations include widespread homosexual conduct among male monastics in later Japanese Buddhism, homosexual conduct among "irregular" Tibetan monks (those who were allowed to play into their sexual desires), and widespread marriage among some Japanese and Tibetan men who would be monks in other Buddhist contexts because of their religious roles and authority. Laymen are prohibited from other forms of sexual activity, including having sex in an inappropriate physical location, such as a shrine, at the "wrong" time, or "too often." As is common in religious literature composed mainly by men for men, definitions of female sexual misconduct are much less discussed.

Did sexual orientation affect access to monastic ordination? Modern ideas about sexual orientation do not seem to have been the norm in the times and places in which traditional Buddhist texts were written. Nevertheless, there was a category of person for whom monastic ordination was unavailable or who could be expelled from the monastic community if such a person had already been ordained by oversight. The Sanskrit/Pali term for such people has been translated variously, but most scholars say the common translation "eunuch" is incorrect because physical removal of the testicles was not necessarily involved. Rather, such people seemed to have been anatomical males who could not or would not engage in culturally defined standards of masculinity. They were said to "lack manliness" and sometimes engaged in what today would be considered homosexual activity. Thus, in modern terms, a *celibate* person with a "homosexual orientation" would not be barred from monastic ordination. There is no corresponding category for women in traditional contexts.

Given that sex was forbidden only for monastics and rules about sexuality for laity were much less precise or universal throughout the Buddhist world, what about homosexuality among laypeople? Many modern people would ask if sexual misconduct necessarily includes non-heterosexual sexual activity. It is far from clear to Buddhists that consensual non-heterosexual sexual activity is harmful to anyone. This is another arena for which scholarship is lacking and there is widespread cultural variation.

In the oldest texts pertaining to rules of monastic discipline, there are a few unclear references to sex change. What should the community do if a former monk suddenly becomes a woman or vice versa? Such changes seem to be spontaneous, not the result of a transgender identity. The answer is that the former monk should now observe the rules for nuns and vice versa.

Because of the core belief in rebirth among traditional Buddhists, another avenue for sex change was possible even though sexual identity was usually thought to remain stable, even when a former human was reborn as an animal. For example, in his many prior rebirths as an animal, the historical Buddha was always reborn as a male. Many Buddhist women born into patriarchal conditions have been promised future rebirth as a male as compensation for their sufferings as women living under male dominance. The motif of sex change is quite common in Mahayana scriptures, but it most likely does not relate to what we would call transgender identity today. Most of the changes are female to male and mainly concern male dominance.

ENCOUNTERING LGBTQI ISSUES

Many lesbians and gay people are found in North American Buddhist communities. While some experience a less than full welcome, many lesbian, gay, and bisexual practitioners are well accommodated, including being able to room with their same-sex partners at various retreat centers. General advice to lay practitioners is to consider sexual misconduct as conduct that would harm oneself or one's partners. Homophobia is often trumped by the insight that same-sex relationships do not fit the definition of harmful sex. Many North American Buddhist centers offer various support groups, special meetings, or retreats for people of same-sex orientation. As early as the 1970s, many ministers with the Buddhist Churches of America began performing same-sex marriages. Some who are authorized to solemnize marriages are in same-sex committed relationships themselves.

Several prominent Asian Buddhist teachers have made their viewpoints on same-sex relationships and marriage known. Thich Nhat Hanh, in his well-known interpretation of the Five Lay Precepts (of which avoiding sexual misconduct is the third), focuses on mutual commitment, rather than on more conventional mores, as the essence of avoiding sexual misconduct. He stresses mutual long-term commitment a great deal in his comments on marriage. Regarding sexual orientation, Thich Nhat Hanh relies more on theistic language, stating that "God is a lesbian, but also a gay, a black, a white, a chrysanthemum."[2] Despite the theistic language, his comment is consistent with Buddhist teachings. The Dalai Lama has put forward a similar view, but one that some find inconsistent. Regarding both same-sex marriage and homosexual sexual activity, he comes out in favor of both so long as the relationships are consensual and no abuse is involved. Overall, the Dalai Lama has declared that individuals should follow the teachings or practices of their own religion. Thus, relying on the traditional rules about orifices and organs cited above, the Dalai Lama wants Buddhists, as Buddhists, to refrain from same-sex activities, though he has always said that celibate gay or lesbian Buddhists should not be discriminated against in any way.

North American Buddhist and Buddhist scholar Jeffrey Hopkins, who identifies as gay, has written a provocative and very courageous book titled *Sex, Orgasm, and the Mind of Clear Light: The 64 Arts of Gay Male Love.* It is modeled on several Indian and Tibetan manuals that assumed heterosexuality and draws on a Vajrayana tradition that evaluates certain sexual practices as skillful meditative practices if done with the proper state of mind. Hopkins stated that he wrote the book "in order to support one of my communities—an important one."[3] No form of Buddhism disputes the appropriateness of sexual activity within the bounds of non-harming for lay practitioners, nor is Buddhism particularly sex averse in such contexts. However, the practice of "sexual yoga," for both monastics and laypeople, is found in only a few contexts, Indian and Tibetan, and even in those contexts it has always been quite controversial. Even those who accept and promote it also emphasize, as does Hopkins, that merely engaging in sexual activity does not qualify as sexual yoga and is not spiritually effective. The proper, clear, mindful, stable state of mind, which usually requires proper training and is considered to be quite difficult to attain, is essential in order to engage in sexual yoga. If sexual activity can be appropriate for or helpful to some Buddhists, on what grounds is heterosexual activity to be evaluated as somehow more appropriate than homosexual sex? One would have to rely on the "organs and orifices" arguments and on acceptance of conventional prejudices.

While general acceptance of homosexuality and same-sex marriage is quite high among North American Buddhists, this is not always the case. For instance, an interview with Hopkins in a Buddhist periodical about his ideas and scholarship drew an unusually large response of largely negative letters to the editor, with several requests for subscription cancellation.[4] This response continued on for two issues, after which *Tricycle's* then editor expressed her dismay at this response from "the politically correct, mostly white, mostly liberal, so-called Buddhist community."[5] This exchange occurred nearly twenty years ago, and the response would probably be different today. Regardless, Hopkins's book has since been widely circulated among North American Buddhists and has most likely helped shift some students' and teachers' thoughts on same-sex yogic practice.

Except in a few cities, there is much less experience and information available for and from Buddhists regarding transgender identity. Because North American Buddhist communities strive to be welcoming and inclusive, people who identify as transgender would typically be welcomed to the same support and practice groups that welcome those who are gay, lesbian, and bisexual. However, in terms of Buddhist teachings, identifying as transgender has been much less discussed and raises significant questions.

In any case, both homosexual and transgender people have been accepted as highly renowned teachers in several important North American Buddhist communities.[6] In my work on Buddhism and gender, I have always stressed how critical for Buddhism is the success and acceptance of teachers outside the male heterosexual orbit that has dominated the ranks of accepted Buddhist teachers from Buddhism's beginnings. By this test, North American Buddhists are ahead of the curve for Buddhism historically and for Buddhism worldwide today.

The growing awareness of transgender identities and the possibilities for affecting Buddhism raise new questions for Buddhist scholars, teachers, and students. These questions have not been entertained globally and have barely been addressed in North America, even though there are many transgender Buddhists and some transgender teachers among North American Buddhists. Given the sensibilities of North American Buddhists in general, it is unlikely that transgender people will be excluded or discriminated against in North American Buddhist communities.

For Buddhism, the issues brought up by transgender possibilities must be considered in the context of Buddhist teachings about identity and gender identity. These are more long-standing and have the potential to create greater impact on Buddhism than questions about conventional sexual ethics brought up by gay, lesbian, or bisexual practices, as these are relatively easily resolvable.

What is sometimes called "identity view" in Buddhism is a serious matter that Buddhists have long discussed and is often seriously misunderstood by outsiders. Identity views are often expressed by statements beginning with the words "I am." From the earliest times, "identity view," often translated into contemporary English as the Buddhist claim for "egolessness," has drawn forth significant commentary and questions. Buddhists consider holding a strong identity view or holding it with any attachment, clinging, or personal investment as problematic. In some spiritual traditions, the primary discipline is to explore the question "Who am I?" One of the innovations introduced by the historical Buddha was to answer that question by suggesting that clinging to any belief in a permanent or unchanging identity kept one imprisoned in cyclic existence, with all its unsatisfactory downsides. There are two issues: the psychology of clinging and the belief in a permanent or unchanging identity. The suffering brought about by impermanence and the resistance to impermanence is an important topic for contemplation by Buddhists. Identity belief is the notion that there is a permanent, enduring core of selfhood underlying all the change and impermanence, a belief that is common in many religions but always denied by Buddhists. Buddhist defenses of their claims are too complicated to explore here, but a point many commonly make is that both empirical and rational demonstrations of the existence of such an underlying or permanent self-core are weak. A deeply held belief that "this is who or what I am and this is of supreme, ultimate importance to me" is usually discouraged in Buddhism, although a lightly held awareness of everyday relative identities that are subject to constant fluctuation is not deemed problematic.

In my work on Buddhism and gender, I have often emphasized that for most people, gender identity is one of the most tempting identities to which people cling, both in terms of what they think it means for themselves and in terms of what it means for/about others. It is one of the identities most easily taken to be truly "real" rather than merely appearing as such. However, classical Buddhist thought has done little to link thinking about how identity view and gender identity correlate.

How Buddhists will evaluate transgender issues depends in part on how Buddhists have classically understood gender identity. Buddhists have divided beings dualistically into two categories, male and female, on the basis of the appearance of external genitalia. But what else can be said of these distinctions? This is a topic about which there can be considerable disagreement among Buddhists. As with sexual ethics for lay practitioners, Buddhists have largely followed the guidelines of the cultures in which they live. Thus, throughout history Buddhists have lived with a fairly rigid set of gender roles, which many North American Buddhists are now questioning even as others still uphold this set of gender roles. At the same time, Buddhists have also claimed that gender is relatively irrelevant, that enlightened mind is beyond gender, neither male nor female. Thus, gender is conventional or relative, not ultimate or truly existing. For Buddhists, with our fine-tuned distinctions between appearance and reality, this is very important. The distinction between appearances and reality can be difficult for non-Buddhists to understand, but it is essential for Buddhist practitioners. Appearances are subject to causation and impermanence, while what is truly real exists without conditionality or change. In the Vajrayana tradition this is often called the unborn, natural state of mind.

Buddhists have long contemplated the possibility of sex change, usually from one life to another, and usually from female to male so as to overcome injustices suffered in a life as a female in a patriarchal society. Other more magical instances of sex change can be found in various Buddhist traditions, especially in Mahayana texts. However, I do not believe these traditional stories have any relationship to contemporary notions of transgender identity.

In my work on feminism and gender, I have focused on what I call "the prison of gender roles," the sex-specific behaviors and stereotypes that dictate so much of people's lives and that depend on the shape of their external genitalia, while ignoring their intellects, longings, abilities, and spiritual capacities. I have emphasized how much suffering this prison causes people.

Transgender people express much the same sense of suffering at being forced to conform to gender standards and stereotypes that they find ill-fitting and painful. Given that Buddhism regards gender as relative rather than ultimate and that it has always entertained the possibility of sex change, why not simply endorse the transition from gender to gender that transgender people sometimes seek? However, there are other questions. Does or can such a solution simply fall into identity view, which would ascribe reality to one's gender or gender identity? What is at the root of transgender dissatisfaction? Does it lie with one's biological gender or with what one is constrained to do or refrain from doing because of one's biological sex? I would argue that the construct of gender is at fault. The problem lies with the prison of gender roles, rather than with gender itself. Ultimately, due to the Buddhist emphasis on compassion, the only choice is to offer empathy and support, no matter how different individuals cope with their suffering.

The transgender phenomenon casts an interesting light on gender. On the one hand, it demonstrates how artificial, ephemeral, and constructed gender really is, expressed in large part through hairstyles, gender-specific clothing, and mannerisms that are learned. On the other hand, when transgender people so successfully imitate the conventional appearances and mannerisms usually exhibited by the biological sex they wish to join, are they diminishing the prison of gender roles or being locked up in it? What has changed by altering superficial appearances? To think that one has become a man or a woman would be to assume that there is a gender essence, a "female nature" or a "male nature." While some Buddhists affirm such a notion, it is questionable from the point of view of Buddhist thinkers who take teachings on egolessness and emptiness as normative. Are attempts to change physiological sex based on a belief in a gender essence or based on the hope or belief that changing superficial appearances can bring true lasting happiness? This last question is the most serious. While rational changes in one's relative identities are not problematic from a Buddhist point of view, it is very easy to expect more from such changes than they can deliver.

In its 2015 spring issue, the Buddhist periodical *Buddhadharma*, in its regular column "Ask the Teachers," entertained a question from a practitioner: "Does my transgender identity conflict with the teachings on no-self?" (perhaps the most serious question about transgender possibilities for Buddhists).[7] All the teachers in some way emphasized that all relative identities are just that—relative, since there is no truly existing self. Therefore, wishing or thinking one could have some other relative identity—national, gender, racial, class, or whatever—matters little, since all these identities are ephemeral, apparent, and ultimately unreal. One teacher probed, wondering if there was a deeper longing cloaked in the inquiry. The teacher acknowledged the suffering behind the question but then pointed out that "your longing for change points to something even deeper.... Your question suggests to me that you're homesick for the absolute and that homesickness is expressing itself in this relative way." The teacher then suggested that sex reassignment might be part of finding the ultimate the searcher is seeking for but asked him to be careful, since no matter what relative identity we adopt, if we cling to it, we are still "victims of a primordial identity theft." The teacher also advised the student to identify with the space between the thoughts "I'm a woman" or "I'm a man," absolutizing neither. This combination of dharmically based caution and support is one Buddhist approach to transgender identity.

TRADITION AND TRANSFORMATION

Religions that survive are constantly changing. That is why they are still living religions. As an old religion that has flourished in many cultures, Buddhism has accommodated many changes as it has become internally diverse. Because of this, accommodating change has not usually meant that Buddhism as a whole changes, but that new varieties of Buddhism become established. Even major new movements, such as Mahayana or Vajrayana, were never successful at becoming "the" new Buddhism, but only at becoming major denominations within Buddhism. The older movements also continued to flourish.

From where does the inspiration for such change come? Like members of other religions, Buddhists have mechanisms for attributing such innovations to trans-historical sources, "revelation" of some variety, and many more pious or traditional Buddhists still accept such accounts of change. In fact, such believers often either decry changes as dangerous deviations from the "true faith" or support them wholeheartedly, often condemning older schools in this process.

By contrast, scholars of religions point out that such changes are usually initiated by individuals who are deeply committed to the tradition but also feel strongly motivated about what they are proposing, often claiming that such propositions represent the true heart of the tradition, insights that the founder himself taught or intended. If enough practitioners of the tradition are convinced, then this new founder and his or her followers will have established a new denomination within Buddhism. Eventually, followers of this teacher may claim that he or she also acted outside the processes of history.

LOOKING FORWARD

There is no reason why those who want to see Buddhism become more accommodating to a variety of sexual orientations or transgender identities will not have similar long-term success. Already some voices are claiming that their teachings and practices, if not "traditional," are completely compatible with "what the Buddha taught." At least in North America, they are well on their way to such acceptance.

SUGGESTED RESOURCES

Cabezon, Jose Ignacio, ed. *Buddhism, Sexuality, and Gender.* Albany: State University of New York Press, 1992.

———. "Homosexuality and Buddhism." In *Homosexuality and World Religions*, edited by Arlene Swidler, 81–101. Valley Forge, PA: Trinity Press International, 1993.

Corless, Roger. "Coming Out in the *Sangha*: Queer Community in American Buddhism." In *The Faces of Buddhism in America*, edited by Charles S. Prebish and Kenneth K. Tanaka, 253–65. Berkeley: University of California Press, 1998.

Hopkins, Jeffrey. *Sex, Orgasm, and the Mind of Clear Light: The Sixty-Four Arts of Gay Male Love.* Berkeley, CA: North Atlantic Press, 1998.

Leyland, Winston, ed. *Queer Dharma: Voices of Gay Buddhists.* 2 vols. San Francisco: Gay Sunshine Press, 1998–2000.

The Church of Jesus Christ of Latter-day Saints (Mormon)

John Gustav-Wrathall

[President Jeff Clark of the Palmyra Stake] said he wished that every single one of us were members of his stake; that he wished every member of the Church had the quality of testimonies he had heard shared among us; that we had had to work and struggle against opposition and doubt to come to a deeper understanding of the Gospel, and find our place in it, and he wished for every member of his stake to work at claiming their faith as authentically as we had.[1]

—Report on the May 2015 Affirmation Leadership Retreat

LAYING THE GROUNDWORK

The Latter-day Saints (LDS) movement began in upstate New York in the late 1820s. Early believers gathered around the prophet Joseph Smith Jr., who claimed to have received a series of divine visitations and visions and to have translated a new book of scripture from ancient records known as the Book of Mormon. The Church of Jesus Christ of Latter-day Saints was formally organized in 1830.

John Gustav-Wrathall is an adjunct professor of American religious history at United Theological Seminary of the Twin Cities, and a member of the board of Affirmation: LGBT Mormons, Families & Friends. He has published extensively on being gay and Mormon and is the author of *Take the Young Stranger by the Hand: Same-Sex Dynamics and the Young Men's Christian Association*, articles in *Sunstone* and *Dialogue*, and the *Young Stranger* blog. Though excommunicated from the LDS Church, Gustav-Wrathall has a testimony and has been active in his south Minneapolis ward since 2005.

Early Mormons were part of a broader "restorationist" movement and, like many Americans at that time, believed that no true church of Jesus Christ existed on the earth, but required a restoration through divine intervention.[2] Early Mormons believed in and experienced divine gifts of the Spirit, such as speaking in tongues, healing, visions, and other outpourings of the Holy Spirit. They believed in a God who actively intervened in the affairs of human beings and who would guide his church through modern-day prophets.

Like other utopian sects of the day, early Mormons practiced various forms of communitarian living. Because of their unconventional beliefs, their insistence on gathering in a single centralized community, and, later, their practice of polygamy, Mormons experienced increasingly intense persecution. Growing persecution in Illinois and, later, the assassination of the prophet Joseph Smith led the largest body of Latter-day Saints to immigrate to Utah under the leadership of Brigham Young.

In the latter half of the nineteenth century, the Church of Jesus Christ of Latter-day Saints publicly announced that they were practicing plural marriage, leading to a period of extended conflict with the federal government. By the turn of the century, however, the church had formally renounced the practice of polygamy, leading to growing acceptance by mainstream American society.

Since the 1830s, Mormon missionaries had traveled to disparate areas throughout North America and eventually to western Europe and the Pacific Islands. After the 1950s the LDS Church increasingly encouraged its members not to immigrate to Utah, but instead to remain where they lived and to build up the church in their native regions, resulting in the growth of a worldwide LDS Church.

Members of the Church of Jesus Christ of Latter-day Saints today continue to believe in modern-day revelation. Mormons believe that marriages and families are eternal, and Mormon temple practices focus on "sealing" marriages and families, and performing sacred ordinances such as baptism and marriage on behalf of those who have died without being able to receive them. Individual Latter-day Saints seek to live lives of holiness, faith, and charity and believe that they should devote a substantial portion of their time and resources to building up the church and "Kingdom of God." In addition to revering the Bible and the Book of Mormon as scripture, contemporary

Mormons also look to the Doctrine and Covenants and the Pearl of Great Price and the teachings of "modern-day prophets" as the Word of God as well.

Today there are three major branches of Mormonism. The largest branch is the Church of Jesus Christ of Latter-day Saints, based in Salt Lake City, Utah, with over fourteen million members throughout the world, a majority of whom are non-English speakers living outside the United States. Mormon congregations exist in almost every country of the world, except in Muslim-majority countries where non-Muslim religious practice is proscribed. Utah and other parts of the Intermountain West have Mormon majority populations, but Mormons are not more than 1 to 2 percent of the population in areas anywhere outside the Intermountain West.

The next largest branch of Mormons is the Community of Christ, based in Independence, Missouri, with about 250,000 members worldwide. The Community of Christ was formed from groups of Mormons who rejected the practice of polygamy and the type of temple worship and practice that was embraced by the Church of Jesus Christ of Latter-day Saints. The Community of Christ today strongly emphasizes global peace and justice and allows the ordination of women and openly gay and lesbian leaders. Finally, there are a few thousand "fundamentalist" Mormons living mostly in the Intermountain West who continue to practice polygamy. There is no formal relationship between the Church of Jesus Christ of Latter-day Saints and the Community of Christ or other smaller (mostly fundamentalist) offshoots of Mormonism.

Outside of academic circles there has never been significant interaction among these three main branches of Mormonism. Each has evolved very different approaches to the issue of homosexuality. The focus of this article is on the largest branch, the Church of Jesus Christ of Latter-day Saints, which accounts for approximately 98 percent of Mormons worldwide.

FOUNDATIONAL NARRATIVES

To the extent that the Mormon textual tradition expands upon the biblical tradition, Mormons have a fundamental understanding of human beings as spirit children of God the Father, and of God the Father as a glorified and exalted man, a "Heavenly Father." Key texts developing this theology can be found in the Pearl of Great Price, in Moses 1, which discusses God's purpose in creation to bring to pass the "immortality and eternal life of man," and in Abraham 3, which discusses the pre-mortal existence of human beings. Doctrine and Covenants, section 132, discusses the role of marriage as a prerequisite for sons and daughters of God to be exalted and to become like God.

While these doctrines generally take a very positive view of human nature in the sense that they insist upon human beings' divine nature as literal children of God, they pose a challenge for gays and lesbians in that they posit a male-female coupling as essential in order to experience exaltation in the world to come. Church leaders currently insist that if an individual is unable to marry heterosexually in this world, he or she must remain celibate for life, in order to qualify for exaltation in the next world.

Mormons have occasionally relied upon certain biblical texts such as Genesis 19, Leviticus 18 and 20, Romans 1, 1 Corinthians 6, or 1 Timothy 1 to condemn homosexual behavior outright as a sin and an "abomination." However, because of the Mormon belief in dispensationalism[3] and modern-day revelation, and because they believe in the primacy of the teachings of modern-day prophets over the teachings of dead prophets, Mormons generally are less concerned with textual arguments about homosexuality than they are about what current leaders teach and require of church members. Mormon discourse about homosexuality generally overlooks these biblical texts. Mormons could easily be convinced, for instance, that the Levitical proscriptions on homosexual behavior no longer apply. But if modern-day prophets have condemned homosexuality, for them the argument over biblical texts is moot.

Since 2000, Mormon leaders have avoided the use of Old Testament terms like "abomination" to describe homosexuality. The previous church president, Gordon B. Hinckley, began a trend of speaking about homosexuality in more neutral, accepting terms and of distinguishing between homosexual orientation (not chosen) and homosexual acts (from which individuals should abstain).

Most Mormons today would not be willing to preclude the possibility of a future revelation that would bless homosexual relationships. At the same time, most Mormons today would also find it difficult to imagine how such a future revelation would fit within current Mormon beliefs about the nature of marriage, particularly based on the teachings about marriage contained in Doctrine and Covenants section 132.

Mormon views of transgender people have also been shaped by the same Mormon scriptural texts and beliefs about gender, marriage, and the role of the physical body in exaltation that have shaped Mormon views of homosexuality. Gender variance has been poorly understood by most Latter-day Saints. Church leaders have occasionally used the term "gender confusion," a term that has been applied as much to gay, lesbian, and bisexual individuals as to transgender individuals. "The Family: A Proclamation to the World," a formal statement released by the LDS Church in 1995 under the presidency of Gordon B. Hinckley, described gender as an eternal characteristic of sons and daughters of God. Though not officially canonized, the statement is treated as canonical by many Mormons, who tend to assume that it would be impossible for one's eternal gender to be different from the physical sex into which one's spirit is born. The Church Handbook of Instructions allows, though does not prescribe, excommunication of individuals who undergo surgical procedures to confirm their understanding of gender identity and expression. Gender confirmation surgery also has an impact on one's ability to hold the priesthood and to have one's marriage sealed in the temple. Only biological males who have not undergone gender reassignment surgery may hold the priesthood, and only biologically heterosexual couples may be sealed in the temple.

ENCOUNTERING LGBTQI ISSUES

Following a number of very high-profile statements made by LDS Church leaders in 2006, emphasizing that homosexuality is not chosen and is generally not amenable to change and that homosexual orientation in itself should not be condemned, the general church membership has been evolving toward a more open and accepting attitude toward LGBTQI individuals. The recent 2013 release by the church of its MormonsAndGays.org website has signaled new openness to dialogue and inclusion, though the standard of celibacy outside of heterosexual marriage is still upheld.

Rank-and-file Mormons are currently expressing a range of opinions toward homosexuality. Some still cling to old attitudes, viewing homosexuality as an abomination and expressing extreme antipathy toward homosexual individuals. The majority are adopting the LDS Church's currently stated position of non-condemnation of homosexual orientation, emphasis on the standard of chastity outside of heterosexual marriage, and opposition to same-sex marriage. In many regions of the church there is growing tolerance of those who choose to enter into same-sex relationships, including, in some locales, church leaders who refrain from the previously almost universal practice of excommunicating such individuals.

In 2008 the Mormon Church played a major role in the passage of Proposition 8 in California, which established that only marriages between a man and a woman would be recognized, contributing more than half of the funding for the campaign and large numbers of volunteers. Although the church remained on the sidelines in recent same-sex marriage related campaigns in Minnesota, Maryland, Maine, and Washington, in 2013 it filed an amicus brief on behalf of the Proposition 8 appeal going before the Supreme Court. Local church leaders in Hawaii—the state with the second highest percentage of Mormons in the United States (after Utah)—spoke out in opposition to the legalization of same-sex marriage there in late 2013. There were some locally organized lobbying efforts, though nothing on the scale that took place in California around the time of Proposition 8. When a federal judge overturned the constitutional amendment banning same-sex marriage in Utah in December 2013, the LDS Church issued a public statement expressing disappointment with the ruling and reaffirming the church's commitment to marriage between a man and a woman. After the Supreme Court ruling in *Obergefell et al. v. Hodges* in 2015, LDS Church leaders issued a statement that was read in all LDS congregations in North America reiterating the church's opposition to same-sex marriage, clarifying that LDS Church property could not be used for same-sex weddings and that LDS Church leaders could not use their ecclesiastical office to perform them. The letter also acknowledged differences of opinion among Mormons about this issue and urged members who were wrestling with it to study, pray about it, and seek guidance directly from God as well as from local church leaders.

A growing minority of Mormons have expressed support for full equal marriage rights for same-sex couples and even for church acceptance and blessing of such relationships. In the aftermath of the Utah same-sex marriage ruling, for example, polls showed that 32 percent of Utah Mormons supported full marriage equality for same-sex couples, and 65 percent supported extending some form of legal recognition (such as civil unions) to same-sex couples.[4] This represents a dramatic increase in mainstream Mormon support for marriage equality.

With the growing understanding and acceptance of gay and lesbian individuals has come a corresponding openness toward and understanding of transgender individuals. Mormons are discussing transgender issues openly, and a small but growing number of local church leaders are welcoming gender-nonconforming individuals to remain formal members of the church and to participate in congregational life. Transgender church members are, however, still subject to the restrictions on priesthood holding and temple marriage that are prescribed by the Handbook of Instructions.

The first organization of gay and lesbian Mormons, Affirmation, was founded in the late 1970s. Affirmation has tended to view homosexuality in nonjudgmental terms and to affirm same-sex relationships, and historically its membership has ranged from those who have sought a positive relationship with the church to those who have cut their ties to it. An analogous organization was founded in the Community of Christ in the 1980s, called GALA, or Gay and Lesbian Acceptance. Also in the 1980s, Evergreen International was founded, an organization for Mormons with "same-sex attraction" who sought to overcome their homosexuality through various forms of counseling and reparative therapy. LDS support for Evergreen has declined dramatically in recent years, likely as a result of church leaders' statements accepting that sexual orientation may not be subject to change and denouncing reparative therapy or heterosexual marriage as a "therapeutic step" for homosexuals. In early 2014, Evergreen International announced that it would merge with North Star, a group that came into being in the past decade, which seeks to support LGBTQI individuals in remaining in good standing in the church, but which takes no formal position on the merits of reparative therapy. None of these groups is formally sponsored by the LDS Church.

Other groups that have come into existence within the last decade include Mormons for Equality (mostly straight Mormons who seek dialogue in the church about the issue of same-sex marriage and who have organized nationally and locally to support full legal equality for LGBTQI people); Mormons Building Bridges (an organization of straight active Mormons who are seeking to promote greater understanding of homosexuals within the church); and the Mormon Stories community, which has organized a series of online forums and conferences, such as "Circling the Wagons," where there could be open dialogue about homosexuality and the church.

In recent years there has been increasingly open and robust dialogue about transgender issues in groups like Affirmation, North Star, and Mormons Building Bridges. Furthermore, transgender Mormons have taken advantage of social media to create dynamic online support communities specifically for transgender Latter-day Saints.

TRADITION AND TRANSFORMATION

In evaluating the likelihood of changes in policy, teaching, and/or general attitudes toward homosexuality in the LDS Church, Mormons typically look to two major historical examples of change within Mormonism: the Mormon Church's renunciation of the practice of polygamy at the end of the nineteenth century and the end of the church's ban on the ordination of blacks to the priesthood in the late 1970s.

In the first instance, extreme external pressure was brought to bear on the Mormon Church to force Mormons to abandon polygamy. Federal laws were passed making it illegal. Mormon leaders and members who practiced polygamy were jailed or forced underground or into exile. Church lands were confiscated, Mormons were politically disenfranchised (denied the vote), and Utah was denied statehood. Mormons appealed to the Supreme Court and, in *Reynolds v. the United States* (1879), the Supreme Court denied Mormon polygamy the First Amendment protection of freedom of religious practice. Eventually the church, having exhausted its legal and political options, accepted federal law and abandoned polygamy. In 1890, church president Wilford Woodruff sought and received a revelation from God releasing the Latter-day Saints from the obligation to practice polygamy (though the teachings and doctrines allowing polygamy were not abandoned).

Some historians have observed that external opposition may have intensified Mormon commitment to the practice of polygamy.

Specific federal campaigns against polygamy appear to have coincided with peaks in the numbers of polygamous marriages contracted. Even though polygamy was not popular among Mormons and seemed to be dying out due to internal social and demographic pressures, Mormons may have felt obligated to uphold the practice as an expression of faith in the face of persecution. The church's formal abandonment of polygamy resulted in the growth of a "fundamentalist Mormon" movement, which believed that the church had erred in capitulating to the federal government and abandoning the practice, insisting that faithful adherence to the tenets of Mormonism required its continuation no matter what the political or social cost.

Among Mormons today, polygamy is a difficult topic. The vast majority of practicing Latter-day Saints know little about its history and would probably oppose efforts to reinstitute it. The LDS Church has, at various times in the twentieth century, cooperated with the federal government in its efforts to prosecute "fundamentalist Mormons" who still practice polygamy to this day.

The 1978 change in policy banning black men from the priesthood also came after a period of extended pressure on the LDS Church both from outside the church and from within it. Many churches had similar discriminatory practices, but changed their practices and policies in the 1960s and '70s in response to protest by black civil rights activists. In the case of the ordination of blacks to the priesthood within Mormonism, there was no interference by the federal government analogous to the pressure brought to bear in relation to polygamy. Furthermore, though many Mormons in Utah and the Intermountain West held intensely racist attitudes and believed segregation to be divinely ordained, Mormons in many other parts of the United States and throughout the world had come to embrace a more inclusive vision of the church.

Scholarly research demonstrating that there had been no ban on ordination of black men to the priesthood in the early Mormon Church was influential in helping church leaders reevaluate the ban, which had been instituted by Brigham Young in the 1850s. Also, church leaders had to deal with the fact that the LDS Church was growing rapidly in countries like Brazil and Nigeria, where the ban was creating extreme administrative inconvenience and embarrassment. In 1978, LDS president Spencer W. Kimball unveiled a revelation he had received granting all worthy individuals in the church access to ordination to the priesthood and temple ceremonies without regard to race. When he unveiled it, many church members gratefully embraced it, having already come to a place of desiring an end to racially exclusionary policies in the church.

LOOKING FORWARD

The Church of Jesus Christ of Latter-day Saints has units in every country and in every U.S. state where same-sex marriage is legal. Insufficient study has been done to determine what effect the legalization of same-sex marriage has had on Mormon attitudes toward homosexuality in cultures where there appears to be growing acceptance. Mormonism continues to grow rapidly as a religion both in Latin America—where there is growing acceptance of same-sex marriage—and in Africa—where there is still intense antipathy toward homosexuals and where there are significant legal proscriptions against homosexuality. Even though the Church of Jesus Christ of Latter-day Saints was founded in the United States and is headquartered in Utah, a majority of U.S. Mormons are non-Utah residents, and a majority of Mormons are non-U.S. citizens and non-English speakers. Like the Catholic Church, another worldwide, hierarchically structured church, the LDS Church will increasingly need to take into account cultural dynamics in other regions where the church is organized, which may in some places work for LGBTQI acceptance and in others against it.

Mormons generally believe that any major policy change in the church has to have the sanction of a formal revelation, even—as in the case of the black priesthood issue—when the policy had never been initiated through a formal revelation. By the same token, church leaders are unlikely to seek or promote a revelation if they do not believe that the general church membership is ready to receive it.

Changes in policy related to the role of LGBTQI individuals in the church is complicated by the fact that their status is deeply affected by popular Mormon beliefs about the nature of marriage, which is seen as close to the heart of Mormon beliefs about the nature of God and the nature of humankind. Mormons may find it difficult to make theological space for same-sex marriage for much the same reasons they found it difficult to abandon polygamy. Nevertheless, the religious experience of LGBTQI people, who are beginning to document spiritual experiences of acceptance by God of their identity as gay or transgender and of their loving same-sex relationships, may prompt searching on the part of Mormon members and leaders for greater understanding of the place of sexual and gender diversity within creation and within the "plan of salvation."

Current trends show LDS Church members are more ready than ever for dialogue about the place of LGBTQI people in church and society, though there are still strong reservations among the majority of LDS Church members regarding the acceptance of same-sex relationships.

SUGGESTED RESOURCES

Affirmation, www.affirmation.org. Reaches out to LGBT Mormons, providing support and advocacy.

Far Between, http://farbetweenmovie.com. Interviews with LGBTQI Mormons, with links to influential research projects on the LGBTQI Mormon experience.

"Love One Another: A Discussion on Same-Sex Attraction," Church of Jesus Christ of Latter-day Saints, http://mormonsandgays.org. The LDS Church's own recently launched forum for "kind and reasoned conversation," with interviews from a variety of perspectives within the church.

North Star, http://northstarlds.org. An organization for helping LGBTQI Mormons explore how to live in harmony with the LDS church and to feel supported and valued.

Understanding LDS Homosexuality, http://ldshomosexuality.com. General and academic information, along with personal stories, to promote conversation and understanding in the church.

The Episcopal Church

Rev. Dr. Cameron Partridge

Jesus redefined both home and family. Home is not so much *where* as *when* we're with God. Family is not so much *who* as *whoever* does the will of God. Which still leaves us with this adventure we call life. It is God's gift to us. It's the journey from God and to God.... It's rage and grief and joy and wonder and sorrow and hope and love. It's marrying the person we love and are committed to and want to spend our entire lives with. It's leaving home and returning home.[1]

—Bishop Mary Glasspool, 2015 General Convention
of the Episcopal Church

LAYING THE GROUNDWORK

The Episcopal Church is a Christian denomination with a membership numbering just under two million people.[2] Sometimes described as both Reformed and Catholic, it is descended from the Church of England. It is a church both located in a U.S. context and mindful of its multiple connections across various national and continental borders. Its 109 dioceses (regional areas) center on the United States while also stretching across seventeen countries.[3] The Episcopal

---

Rev. Dr. Cameron Partridge is an Episcopal priest, theologian, and openly transgender man. He is the Episcopal chaplain at Boston University, lecturer and counselor for Episcopalian/Anglican students at Harvard Divinity School, and adjunct lecturer at Episcopal Divinity School. He has contributed to *The Open Body: Essays in Anglican Ecclesiology* and *Looking Forward, Looking Backward: Forty Years of Women's Ordination*, and he is co-editor with Zachary Guiliano of *Preaching and the Theological Imagination*.

Church is also a member of the worldwide Anglican Communion, which numbers approximately eighty million people.[4]

The Episcopal Church formally came into being after the Revolutionary War, becoming independent of the Church of England while honoring its roots and ongoing communion with that wider church, claiming its "Anglicanism." One of the chief marks of that Anglicanism is worship according to the Book of Common Prayer, a collection of worship services that range from rites of baptism and confirmation to the Daily Office and Holy Communion (also called the Eucharist, the Mass, or the Lord's Supper). Significant to Episcopal and wider Anglican practice is an understanding of ministry as practiced in various ways by both laity and clergy, with clergy consisting of bishops, priests, and deacons. The presence of these orders of ministry as well as the centrality of Communion in weekly worship underscore the tradition's catholic, sacramental bent. At the same time, its long-standing emphasis on lively, critical biblical interpretation and preaching points toward Anglicanism's roots in the English Reformation.

Distinctive to the shape of the Episcopal Church is its shared system of governance that has both democratic and hierarchical qualities. The Greek word *episkopos*, "overseer" or "bishop," points to that hierarchical dimension. At the same time, the Episcopal Church's highest level of authority is located in its General Convention, an elected congress that meets every three years. Because of its critical place in the overall structure of the church, the General Convention has long served as an important arena for addressing LGBTQI concerns.

FOUNDATIONAL NARRATIVES

Biblical texts that have historically played a part in Episcopal Church conversations on LGBTQI people come from both the Hebrew Bible and the Christian Scriptures. Some of these texts have inspired critique of or debate about sexual and gender minorities, while others have served as springboards of inspiration and hope. Theological writings from a wide historical sweep of Christian tradition also inform the church's conversation in important ways—not least because of how they have interpreted biblical passages.[5] Finally, because of Anglicanism's strong emphasis on worship, and particularly upon the

Book of Common Prayer, that text and other liturgical texts continue
to play key roles in churchwide conversation.

In the Hebrew Bible, the story of Sodom and Gomorrah (Genesis 19:1–26) has historically formed one well-known touchstone in
church debate about LGBTQI people. The story tells how the men
of Sodom seek violent access to two angelic visitors staying at Lot's
house to "know" them (19:5). Divine punishment for this threatened
crime, apparently a pattern among Sodom's population, is annihila-
tion. But how to understand the nature of this sin, exactly? Was it
primarily about potential same-sex contact, the threat of violent sex,
the violation of hospitality customs, or some combination of these?
In another example, the prohibition against "[lying] with a male as
with a woman" (Leviticus 18:22 and 20:13) has generated questions
about the links between sexual practices and gender norms. What
does it mean for a man to lie with a man as if with a woman? And
if this "lying" references active and passive sexual partnership, does
this text condemn both equally or one more than the other? Most
importantly, what might these stories have to do with contemporary
LGBTQI people? In congregational conversations and wider forums,
Episcopalians often question the simple application of these texts to
contemporary LGBTQI people. They tend to appreciate the complexity, the variety of ways in which personhood has been constructed
and narrated in historical contexts between ancient and contemporary worlds.[6]

In recent years the creation stories of Genesis 1–3 have become
important in Anglican conversations about not only sexuality but also
gender identity. More conservative interpreters have read references
to male and female in these creation accounts as establishing a strict
sexual binary of male and female, an idea often termed sexual or
gender "complementarity." Key phrases in this approach include the
declaration "male and female he created them" (1:27), "be fruitful
and multiply" (1:28), and "therefore a man leaves his father and his
mother and clings to his wife, and they become one flesh" (2:24). Heterosexual marriage, in this interpretive tradition, upholds the male/
female sexual binary. Deviation from it potentially signals not simply sexual sin but gender confusion.[7] This approach has increasingly
anchored conservative critiques of same-sex marriage.[8] At the same
time, similar arguments have undergirded critiques of transgender

people in the Episcopal Church and Church of England, suggesting that transgender people implicitly reject the "givenness" of their bodily creation.[9] This turn to the Genesis creation stories in both marriage equality and transgender contexts signals a clear and often overlooked theological intersection between transgender and cisgender gay and lesbian concerns, while bisexuality and intersexuality have not yet received concentrated attention in wider church conversations.[10] Existing areas of conversation tend to be framed through distinct categories (sexual orientation on the one hand, and gender identity and expression on the other), yet implicitly and explicitly all of these groups contest rigid ideas of complementarity and can inspire richer theological accounts of the human person.

As in other Christian traditions, certain scriptural texts have inspired critique of LGB people. Paul of Tarsus, the "apostle to the gentiles," authored several such passages. Chief among them is the first chapter of his letter to the Romans (especially Romans 1:26–27), in which he speaks of an "exchange" of "natural" for "unnatural" sex among both women and men. God has observed this exchange, he argues, and has condemned such people ("for this reason God gave them up to degrading passions"). Recent biblical scholarship has pointed out that the primary issue in Romans 1 is idolatry (as Romans 1:23 conveys: instead of honoring "the glory of the immortal God" the people at issue worshipped "images resembling a mortal human being or birds or four-footed animals or reptiles"). Such scholarship is also attuned to patterns of androcentrism and misogyny, how male bodies were constructed and reinforced as dominant in the ancient world, and how women's bodies were constructed as passive, fluid, and dangerous.[11] Contemporary critiques of such bodily construction, as well as of the definitions of "natural" and "unnatural," have pushed back against the use of this passage as a text of judgment, particularly against cisgender gay and lesbian people.

Churches have used another Pauline text, 1 Corinthians 6:9–10, in a similar manner. Among a list of people who "will not inherit the kingdom of God," two Greek terms, *arsenokoites* and *malakos*, have in recent decades been translated in relation to the modern category of homosexuality. As with Romans 1, a critical inquiry into the construction of normative male embodiment forms a crucial response to this text. The latter term, *malakos,* points to the gendered, ideological dimensions of Paul's slur: an effeminate man. As Dale Martin points out in *Sex and the Single Savior,* effeminacy was an entire way of being in the world, a whole set of gendered practices. The term *arsenokoites* is yet more difficult to pin down. Perhaps, as Martin has explored, it may point to a link between economic exploitation and sexuality.[12]

Yet, while the above-referenced passages have been important to Episcopal Church conversation, they do not necessarily rule the day. Rather than reacting to texts cited in judgment, Episcopalians are increasingly retrieving what theologian Jay Johnson has described as the "rich diversity" of both biblical texts and their theological elaboration in various historical periods.[13] They are turning proactively to Jesus's ministry of healing and transformation among the most marginal of the marginalized. Episcopalians are increasingly inspired by passages that call all Christians to be agents of transformation in the church and in the wider world.

Paul's idea of a "new creation" is one such source: "If anyone is in Christ there is a new creation; everything old has passed away; see, everything has become new!" (2 Corinthians 5:17). So, too, Paul's baptismal formula from Galatians 3:28 speaks to a breaking down of taxonomies and barriers and a movement toward transformative union in the collective body of Christ: "There is no longer Jew nor Greek, there is no longer slave nor free, there is no longer male and female; for all of you are one in Christ Jesus." Paul's discussion of individual incorporation into the collective body of Christ in Romans 11:17 speaks to this transformation as a productively jarring process. His image of grafting envisions gentile Christians being spliced *para physis,* or "contrary to nature" (Romans 11:24), onto the ancient promise originally given to Abraham. Similarly, the tenth chapter of the Acts of the Apostles has become an inspiration for LGBTQI Episcopalians. There, Peter has a strange dream in which a sheet unfolds before him, holding all manner of animals that, by law, he was forbidden to consume. Yet, he hears a divine voice calling him to do just that, declaring, "What God has made clean you must not call profane" (Acts 10:15).[14]

The signaling of transformation, of an altered concept of taboo and impurity, can inspire a more expansive understanding of sexuality and gender identity. But perhaps most important of all these biblical themes that inspire the embrace of LGBTQI people in the Episcopal

Church is what theologian Patrick Cheng has called "radical love." A love that stems from the God who is love (1 John 4:8) infuses the heart of the Christian message itself: "A God who, through the incarnation, life, death, resurrection, and ascension of Jesus Christ, has dissolved the boundaries between death and life, time and eternity, and the human and the divine."[15] This same love, in turn, can challenge and open up preconceived, binary understandings of sexuality and of gender identity.

These readings are beginning to affirm the lives of intersex as well as transgender Episcopalians. Isaiah 56:3–5 implicitly engages and transforms the earlier prohibition against men with crushed testicles being able to enter the assembly (Deuteronomy 23:1). Instead of reinforcing this critique of an "imperfect" male body, Isaiah declares, "Do not let the eunuch say, 'I am only a dry tree.'" Those eunuchs who "keep my sabbaths, who choose things that please me and hold fast my covenant" will instead receive "a monument and a name better than sons or daughters," indeed "an everlasting name that shall not be cut off." Taboo is transformed. A body thus changed, whether by birth, accident, or design, is welcomed and honored.

Similarly, the Christian Scriptures also reference eunuchs in a positive light.[16] In the context of a discussion about marriage and divorce, Jesus acknowledges that not everyone is called to marriage. He then cites eunuchs (Matthew 19:11–12). In the Acts of the Apostles, a eunuch who was a court official of the queen of Ethiopia comes to signal the radical transformation of the good news as he travels in a chariot along the road from Jerusalem to Gaza. Receiving instruction from the apostle Philip on the prophetic writings of Isaiah, the eunuch sees some water along the road, stops his chariot, and asks Philip to baptize him. Much ink has been spilled by contemporary scholars of early Christianity on these passages and on the social construction of eunuchs and of masculinity in the ancient world.[17] While it would be inaccurate to claim any simple equivalence between this ancient category and contemporary gender minorities, Jesus's naming of a people whose gender was not normative, whether by birth, by accident, or by design—including self-chosen ("those who have made themselves eunuchs for the sake of the kingdom of heaven" [Matthew 19:12])—signals a transformative possibility. And that message is that sexual difference itself is not simply, statically, and only binary, male or female alone. Here Jesus voices *both* that sexual differ-ence can be ambiguous *and* that it can be transformed.

Reflecting Anglicans' penchant for doing theology liturgically, the Book of Common Prayer also serves as a formative textual touch-stone. Crucial to the theology of the Book of Common Prayer is the service of Holy Baptism, which is celebrated publicly in the midst of the whole congregation. Within that service is a covenant begun by candidates for baptism and their sponsors and joined by the whole congregation. It asks, "Will you seek and serve Christ in all persons, loving your neighbor as yourself?" and "Will you strive for justice and peace and respect the dignity of every human being?" These may well be the words most often cited in Episcopal Church conversation about LGBTQI people. The call to respect the human dignity of LGBTQI people and to strive for justice on their behalf is considered by many Episcopalians to be fundamental to their baptismal identities.

Another set of emerging texts in the Episcopal Church LGBTQI conversation, also liturgical, centers on Christian marriage, or "holy matrimony." At the beginning of the 2015 General Convention, Epis-copalians had three services of Christian marriage in the Book of Common Prayer.[18] These texts refer to the married couple as male and female and link holy matrimony to three divinely intended "goods": the "mutual joy" of the couple; "for the help and comfort given one another in prosperity and adversity"; and, finally, "when it is God's will, for the procreation of children and their nurture in the knowledge and love of the Lord." As debate about opening up holy matrimony to same-sex couples has unfolded, several questions have come to the fore: How to interpret that qualifying phrase "when it is God's will"? How to understand the concept of procreation? How strongly must procreation rely upon a binary understanding of male and female? Is there not a broadly spiritual Christian theology of fruitfulness, and indeed of adoption—the very mechanism of baptis-mal incorporation into the body of Christ—that couples can and do fulfill regardless of whether they have children?[19]

In response to a resolution passed at the 2009 General Conven-tion, a liturgy was designed for same-sex couples to have services of blessing in dioceses where that was authorized.[20] Some dioceses with civil marriage equality adapted that rite into a service of Chris-tian marriage, while the wider church worked toward full liturgical marriage equality. Between 2012 and 2015, proposals emerged to remove gender-specific language from the marriage canon as well as to create services of holy matrimony that were flexible enough to be used by all couples.[21] These texts, along with the canon change proposals, were designed to move the Episcopal Church closer to liturgical marriage equality. Full marriage equality in the Episcopal Church will arrive only when the marriage rites of the Book of Common Prayer contain these (or other adapted) rites. Because prayerbook revision takes many years, the church has voted to live into that process by authorizing the new marriage liturgies, as well as the previous official blessing liturgy, so that all couples may access marriage in the Episcopal Church. While, by canon, clergy remain free to refuse to perform marriages with which they are uncomfortable, any dioceses, parishes, or clergy who are unwilling to facilitate the marriages of same-sex couples must create a pathway to accommodate them.[22]

ENCOUNTERING LGBTQI ISSUES

As the previous discussion suggests, the Episcopal Church's official current stance is broadly supportive of LGBTQI persons, even as there remain some dioceses and individuals who oppose the ministerial leadership and liturgical celebration of LGBTQI people. The work of fully incorporating LGBTQI people in the Episcopal Church has come a very long way, even as much work remains to be done and even as some branches of the Anglican Communion critique the church's progressive shift.

Since the mid-1970s the General Convention has passed numerous resolutions decrying anti-LGBTQI patterns both within and outside the borders of the church.[23] IntegrityUSA, an organization founded by Louie Clay (née Crew) in 1974, marked the earliest organized grassroots efforts in support of sexual minorities in the Episcopal Church. In 1976 the General Convention passed a landmark resolution (1976-A069) declaring: "Resolved, that it is the sense of this General Convention that homosexual persons are children of God and have a full and equal claim with all other persons upon the love, acceptance, and pastoral concern and care of the Church." As Rev. Michael Hopkins has remarked on this resolution, "For the first time in its history, the Church had spoken the name of homosexual people without condemnation.... It was a Red Sea crossing experience."[24]

Another watershed moment followed in 1977 when Bishop Paul Moore ordained an openly lesbian woman, Rev. Ellen Barrett, in the Diocese of New York.[25] The well-known priest and civil rights advocate Rev. Malcolm Boyd put another face on the reality of cisgender gay and lesbian clergy in the Episcopal Church when he came out a year later in his book *Take Off the Masks*.[26] So, too, did Rev. Dr. Carter Heyward in 1979, already well known as one of the first women ordained in the Episcopal Church five years earlier.[27] The 1989 ordination of Rev. Robert Williams, an openly gay man, by Bishop John Shelby Spong, intensified the church's ongoing debate.[28] Then, in 1994 Bishop Walter Righter was acquitted in a heresy trial that sought judgment upon his ordination of another openly gay man, Rev. Barry Stopfel, in 1990.[29] As a result of that trial, questions of human sexuality were deemed not to be matters of "core doctrine." In the years after that acquittal, controversies over cisgender openly gay and lesbian priests and deacons seemed to die down, while new touch points emerged: the episcopate (bishops), liturgies of blessing (later of marriage) for same-sex couples, and ministry of and with transgender people.

Thus, in 2003, when a partnered, openly gay man, Rev. Gene Robinson, was elected bishop by the Diocese of New Hampshire, conversation about sexuality in the Episcopal Church was by no means new. Yet, in crossing this particular threshold of leadership and representation, that conversation suddenly skyrocketed into a worldwide debate within the Anglican Communion. Prior to Bishop Robinson's election, there had indeed been some groups who had left the Episcopal Church; they left over the emergence of the current, 1979 edition of the Book of Common Prayer and over the ordination of women in the mid-1970s. This time divisions unfolded in closer connection to more conservative branches of the Anglican Communion. Given that the Anglican Communion has never been bound together as closely as other worldwide churches in the Christian tradition other parts of the communion sought ways to regulate Episcopal Church membership in the communion.[30] Within the Episcopal Church itself, a quasi-moratorium on the election of further openly LGBTQI bishops was passed at the 2006 General Convention, but it was essentially overturned in 2009. The 2010 consecration of Bishop Mary Glasspool, an openly lesbian woman who became a bishop for the Diocese of Los Angeles, marked its definitive end.[31]

During these same tumultuous years, transgender Episcopalians began to organize to seek structural, canonical changes to aid in the growing work of supporting transgender people in all facets of church life. Although transgender clergy and lay leaders were already present in the Episcopal Church, as well as in the Church of England, dating at least to the late 1990s, many experienced a sense of isolation, which began to dissipate through the founding of the group TransEpiscopal in 2005.[32] Working in coalition with several other Episcopal peace and justice groups, including the Consultation, IntegrityUSA, and the Chicago Consultation, the group advocated for the addition of "gender identity and expression" to the church's nondiscrimination canons regarding access to both lay and ordained ministry.[33] That goal was achieved at the General Convention in 2012. Amid that effort, the 2009 General Convention went on record decrying anti-transgender violence and calling for the passage of a fully inclusive federal Employment Non-Discrimination Act. As of this writing, the Episcopal Church has some of the most progressive policies regarding transgender people among faith traditions in the United States. It has several openly transgender clergy, transgender people are increasingly coming into its congregations, and at least two diocesan cathedrals annually host Transgender Day of Remembrance observances on November 20, standing in solidarity with the wider transgender community in the face of an ongoing epidemic of violence, particularly against transgender women of color. At the same time, the hard work of fully living into the values it has proclaimed in a consistent way across dioceses and congregations remains before the Episcopal Church. This is the call to greater education and to sensitive pastoral support for transgender youth and their families as well as for transgender people who are themselves parents. It is a call to deeper conversion, to opening the church's eyes more widely to the mystery of the human person and to the ways in which people so often seek to contain or squelch that mystery.

That call continues to reverberate as well in the Episcopal Church's ongoing work to open more widely LGBTQI access to its worship life. In addition to taking steps on liturgical marriage equality, the 2015 General Convention also approved a plan to add a name-change liturgy to its revised and expanded *Book of Occasional Services*. As of this writing, the Church of England is soon to have a discussion at its General Synod about developing a name-change rite specifically for transgender people.[34] The convergence between these two branches of the Anglican Communion on this topic is striking, particularly since the Church of England does not yet officially affirm openly gay, lesbian, and bisexual partnered clergy, nor does it have liturgical marriage equality. It also just appointed its first women to serve as bishops in 2014, having opened up ordained ministry to women in 1994.[35]

TRADITION AND TRANSFORMATION

The Episcopal Church's own history of social change regarding women in ministry and its engagement in the civil rights movement are both linked in important ways to its more recent moves in support of LGBTQI people. Its work on civil rights and its ongoing conversation about the structural sin of racism stretches beyond the civil rights movement of the 1950s and '60s to much earlier chapters of the church's life.[36] The conversations have been severalfold, seeking over time to incorporate people of all races in congregational life; to lift up and empower communities of color, including via ordained leadership; and to continue illumining and critiquing the church's struggle with racism, including its direct participation in slavery and in the broader economic system of the slave trade. Thus, in its liturgical celebrations of the saints—which the Episcopal Church defines more broadly than do other Christian traditions—the church uplifts historic leaders such as Rev. Absalom Jones, who was the first African American Episcopal priest, as well as Rev. Pauli Murray, the first African American woman priest.[37] It remembers ministers like Rev. Deacon David Pendleton Oakerhater, who served Indigenous Episcopal communities in Oklahoma.[38] And in recognition that such celebration does not, in and of itself, eradicate the ongoing sin of racism, it has issued pastoral letters and instituted anti-racism trainings.[39] As the systemic evil of terrorist white supremacy showed its full horror just prior to the 2015 General Convention, with burnings of black churches unfolding even as deputies and bishops began their work, the convention offered a formal acknowledgment "of our historic and contemporary participation in this evil and repent of it."[40] In the midst of this, the convention also elected with great elation its first African American presiding bishop, Rt. Rev. Michael Curry.[41]

Bishop Curry's election follows that of the first woman presiding bishop, The Most Rev. Katharine Jefferts Schori, whose nine-year term from 2006 to 2015 brought the Episcopal Church's ongoing conversation about women's leadership to a new level.[42] That conversation emerged from the civil rights movement, as a number of those involved in the latter used some of the same tools of engagement and resistance to help bring the church into a new era in recognizing the gifts of women at all levels of church life. In 1970 women were officially admitted as deputies to the General Convention, albeit as laity only.[43] The same convention also affirmed women as able to be ordained fully into the order of the diaconate, and not kept in the second-class category of deaconesses.[44] In July 1974, after years of organizing for women's equality in the Episcopal Church, eleven women were ordained in Philadelphia as priests. Through the controversy that ensued, the Episcopal Church was catapulted forward in recognition both of its emerging women leaders and of the ongoing presence of sexism and misogyny in its midst.[45] The Rt. Rev. Barbara C. Harris was consecrated the first woman bishop in the Episcopal Church in February 1989.[46] Bishop Harris, an African American woman and longtime social justice leader in the Episcopal Church, continues to challenge the church to fight systemic racism, sexism, classism, homophobia, and transphobia in its own life and in the wider world. The willingness of these most recent leaders to challenge the church to support sexual and gender minorities, as well as to point out the interlocking character of systems of oppression, has added crucial momentum to the Episcopal Church's efforts in support of LGBTQI people.

LOOKING FORWARD

Emerging trends in the Episcopal Church are hinted at in the passage of two resolutions at the 2015 General Convention. One is the continuation of a task force on marriage charged with exploring constructions of family and sexual ethics, particularly for those who are not married and do not necessarily discern a call to marriage.[47] How might the Episcopal Church produce resources for having real, theologically grounded conversations about sexuality that are not stifled in advance by the position that sexuality can only be legitimately discussed in relation to celibacy or marriage? How might Episcopalians honor much more fully the gifts of bisexual Episcopalians, whose existence has barely been acknowledged in conversations to date? The further emergence of transgender Episcopalians is another anticipated trend, particularly genderqueer or gender non-binary people, whose gender identities and expressions exceed and complicate the duality of male and female. How might the church recognize more fully and respond to the disproportionate transphobic and transmisogynistic violence directed at transgender women, particularly transgender women of color? How might the church begin to recognize and alleviate the exclusionary forms of second-wave radical feminism that have sought to exclude transgender women from women's spaces? A further area of emergence is in the support of LGBTQI youth. How might congregations and youth groups support youth who are coming out as gay, lesbian, bisexual, queer, or asexual? As intersex, transgender, gender non-binary, and/or genderqueer? These are just some of the ways in which the Episcopal Church can take up more fully the baptismal call to strive for justice among all people and to respect the dignity of every human being—indeed, to grow more fully into the stature of Christ.

SUGGESTED RESOURCES

The Archives of the Episcopal Church, www.episcopalarchives.org.

Cheng, Patrick. *Rainbow Theology: Bridging Race, Sexuality, and Spirit.* New York: Seabury Books, 2013.

Curry, Michael B. *Crazy Christians: A Call to Follow Jesus.* New York: Morehouse, 2013.

Holmes, Urban T. *What Is Anglicanism?* Anglican Studies Series. Harrisburg, PA: Morehouse, 1982.

Sedgwick, Timothy F. *Sex, Moral Teaching, and the Unity of the Church: A Study of the Episcopal Church.* New York: Morehouse, 2014.

First Nations (Native American)

Alex Wilson, EdD

I am a mother—a lesbian mother. I am a grandmother—a lesbian grandmother. I am the lesbian daughter of my mother and father. I am the lesbian lover of women. I am the lesbian partner of Denise. I am the lesbian being who welcomes Heron, Turtle and Moose into my life. I am the lesbian being who prays with words, heart and body. I am a Two-Spirit woman of the Mohawk Nation. I am a lesbian who listens to the spirits who guide me. I am a Two Spirit who walks this path my ancestors cleared for us.[1]

—Beth Brant

LAYING THE GROUNDWORK

Indigenous peoples across what we now call North America are diverse, each group with its own distinct culture, language, and spiritual understandings, beliefs, and practices.[2] At the same time, there is commonality in some aspects of our cultures and spirituality and in our historical and present-day experiences. For example, we understand that we have been on this landmass continuously for fifty

Alex Wilson, EdD, of the Opaskwayak Cree Nation, is an associate professor and the academic director of the Aboriginal Education Research Centre at the University of Saskatchewan. Her scholarship has greatly contributed to building and sharing knowledge about two-spirit identity, history, and teachings; Indigenous research methodologies; anti-oppressive education; and the prevention of violence in the lives of Indigenous peoples. As a community activist and Idle No More organizer, her work also focuses on interventions that prevent the destruction of land and water.

thousand years or more, and, as our origin stories tell us, we evolved from these lands and waters.[3] Our sense of ourselves in the world is, and has always been, inseparable from the land and waters that birthed and now nurture and sustain us.

In traditional Indigenous spiritualities, we do not look to an individual or specific people as the founder(s) or leader(s). Rather, we find guidance in a Great Mystery—the recognition that while we cannot know everything, we are connected to everything by a spiritual energy, joining us in a circle that reaches out as far as the stars, constellations, and cosmos and that encompasses the whole of our past, present, and future. We are all related.

This understanding shapes and is reflected in our languages. The Cree language of my community is ordered, organized, or gendered around whether something is animate—meaning that it has a spiritual purpose and a spiritual energy—or inanimate. The Cree term *aski* expresses our relationality—it means "land" and all of the relationships connected to land, including water, air, and so on. It expresses our understanding of what land means; we, the land and waters, the plants, animals, and other living creatures are all related. The term *mino pimatisiwin* refers to our relational accountability, that is, our responsibility to live in conscious connection with the land and living things in a way that creates and sustains balance—or, as my father translates from our dialect, to live beautifully.

A form of humility comes along with knowing that, as people, we are part of something bigger. None of us is endowed with absolute authority or knowingness. We recognize Elders, pipe carriers, Sundance leaders, and others who have significant or special understanding, knowledge, or experiences that others do not have. We also understand that everyone comes into the world with gifts or talents, perhaps, for example, the ability to paddle, the ability to communicate and work with animals, or the ability to connect with the spirits. A person's gifts may simply emerge as experience calls them forth, or they may be discovered or developed by working, whether for years or for a lifetime, with a mentor, an Elder, or another person from whom they can learn.

In Canada and the United States, every First Nation or Indigenous nation has gone through colonization and, with that, sustained attempts to assimilate its citizens. The historical era, extent, and manner in which colonization was imposed and the impacts of these experiences differ within and across nations, but as part of this process, the practice or expression of traditional spirituality was made illegal in both Canada and the United States.

Over this time, traditional spirituality went underground, and many of our people were forced or chose to adopt or adapt Christian practices. Even after the prohibition was lifted and it again became legal to practice traditional spirituality, people were still affected by the disruption of the continuity of their spiritual practices. Many who had adopted Christianity continued to worship in those churches, although Christian practice in our communities is often infused with traditional spiritual practices. For example, Catholicism is practiced in many Pueblo communities, but in some of these communities, traditional ceremonies, led by Pueblo head persons or by Catholic priests, have been adapted to celebrate Catholic holidays. The Native American Church mixes traditional practices from midwestern and southwestern Indigenous peoples with Christianity. As with other aspects of our traditional cultures, we find ways to reconnect or maintain our connections to traditional spirituality.

FOUNDATIONAL NARRATIVES

Historically, if there was an equivalent to the Bible, Qur'an, or other authoritative text in traditional Indigenous spirituality, it was the land. In all Indigenous nations in Canada and the United States, knowledge that we gathered on the land was transferred orally in stories, songs, chants, or recitations of family lineages. These are the foundational narratives that tell us who we are, why we are here, and how we can be in this world. A main character in Cree traditional stories is Weesageychak, a trickster, who, when the story was told in our language, was not assigned a gender. The implicit understanding of gender and sexual diversity communicated by the absence of gender-distinct words in Cree is lost, however, when the story is told in modern settings or translated into English, which requires gender attribution. In these retellings, Weesageychak is transformed into a male, and new meanings that reflect the semantic burdens of Christianity and heteropatriarchy that the English language carries are ascribed to these very old stories.[4]

In this sense, the main texts that are now brought to bear on Indigenous LGBTQI personhood include the Christian Bible, dictionaries, and the Indian Act. The Bible has become authoritative, in part, because it has been translated into every Native language in the world and published in Canada not only in Roman orthography but also in syllabics, an orthography created by a missionary while he was working to Christianize and assimilate Indigenous peoples within the traditional territories of the Swampy Cree. Syllabics were also used in dictionaries of the Cree and other Indigenous languages, texts written primarily by ministers or priests from Catholic or other Christian denominations. These dictionaries were carefully censored, eliding from our languages any terms or concepts that challenged a Western worldview, such as spiritual understandings about sexual and gender diversity, or our responsibility to care for and nurture the well-being of the land, waters, and living things. Today people in my community who are trying to learn or recover our language rely on those texts, the dictionaries and Bibles that were written to assimilate us into a Christian, heteropatriarchal, and hierarchic worldview.

The Indian Act was passed in 1876, nine years after Canada was formed. The act placed control of the everyday lives of Indigenous peoples and communities in Canada in the hands of the federal government. With the Indian Act's passage, government agents traveled through our settlements and communities and developed lists that identified who among our people it would now recognize as Indigenous ("status Indians," a category of being that now belongs only to some descendants of the people included in the agents' lists). Those of us whom the agents did not find and add to their lists suddenly were no longer, in a legal sense, who we knew ourselves to be. Those of us who were (un)lucky enough to be identified as "status Indians" became legal wards of the state. We were confined to small reserves, typically located within our larger traditional territories on tracts of land that were considered undesirable in the new settler economy, and our well-developed governance systems were replaced with a chief and council system designed and overseen by the government.

The purpose and intent of the Indian Act was to assimilate Indigenous peoples out of existence. Removing and controlling our access to the vast expanses of our traditional territories was a way to remove and control our access to our identity, our sense of ourselves that is shaped by the spiritual values of relationality and relational account-ability to the land, waters, and living things. The act's regulations and descriptions of Indian identity were deeply heteropatriarchal. Until 1985, if a woman with "Indian status" married a person who was non-Indigenous or Indigenous without status, the government would legally strip her, and her children, of status. Without status, she would lose the right to live on her reserve. The obverse was true for men with status: if they married an Indigenous or non-Indigenous person without status, she would gain status.

This and other aspects of the Indian Act introduced regulation of the body (and the heart) into Indigenous communities, leaving little room for the acceptance of diverse gender and sexual identities that had once been common in our communities. The act has been revised repeatedly, carefully fine-tuned to meet the needs of main-stream society at any given time and steadily chipping away at the cul-turally distinct values and ways of being of Indigenous peoples. It was the legal tool that enabled the government to prohibit, for a seventy-five-year period that did not end until 1951, ceremonies such as the Sundance and the Potlatch, ceremonial dances, and other spiritual practices that express our fundamental spiritual principles of rela-tionality and relational accountability.

ENCOUNTERING LGBTQI ISSUES

There is a long history of acceptance of gender diversity and sexual diversity within Indigenous nations of North America. We know this, in part, because it was recorded in texts produced by Europeans at the time of first contact and then later by anthropologists who cata-logued our cultures. More significantly, we also know this from the more authentic records of our own people—our stories, ceremonies, languages, and ways of being. As discussed earlier, all Indigenous peoples in Canada and the United States have experienced coloniza-tion and parallel attempts at assimilation. This disruptive and invasive dynamic has corrupted and relegated as inconsequential Indigenous peoples' traditional knowledge and spirituality and made room for values and practices from settler culture to seep into our cultures.

For Indigenous LGBTQI people, this means we are now subject to racism, sexism, misogyny, homophobia, and transphobia both in mainstream society and in our home communities. The extent to which these interconnected oppressions are manifested and normalized in our communities depends on several factors, including the number and kinds of churches in a community and the extent to which spiritual leaders, both inside and outside the churches, promote or challenge these various forms of oppression. For example, in the early 1980s, queer Indigenous peoples were hit hard by the HIV and AIDS epidemic, and over a short period, many died. In Canada, a federal law was in place that prevented anyone who died from HIV/AIDS-related illnesses from being buried on a reserve, the home community of many people with HIV or AIDS. In some communities, active resistance developed around this issue, as family members (in particular, mothers, aunties, and grandmothers) recognized the homophobia and AIDS phobia that drove the law. Ultimately, a group of women lobbied the federal government, and the law was changed so that their relatives could be buried with their other family and community members. That experience generated a significant positive shift in thinking in many communities, including my own.

Although they are manifested less openly than they were a few decades ago, homophobia and transphobia still linger in our communities. In combination with the ongoing racism directed at Indigenous people, the misogyny and sexism directed at women and transgender people, and the seemingly insoluble poverty that prevails in our communities, Indigenous LGBTQI people—youth in particular—continue to be at risk. Homelessness is increasing for Indigenous youth, and school dropout and forced-out rates, HIV infection, and suicide rates are elevated within this group. Transgender Indigenous youth often leave school around the time that they recognize and name their identity and, following this, are often forced out of or feel that they have to leave their families or homes and so become homeless.

TRADITION AND TRANSFORMATION

In response to their experiences of multiple forms of oppression, Indigenous LGBTQI people are finding strength in their culturally distinct identities. In the 1990s, a relatively small group of LGBTQI people from several Indigenous nations throughout Canada and the United States recognized the need for a term to describe themselves that would acknowledge and affirm their Indigenous identity, their spiritual connection to the land, and the spiritual values that recognize and accept gender and sexual diversity. They, like the Mohawk author Beth Brant, whose words open this chapter, named themselves "two spirit." They also began to explore, ask about, and talk more freely and openly about words from their own language that refer to two-spirit, gender, and sexually diverse people. For example, Dine culture recognizes multiple genders, and there are different forms of Dine language for each of those genders. In other cultures, including my own, a term for queerness does not exist because queer people were simply seen as part of the circle. As part of this cultural resurgence, there is greater understanding of the recognition of and respect for sexual and gender diversity in traditional cultures.

The term "two spirit" emerged as an act of empowerment for both individual two-spirit people and the larger community. It has been embraced widely by Indigenous LGBTQI people, and with that a range of meanings has been attributed to it. "Two spirit" was developed as a term to describe our connection to traditional understandings of sexual and gender diversity, but some have taken it to mean that we are positioning ourselves on a continuum that ranges between "female" and "male." Others see it as an expression of our connection to the land—or the physical and material—and the spiritual worlds. I understand it as a multidimensional and multi-liminal space in which we bring to any moment both our experiences of multiple forms of oppression and our possession of multiple forms of empowered identity, where we are in relationship with the land, the people, our animal and other guardian spirits, the star spirits, and our own souls.

As an invented term that uses the English language to express our identity, "two spirit" encourages non-Indigenous people to acknowledge the complexity of our distinct identity. The term recognizes the importance of spirituality and spiritual traditions, but in claiming our identity as two-spirit people, we are not proclaiming ourselves as people who, by our nature, are extraordinarily spiritually gifted. A young person who is just coming to understand their sexuality typically wants to be part of a community where they are seen and valued as the person they are. As a community, two-spirit people can offer that to each other. Within Western culture, however, two-spirit people are often romanticized, recast in flattening stereotypes excavated from the writings of European explorers and more contemporary anthropologists—strange beings whose sexuality somehow makes them hyper-spiritual. This is not who we are.

There has been considerable discussion within Indigenous communities about who can rightfully call themselves two spirit, and the general agreement seems to be that the term should be reserved for Indigenous people—that is, people who are descendants of the original peoples of these lands. Many of our community members feel that when a non-Indigenous person identifies themself as two spirit, it is an act of cultural appropriation. At powwows and in other contexts, non-Indigenous people may be welcome to come and observe our ceremonies, celebrations, or other aspects of our culture. Non-Indigenous people may also be invited to participate in ceremonies, but this does not typically happen unless we are confident that the person invited will participate in a way that respects the protocols, values, and intent associated with the ceremony. It is particularly important that non-Indigenous people do not impose their own meanings on our ceremonies or spirituality or exploit them for their own personal ends or for profit.[5] Each two-spirit person has their own understanding of what that identity means, but for all of us, our present-day and historical experiences as Indigenous people are an essential component of that identity.

Soon after Indigenous LGBTQI people identified as two spirit in the 1990s, the two-spirit community began to organize gatherings that would offer them a safe space to socialize, share their understandings around sexual and gender diversity, and participate in ceremonies. Two-spirit gatherings quickly became annual events, and today there are many gatherings held each year at locations throughout the United States and Canada. At more local levels, two-spirit people have organized drum groups for ceremonies, powwows, and other significant events such as Pride celebrations. At the two-spirit powwow in the San Francisco Bay Area, the rigid gender categories that have become a standard feature of the powwow circuit have been stripped off, and dancers are welcome to participate in the regalia and steps of their choice. Two-spirit sweat lodges have been built, and there are now Sundances that are led and attended only by two-spirit people. Change has also occurred outside the two-spirit community.

In many of our home communities, our identity has been recognized, and the term "two spirit" appears, for example, in literature produced by local organizations and in casual conversations between community members.

LOOKING FORWARD

Today, some young Indigenous LGBTQI people are searching for a new term to describe their identity. Two-spirit identity has helped to empower Indigenous LGBQTI people and increased understanding of gender and sexual diversity in our communities. From these young people's perspective, however, the term has been described as a placeholder, and what is needed now is a term that makes it clear that gender and sexuality are fluid, flexible, and queer (that is, disinterested in becoming "normal") states of being.

Another exciting change is the emergence of the concept of "coming in." Two-spirit or Indigenous LGBTQI people's stories of how they grew into their identities are often very different from conventional "coming out" stories, which typically feature a declaration of an independent identity: an LGBTQI person gathers up their courage, tells a friend or family member who they are, and, more often than not, are met with resistance, anger, rejection, abandonment, or violence. Coming in is about individual identities while also about collective community building. Our coming in stories are about recognizing ourselves as Indigenous people who are LGBTQI people and then, fully present in that identity, coming in to relationships with our biological, found, or created families and communities. Like the term "two spirit," the concept of coming in fits us well. People are using the term and have developed coming in ceremonies to welcome, embrace, and honor two-spirit people within Indigenous traditional spirituality.[6]

SUGGESTED RESOURCES

Jacobs, Sue-Ellen, Wesley Thomas, and Sabine Lang, eds. *Two-Spirit People: Native American Gender Identity, Sexuality, and Spirituality.* Urbana: University of Illinois Press, 1997.

Malone, Kelly. *Journey of Indigenous Gender Identity.* CKOM, November 9, 2014. http://ckom.com/article/194879/video-journey-indigenous -gender-identity.

Pruden, Harlan. *Two-Spirit Resource Directory.* National Confederacy of Two-Spirit Organizations and NorthEast Two-Spirit Society, September 2013. www.ne2ss.org/wp-content/uploads/2013/10/two -spirit-resource-directory-september-2013-1.pdf.

"Queering Culture." *Awaye!* Australian Broadcasting Corporation. March 7, 2015. www.abc.net.au/radionational/programs/awaye /queering-culture/6280254.

Wilson, Alex. "How We Find Ourselves: Identity Development and Two-Spirit People." *Harvard Educational Review* 66, no. 2 (Summer 1996): 303–18.

Hinduism

Ruth Vanita, PhD

Whatever is done in a hidden manner becomes a wrong act and is treated as a sin. But whatever is done openly does invite criticism for some time but ultimately gains acceptance. Why not give them the liberty to live in their own way, if they are going to do it anyway?[1]

—Pandit Shailendra Shri Sheshnarayan Ji Vaidyaka

LAYING THE GROUNDWORK

The term "Hindu" is used to refer to the many indigenous religious traditions of India that have certain foundational doctrines in common but vary widely in practice. Hinduism's central doctrine of rebirth distinguishes it from the Abrahamic religions; this doctrine was adopted by the other three Indic religions: Buddhism, Sikhism, and Jainism. The term "Hindu" was originally used by West Asian Muslims to refer to all the non-Muslim inhabitants of India, but today Buddhism, Jainism, and Sikhism are considered separate religions.

Unlike all of these other religions, Hinduism has no one founder; the four Veda Samhitas (literally, collections of knowledge, ca. 1500–1200 BCE[2]) are considered its foundational texts, and the Gods worshipped by the inhabitants of the Indus Valley civilizations (flourished ca. 3500 BCE) appear to have much in common

Raised and educated in India, **Ruth Vanita, PhD**, taught at Delhi University for many years and was founding co-editor of *Manushi*, India's first nationwide feminist magazine. She is the author of several books, including the pioneering *Same-Sex Love in India* (with Saleem Kidwai) and has translated major works of fiction and poetry from Hindi and Urdu into English. She recently wrote the entry on gender and sexuality for *Brill's Encyclopedia of Hinduism* and is a professor at the University of Montana.

with later Hindu Gods.[3] The Upanishads (ca. 1200–800 BCE), commentaries on the Vedas, are philosophical texts that adumbrate the doctrines of what later came to be called Hinduism. Central among these doctrines is the idea that both matter and spirit are real (some schools of Hindu philosophy consider them two independent principles, while others consider matter a fluid and ever-changing projection of unchanging spirit) and the idea that everything in the universe is a manifestation of one, or two, principles. Buddhism and Jainism (founded in the sixth century BCE) rejected both the notion of the reality of consciousness or spirit—human or divine—as well as the authority of the Vedas.

Most Hindus consider the many Gods and Goddesses as manifestations of one consciousness, even while the reality of their separate identities is endorsed, just as all individual living beings, both human and nonhuman, are considered not ultimately different from each other even though their individual being is real in the present. In the epics the Ramayana and the Mahabharata (ca. 500–100 BCE; the latter contains the Bhagavad Gita) and the Puranas (story cycles about the Gods, ca. fourth to fourteenth centuries CE), the Vedic Gods and Goddesses develop into a pantheon that is widely worshipped today. The Vedic sacred rituals come to be supplemented by a wide range of devotional practices, wherein any person can offer a variety of items to their chosen God or Goddess without a priest's aid.

Today, the ancient texts, composed in Sanskrit, are little read, but late medieval and modern versions of the epics in several Indian languages (the Indian government recognizes twenty-four official languages) are widely recited and enacted and have been made into popular TV serials and movies. Also, parts of the Sanskrit originals are often recited at life-cycle rituals such as weddings, and tags or phrases from them are popularly known and repeated. There are thousands of sacred books and millions of teachers (gurus) revered by different Hindu communities.

A fundamental tenet of Hinduism is that all devotional paths are valid (though some may be more efficacious than others) and that all lead to the same goal: liberation from the cycle of rebirth. This has helped Hinduism to survive while most other ancient religions were erased by the advance of Christianity, Buddhism, and Islam. It has also enabled the development of syncretic cultures, whereby, for example, large numbers of Hindus worship in Sikh temples, adopt Jain practices, and regularly visit churches and the shrines (*dargah*) of Muslim saints. Many Hindus incorporate icons of Buddha, Jesus, and Mary into their shrines at home.

SIGNIFICANT BRANCHES

With over a billion Hindus worldwide, Hinduism is the world's third-largest religion, practiced by one-sixth of humanity. Most Hindus live in India and Nepal—both secular democracies with Hindu majorities—with significant and mostly prosperous, highly educated communities in Europe, the United States, Canada, Australia, and New Zealand, and small, impoverished groups in Pakistan and Bangladesh. There are also older migrant groups in Indonesia, Fiji, Malaysia, Singapore, and the Caribbean.

Historically, Hindus, like Jews, have not sought converts; this changed to some degree in the twentieth century. The vast majority of Hindus are still of Indian origin, but there is a significant minority of non-Indian Hindus. While some undergo conversion ceremonies, no ceremony is required to become a part of the Hindu religion. Anyone can begin practicing Hindu devotion, and many non-Indians, largely through New Age movements, have incorporated Hindu ideas and icons into their worship. Many American and European celebrities have either become followers of particular gurus or been deeply influenced by exposure to Hindu doctrine and practice; among them are several gay, lesbian, and bisexual people, such as Baba Ram Dass (Richard Alpert), Allen Ginsberg, Andrew Harvey, and Swami Shraddhananda (Sonya Jones).

Hindus are traditionally categorized into Vaishnavas (worshipers of preserver-God Vishnu and his many incarnations, such as Rama and Krishna), Shaivas (worshipers of Shiva and associated deities), and Shaktas (worshipers of Goddesses, such as the mother-goddesses Durga and Kali; the Goddess of learning and the arts, Saraswati; and the Goddess of prosperity, Lakshmi). Every God or Goddess is viewed as incorporating all possibilities, being simultaneously male, female, and neuter, as well as human, animal, plant, and divine. The Gods are able to transform at will; thus, Vishnu has ten incarnations, including human and animal ones, and also takes the form of a woman, Mohini (the enchanting one). This is not cross-dressing; it expresses the truth that Gods are not limited by categories such as gender or species, which are temporary and fluid for all of us, changing from birth to birth. Most Hindus worship many divinities together, and most modern temples accommodate a number of them while generally being devoted to one prominent God or Goddess.

Dualist Hindus believe in the eternal dyad of divinity and devotee. The most visible converts to this type of practice in the United States from the 1960s onwards were members of the International Society for Krishna Consciousness (ISKCON, popularly known as the Hare Krishna movement), still an extremely prosperous and powerful group, with several subgroups.

Non-dualists (Advaita Vedanta) believe that spirit is the ultimate indivisible reality of which all individual beings and objects are manifestations. These Hindus also worship deities, but as stepping-stones to the ultimate reality, which is without name and form. There are several variations on these positions, such as Dvaitadvaita (dualistic non-dualism).

Hindus have no one leader. Renunciants (those of any class, caste, or gender who choose to renounce all worldly categories and concerns and devote themselves to spiritual practice, often visible by their saffron robes) were organized into ten orders by the eighth-century leader Adi Shankaracharya. Spiritual attainment is generally thought to be nearly impossible without a guru. Ordinary Hindus pick their own guru from among the millions available, just as they pick their own *ishta devata* (God chosen for special worship). Today, many lay Hindus have no guru; they simply worship on their own.

Priests who conduct temple worship are distinct from gurus; they are generally married men, while gurus may be either male or female and are usually celibate. There are renowned priestly hierarchies at major temples and pilgrimage centers in India. The head priests of these hierarchies have special but not unique authority.

Gurus meet disciples one-on-one and also establish communities that meet regularly for worship, singing, and discourses. These days, many gurus have communities of lay disciples, which they visit regularly, in numerous places all over India as well as in many other countries. The first major guru to bring Hinduism to the United States was Swami Vivekananda. He was followed by many others. Active lay disciples take on responsibilities of fund-raising, organizing meetings, hosting the guru, and outreach. These disciples significantly influence the direction that the community takes.

Hindus visit temples regularly or occasionally, but most worship at home and at natural sites considered sacred, such as rivers, mountains, trees, and rocks. Some of the most popular Gods take animal or semi-animal forms, and many animals and plants are worshipped as particularly sacred. This is often misunderstood as idolatry, whereas it in fact expresses the Hindu idea that everything and everyone is a manifestation of the divine, the only difference being that some are more fully realized and others less realized manifestations. The home-based nature of Hindu worship, with the shrine traditionally being maintained in the purest place, the kitchen, and daily worship usually being conducted by the woman of the family, made it hard for more centrally organized conversion religions to eradicate Hinduism. Temples and idols could be attacked and destroyed (and rebuilt by worshipers later), but worship in the home and of divinities such as fire could not be as easily erased.

FOUNDATIONAL NARRATIVES

Hindu texts can be divided into three types—those that discuss philosophy, those that analyze society and lay down rules (treatises on medicine, law, and eroticism), and those that tell stories with symbolic and philosophical significance. The philosophical texts, such as the Upanishads (ca. 1200–800 BCE), outline how human beings can achieve the four goals of life: *dharma* (fulfilling the law of one's being), *artha* (material, including monetary, success), *kama* (desire, including sexual desire), and, most importantly, *moksha* (liberation from the cycle of rebirths).[4]

When a being is reborn, all its attributes (species, class, caste, gender, physical appearance, and abilities) may change, but attachments such as love or hatred persist from birth to birth. The Gods can change their sex, species, and other such attributes miraculously. For humans and animals these can change from one birth to the next. But some specially blessed humans can undergo miraculous and perfect sex change within one lifetime. The best-known story of such sex change is that of Princess Amba in the ancient epic the Mahabharata. She strongly desires to be a man in her next birth in order to take revenge on a man she thinks has wronged her. However, she is reborn as a woman, Princess Shikhandini. Her father raises her as a boy and gets her married to another princess. When her wife discovers her sex, a war is about to ensue. Shikhandini manages to exchange her sex with a male forest spirit and becomes a man, Shikhandin. As a man, he is able to father children and also becomes a warrior and kills in battle the person that Amba wished to kill.

There are many lesser known stories of miraculous sex change, such as that of the king Ila (in the ancient epic the Ramayana), who wanders into a forest where Shiva has taken a female form to sport with his wife, Parvati. When Shiva becomes female, every male being in the forest also becomes female. Ila becomes a woman, and his horse becomes a mare. Distressed, Ila prays to the Gods, who agree that Ila will be a man for six months and a woman for six months. Ila is able to produce children both as a man and as a woman.

These stories of sex change demonstrate the philosophical principle that gender—like class, caste, species—is a temporary and ever-changing category. The spirit has no gender and in its physical manifestation can take on many genders.

A wide category of *ayoni*, or non-vaginal sex, appears in many texts. While this type of sex often results in the birth of Gods, heroes, and sages and is thus inscribed as miraculous in narrative texts, it is forbidden for humans. In the fourth-century legal text the *Arthashastra*, it is punishable with the first fine (4.13.236). The first fine is not a severe punishment—it is the lowest fine, payable in grades for robberies of three types of items that are not high in value. Many types of heterosexual vaginal sex are punishable much more severely. Women who have sex with each other have to pay a lower fine than do men who have sex with each other. But a woman who sleeps with an unwilling woman has to pay her a large amount of money. This text treats heterosexual vaginal sex as the norm but makes no particular distinction between oral/anal sex occurring between men or between men and women.

The law book *Manusmriti* (ca. first century BCE) appears even less judgmental in its famous prescription that a man who has sex with a man, with a woman in a cart pulled by a cow, in water, or by day should bathe with his clothes on (11.175). It prescribes that a man who sheds his semen in nonhuman females, in a man, in a menstruating woman, in something other than a vagina, or in water has to perform a minor penance consisting of eating the five products of the cow and keeping a one-night fast (11.174). This is the same penance prescribed for stealing articles of little value. Sex between non-virgin women incurs a very small fine, while a man or a woman who manually deflowers a virgin has two fingers cut off (8.367–69). This last proscription is not based on the gender of the partners but on any act that results in loss of virginity and thus has an adverse effect on a girl's chances of marriage. A virgin who manually deflowers a virgin has to pay double the girl's dowry and is given ten whiplashes.

Mutual manual stimulation or oral sex that does not involve deflowering, although nonjudgmentally described in the near-contemporaneous *Kamasutra,* a sacred treatise on the erotic life, is not mentioned in the *Manusmriti* as punishable.

Medical texts *Sushruta Samhita* and *Charaka Samhita* (ca. first century BCE to first century CE) contain the first known medicalization of same-sex desire. These texts construct categories and terminologies; for example, a man who can have an erection only by sucking the genitals and drinking the sperm of another man is termed an *a'sekya.*[5] This text also notes that if two women have intercourse, and one of them becomes pregnant, a boneless child will be born. Michael Sweet and Leonard Zwilling, writing in the *Journal of the History of Sexuality,* have demonstrated that the concept of a third sex, with various ambiguous subcategories such as *kliba, pandaka,* and *napunsaka* (all varieties of the neutered), "has been a part of the Indian worldview for nearly three thousand years."[6]

While legal texts lay down strict gender-coded rules of conduct, philosophical arguments, sometimes within the same text, remark that the atman, or self/spirit, is the same in all beings and has no gender; therefore, human behavior should not be measured by gender-coded rules. There is thus a contradiction between the social and the philosophical understanding of gendered behavior. The Gods and Goddesses are manifestations of the philosophical understanding, since each one is worshipped as encompassing all possibilities, including maleness and femaleness.

Hindu texts that tell stories of Gods and heroes are today much more widely known than philosophical texts. In these, many deities as well as humans are produced in non-biological ways; for example, they may spring fully formed from the head or thigh of a sage. A set of fourteenth-century devotional texts from Bengal, which I have analyzed elsewhere, narrates the story of the birth of a well-known hero, Bhagi-ratha. He is the son of two co-widows; one of them becomes miracu-lously pregnant after a divinely blessed sexual relationship between them. In some versions of the story, he is born boneless, as prescribed in the ancient medical text, and is cured by divine blessing; in other versions, he is born healthy, because his birth is inspired by the God of love, Kama. The texts provide a folk etymology of his name, relat-ing it to the word "vulva," which is one of the meanings of the word *bhaga*.[7] Here, the texts seem to imagine the possibility of babies being produced in ways other than by heterosexual intercourse.

ENCOUNTERING LGBTQI ISSUES

Hinduism has no history of persecuting gender-variant people or same-sex relations, but in the last two centuries, as a result of internal-izing the attitudes of Victorian British colonizers, many Hindus have become embarrassed about sexuality in general and same-sex sexual-ity in particular. The worship of Kama, God of love (the counterpart of the Greek Eros), a beautiful youth who shoots flowery arrows, has dwindled, and many modern, educated Hindus have grown ashamed of texts such as the *Kamasutra* and temples such as those at Konarak and Khajuraho, which are covered with elaborate sculptural friezes, including many unabashedly heteroerotic and homoerotic ones.

Until very recently, sex has almost never been talked about in public in the modern period, and even married couples almost never display affection in public. Same-sex relations are often viewed as fun or play and tacitly accepted if they do not conflict with heterosexual marriage; many same-sex couples have also lived together and been socially accepted as devoted friends, because Indian society has a long history of elevating and celebrating same-sex friendship.

Stories about same-sex relations and sex change have been lost in the vast corpus of sacred narrative and interpreted as miraculous exceptions to the norm. However, in the last couple of decades, they have also been interpreted to legitimize same-sex relationships; for example, at the wedding of one male couple in Delhi in 1993, the beautiful bachelor God Kartikeya, who is the product of Shiva's semen swallowed by the fire God Agni, was invoked. This transna-tional couple is a good example of how LGBTQI Hindus live in today's globalized world: one partner is Indian, the other British;

they lived for over two decades in San Francisco and recently relocated to New Delhi, where they are raising their twin babies born of a surrogate Indian mother. The mother of the Indian partner was among the earliest parents to go on TV and support her son. Several transnational couples based in the United States have gotten married over the last decade, combining Hindu and non-Hindu ceremonies. Some have received considerable Internet visibility.

Gender-variant people known as *hijras* have traditionally been treated with a mixture of fear, respect, and contempt in India. Although it was popularly believed that all *hijras* were intersexed and that they adopted any child born intersexed, this myth has been disproved by research. *Hijras* are almost all born biologically male; a tiny minority of them may be intersexed. Homoerotically inclined and transgendered men of economically poor communities who are discriminated against in mainstream society often run away to join the *hijras*. Some *hijras* get themselves castrated in an initiation ritual, and others do not, but most take on a female persona, wearing female clothing and taking female names. A few pass as women, but most make their *hijra* identity visible through body language and gestures. This identity helps them earn a living by singing and dancing and by blessing newlywed couples and newborn babies. Some live in long-term relationships with men, and some engage in sex work.[8] As with other traditional occupation-based communities, they tend to be restricted to these occupations, although this is now gradually changing.

Hijras live in their own hierarchically organized communities and have their own religious practices that are a mixture of Hinduism and Islam. They often worship the Goddess Bahuchara, but they also often take Muslim names and are buried instead of cremated. Some try to trace their history to *khwajasarais* (men who were forcibly castrated and who often rose to high positions) in Muslim courts. There is, however, no historical evidence of any connection. Many *hijras* also claim a Hindu third-gender status, linking themselves with stories from ancient narratives, such as that of Krishna temporarily taking the form of a woman to marry Aravan, a hero destined to die in battle whom no woman was willing to marry. *Hijras* (terming themselves *aravanis*) gather annually in large numbers in South India to celebrate the marriage and mourn the death of Aravan, identifying both as his brides and his widows.

These days, some *hijras* are adopting new identities like transgender and transsexual along with their *hijra* identity and have joined the LGBTQI movement. A few who are from educated, middle-class backgrounds have written autobiographies and frequently appear on television shows. Several have successfully stood for election to public office, and several work for nonprofit groups on issues like HIV. Some states, like Tamil Nadu, have for some time recognized *hijras* and other transsexuals as a third gender. Recently, the Supreme Court of India, which has reinstated the anti-sodomy law, nevertheless, in a separate judgment, directed the central government to recognize the rights of transsexuals as a third gender. This means that *hijras* can demand nondiscrimination and even affirmative action in education and employment.

In the last two decades, as the LGBTQI movement has developed and come into the public eye, especially in the mass media and over the Internet, there have been both positive and negative reactions to homosexuality among Hindus. Silence continues to be the norm in most Hindu sects in the United States, with both gurus and lay Hindus accepting gay and lesbian individuals and couples, but not talking about the issue. A few, based in both India and the United States, such as Swami Chinmayananda, Swami Bodhananda, and Sri Sri Ravi Shankar, have responded sympathetically when interviewed.[9] In the recent and continuing public debate about abolishing the anti-sodomy law, introduced in 1861 by British rulers in India, TV talk shows have only been able to find a couple of gurus willing to speak out for or against the law. Most have remained silent. A popular TV yoga teacher, Baba Ramdev, virulently attacked homosexuality, saying he could cure it, but at the same time, Sri Sri Ravi Shankar, a major international guru based in Bangalore, pointed to the ancient texts to insist that everyone has both male and female in them, and there is nothing unnatural or criminal about homosexuality.[10]

Priests have responded in interesting ways. Over the last thirty years, many priests have conducted weddings of female couples all over India and in the United States. When interviewed by journalists, they have often cited rebirth, noting that those who fall in love do so because they were connected in former births and that this love is therefore valid and irresistible. As early as 1975, the head priest of the major temple at Srirangam, interviewed by the author of an early book on homosexuality, had said exactly this and had also said that homosexuality is nature's way of limiting the population.[11] When I interviewed a Shaiva priest who conducted the wedding of two Indian women in Seattle in 2002, he added that according to Hindu texts, the spirit has no gender, and marriage is a union of spirits.[12] These two doctrinal arguments have worked for centuries to legitimize socially disapproved unions.

Since then, many Hindu same-sex weddings (both between Indians and between Indians and non-Indians) have been performed by Hindu priests in the United States. In 2012, as many states were moving toward marriage equality, I spoke to four Hindu priests in the United States, all of whom were willing to officiate at same-sex marriages if it was legally recognized in the state concerned.

Over the last century, several militant Hindu right-wing organizations have come to prominence in India; they are often collectively known as the Sangh Parivar. They are much more political than religious, their main goal being to toughen up Hindus in resistance to perceived attacks by Muslims and Christians; some of their founders were atheists who flouted Hindu conventions. They now have branches in the United States that help fund them and often borrow from U.S.-based right-wing Christian rhetoric.

Some of these organizations are not just homophobic but sex-phobic. One of their most publicized campaigns in India is against Valentine's Day, which they see as the product of decadent Western capitalism and which they combat by attacking dating couples and vandalizing stores and hotels celebrating the festival. They have also attacked a couple of films about lesbianism, most notably the Canadian-made film *Fire* in 1998. Their opposition, however, has not been consistent, as they have not attacked several Indian-made films about gay men, such as *My Brother Nikhil* (2005).

In India, there are no avowedly left-wing Hindu organizations, but there are a few outside India, such as the Hindu American Foundation and the New York–based group Sadhana, which are LGBTQI-affirming. Only a few LGBTQI activists have come out in India as Hindu; due to the dominance of Marxist secular ideology in left-wing circles in India, there is an embarrassment attached to belonging to a majority religion that is often stereotyped as backward, idolatrous, and oppressive of minorities.

However, the few who are out have made major strides. Ashok Row Kavi, a pioneering gay activist, was formerly a monk-in-training at the Ramakrishna mission and has written about his positive experience there, as did Christopher Isherwood much earlier, since his guru Prabhavananda also belonged to this denomination.

A non-Indian Hindu monk in ISKCON has founded the Gay and Lesbian Vaishnava Association (GALVA) in Hawaii, which is influencing this powerful and often homophobic denomination. *Trikone* magazine, founded by Indians in 1986 in San Francisco, played an instrumental role in galvanizing the India-based LGBTQI movement. It had a special issue on Hinduism and homosexuality in 1996 and has carried several articles on the subject since then. The mother of one of its founders was a guru herself, named Ma Yogashakti; initially critical of her son's sexuality, she later came around and conducted his wedding to his partner.[13]

The diversity of present-day Hindu teachers' attitudes to same-sex marriage emerged in interviews conducted at a major pilgrimage destination, the Kumbha Mela, in north India, in 2004 by Rajiv Malik, a journalist from the U.S.-based magazine *Hinduism Today*. Several teachers condemned same-sex marriage—Swami Avdheshananda called it "unnatural, uncommon and unusual"[14]—but others presented remarkable arguments in favor of it. Mahant Ram Puri, who belongs to the same lineage as Swami Avdheshananda, said, "There is a principle in all Hindu law that local always has precedence. In other words, the general rules and the general laws are always overruled by a local situation. I do not think that this is something that is decided on a theoretical level. We do not have a rule book in Hinduism. We have a hundred million authorities."[15]

Equally thoughtfully, Pandit Shailendra Shri Sheshnarayan Ji Vaidyaka pointed out that definitions change over time: "Whatever is done in a hidden manner becomes a wrong act and is treated as a sin. But whatever is done openly does invite criticism for some time but ultimately gains acceptance. Why not give them the liberty to live in their own way, if they are going to do it anyway?"[16]

However, many ordinary Hindus have internalized homophobia without any textual basis. Young people in India and in the United States frequently write about how their parents react with horror to homosexuality, viewing it as polluted and perverted. Indians in general and Hindus in particular tend to live in tight-knit families and communities, where social approval matters more than doctrinal correctness.

Hindus' attitudes are changing slowly as social attitudes change. Several young people have documented how their parents' views have evolved. More interestingly, quite apart from movements and public debates, young, low-income, non-English-speaking women in many parts of India have been declaring their love by getting married or committing joint suicide over the last thirty-five years. Some families persecute such women, driving them to suicide, but others come around to supporting them and participating in their weddings. In the earliest reported case in 1980, two young policewomen got married with family support, and one of their neighbors, a village schoolteacher, said to journalists, "After all, what is marriage? It is a wedding of two souls. Where in the scriptures is it said that it has to be between a man and a woman?"[17]

TRADITION AND TRANSFORMATION

Historically, social change in Hindu society has come about primarily through gradual modifications in social attitudes, consequent on Hinduism's very long-standing assimilative tendencies. Hindus tend to incorporate outside influences and the views of opponents by writing them into texts and into deities (as new Hindu texts and deities are always emerging) and then constructing them with retrospective effect as part of unbroken tradition. For example, after initial severe conflicts with Buddhism, Hindus wrote Buddha into the pantheon by making him one of the ten incarnations of Vishnu, and most Hindus now happily worship Buddha, revere the Dalai Lama, and visit Buddhist shrines.

Similarly, many female as well as so-called low-caste mystics opposed oppressive social customs in the course of the two-thousand-year-long medieval devotional (*bhakti*) movements. Legends of the mystics' lives include their struggles with priests and upper-caste scholars, almost always concluding with the latter undergoing a change of heart after miracles demonstrate the authenticity of the mystics' devotion. Today, Brahman priests have fully incorporated devotional traditions into ritualistic practice by the priesthood, and the two form a virtually seamless whole for most Hindus.

In the late nineteenth and early twentieth centuries, the social reform movement and the national independence movement, led by Gandhi and many others, campaigned for women's equality and caste equality. They accomplished many institutional changes in mainstream Hinduism—for example, allowing admission for so-called lower castes into temples. However, reformist sects themselves also changed, as many of their members reverted to mainstream practices such as icon worship.

Change now occurs through the interaction of these two mechanisms. Changes at the top occur much faster but have little impact on social reality until attitudes change, which they do through the older assimilative mechanism. For example, despite resistance, Hindu laws relating to marriage and inheritance were changed in 1955 by the new government of independent India, while other communities, such as Muslims and Christians, successfully resisted such legal change; however, many Hindus ignore the legal changes and continue traditional practices until attitudes change, which they do much more slowly, in accord with varying socioeconomic conditions and varying traditions among regional Hindu communities.

The younger generation of queer people is very active on social media, and this has internationalized the community. Hindu LGBTQI people of Indian origin in the United States and American LGBTQI Hindus now interact seamlessly with LGBTQI people in India on Facebook and in chat rooms. A few are now openly claiming and transforming religious rituals, creating controversy. For example, in 2012, a female activist couple in Kolkata posted Facebook pictures of themselves observing Karva Chauth, a north Indian festival wherein married women dress and adorn themselves and do no work all day, keeping a daylong fast for their husbands' longevity. Many queer activists derided the women for this observance, claiming that they were imitating heterosexual gender roles, but many rank-and-file LGBTQI people supported them.

As is common in immigrant communities, Indian Hindus in the United States, especially older people, are often more conservative and insular than their counterparts living in India. I not infrequently receive emails and phone calls from young Hindus in the United States, recounting their parents' negative reactions to their coming out; in one case, a young man was dragged to the family guru in the hope of being converted to heterosexuality. On the other hand, several Hindu gay and lesbian weddings have been performed in the United States, with priestly and familial participation. Newsletters and magazines produced by the Indian community in the United States have written sympathetically about LGBTQI movements, and members of Indian groups like Trikone and Salga regularly march in India Day parades and form Indian contingents in Gay Pride parades.

LOOKING FORWARD

Hinduism has survived through millennia by adapting, assimilating, and changing without losing its core identity. Homosexuality has never been unspeakable in Hindu textual traditions, and the discussion around it has ranged from mild disapproval to open celebration. Hindus tend to flourish by absorbing outside influences and creating new hybrid ways of life; for example, Western democratic institutions have been accepted and modified in India with considerable success. Now that the colonizers who imported modern homophobia into the religion have themselves changed their position on the issue, new scholarship is revealing the way same-sex relations have been represented in Hindu texts for centuries without any history of persecution, and LGBTQI movements are widely visible among Hindus everywhere, the future seems bright despite the naysaying of the new Hindu right-wing groups.

SUGGESTED RESOURCES

Gay and Lesbian Vaishnava Association (GALVA), http://galva108.org.

Namjoshi, Suniti. *The Conversations of Cow.* London: Women's Press, 1985.

Vanita, Ruth. *Gandhi's Tiger and Sita's Smile: Essays on Gender, Sexuality and Culture.* New Delhi: Yoda Press, 2005.

———. *Love's Rite: Same-Sex Marriage in India and the West.* New York: Palgrave-Macmillan, 2005.

Vanita, Ruth, and Saleem Kidwai, eds. *Same-Sex Love in India: Readings from Literature and History.* New York: Palgrave-Macmillan, 2000. Updated edition, Gurgaon: Penguin India, 2008.

Islam

Shehnaz Haqqani with Laury Silvers, El-Farouk Khaki, and Troy Jackson

[An Islamic law professor told her class] that she had gone to a Muslim camp, and the males and females had separate tents. There was a lesbian Muslim there who didn't keep her sexual identity a secret. There were too many questions for the other women to let her stay with them. They asked, "Can we show our hair in front of her? Should she be sleeping in the men's tent or the women's tent? How do we behave around her? Should we give her the right to stay with us at the expense of making every other woman uncomfortable?" And, of course, she couldn't stay in the men's tents. They had to kick her out of the camp so that everyone else could be comfortable.[1]

—Orbala, *Freedom from the Forbidden* (blog)

Shehnaz Haqqani is currently pursuing her PhD in Islamic studies from the University of Texas at Austin, concentrating on gender and sexuality in Islamic law. A native Pashtun, she is invested in gender matters among Pashtuns in the diaspora. She blogs on matters pertinent to contemporary Muslims, Islam, and Pashtuns, emphasizing the need for mainstream Muslims to recognize and work toward a gender-egalitarian Islam that embraces feminist and LGBTQI initiatives.

Laury Silvers co-founded the Toronto Unity Mosque, the founding mosque of el-Tawhid Juma Circle, along with Troy Jackson and El-Farouk Khaki. She is presently a sessional instructor at the University of Toronto in the Department for the Study of Religion. **El-Farouk Khaki** is a refugee lawyer who spearheaded within Canada's refugee system the representation of LGBTQI+ people and women fleeing gender-based violence and is founder of Salaam: Queer Muslim Community and co-founder of el-Tawhid Juma Circle. **Troy Jackson** is president and co-founder of the el-Tawhid Juma Circle and Toronto Unity Mosque.

LAYING THE GROUNDWORK

Every religion and secular ideology has had its profoundly difficult moment in history. Islam's moment is now. It is particularly difficult to discuss the complex social and historical realities of Islam as well as the profound diversity of experiences of Muslims in the present political climate.

There is no such thing as "Islam," meaning there is not now and never has been a monolithic religious community of people identified as followers of the Prophet Muhammad. The assumption that Muslims all think and act in unison is reinforced by the bombardment of images in the media of worshipers bending over uniformly in prayer around the world. Muslims live in every populated region of the world; so, yes, given the timing of the five ritual daily prayers to the rising and setting of the sun, some Muslims somewhere are always facing Mecca and bending in prostration in worship of God. But look more closely and one might recognize the diversity in dress, in ritual form both in how the body moves and what one recites, and in spaces used for prayer. More closely still and one might hear the unique inward attitudes and experiences of worship, especially in the context of LGBTQI Muslims.

FOUNDATIONAL NARRATIVES

Muslims are followers of the Prophet Muhammad, whom they believe brought a revelation from God in the form of recited verses and then a written book, the Qur'an. In short, the message of the Qur'an is that there is only one God, the God of Muhammad and all the prophets who have come before, who calls people to live an ethical life through submission to God's will; they will be judged in the afterlife for the degree to which they have submitted or not to God's will. Muhammad received his first revelation in the year 610 CE while he was meditating in a cave near Mecca, in present-day Saudi Arabia. He continued to receive them for another twenty-three years, when he shared the final verses with his community just prior to his death. The recitation is understood to have so overwhelmed him that his character became the living embodiment of the Qur'an itself. The transmitted memories of his embodied understanding of the Qur'an are called the Sunna, or the Prophet's "Way." Those individual memories are known as hadith, or "reports," of what Muhammad said, did, accepted, or rejected.

Muslims understand full well that many of those memories are either misremembered or outright fabricated, but those stories remain important to the ways that individual Muslims and communities imagine the person of the Prophet. For instance, in a well-known story of a cat that fell asleep on Muhammad's cloak, he cut the cloak rather than disturb the cat. Whether or not it is true, most Muslims certainly prefer to remember this and other numerous accounts of his acts of kindness to all creatures, including human beings, whereas others prefer to remember him as made of much sterner stuff—kind to cats perhaps, but uncompromising when it came to other matters. How any one Muslim or Muslim community remembers him guides how that person or community understands the Qur'an and thus God's will for Muslims. Most Muslims find it impossible to believe that one could read the Qur'an and find any justification for the violence of terrorism, whereas others find it everywhere they look. The plea made by many Muslims that "Islam is peace" is not a lie to those who say it. It is an honest expression of their unqualified love of the Prophet's peaceful character and thus their understanding of the core message of the Qur'an. LGBTQI Muslims, likewise, have diverse understandings of the Qur'an and Muhammad, some seeing the well as poisoned, while others find it the very source of their life and faith.

Muslims typically present their textual tradition as a simple matter. They read the Qur'an and look to the Prophet for guidance in understanding it. But as mentioned above, readings are indelibly tied to differences in social and historical contexts. Thus, differences in understanding the message began even in Muhammad's community. This is most often articulated through the depiction of the different members of the Prophet's family and companions. For instance, Ali is characterized by his great nobility and inner restraint; Abu Bakr is characterized by his gentleness and forethought; and Umar by his rash temper and his skills as a military and imperial leader. All were attentive followers of Muhammad's example, yet all embodied his example in distinct ways in keeping with their distinct personalities.

SIGNIFICANT BRANCHES

Major political divisions arose after Muhammad's death in 632 CE and ultimately divided the community into distinct sects known as the Sunni and the Shia. But the groupings of Sunni and Shia encompass myriad subgroups, each organized around different religious leaders, theology, and schools of religious law. Among the Sunnis the extant groups are the Hanafi, the Maliki, the Shafi`i, and the Hanbali schools; among the Shia are the Ja`fari, Zaidi, and Isma`ili schools. The division between Sunnis and Shia is conventionally attributed to a lack of certainty over Muhammad's intentions for a successor. Those who would become known as the Sunnis gathered to choose a successor among themselves, selecting Abu Bakr, the Prophet's father-in-law, as the next leader. Those who would become known as the Shia believed that leadership was inherited and so they supported Ali, the Prophet's son-in-law and cousin. Globally, Sunnis are the majority, and the various Shia groups are the second largest Muslim community, followed by the Ahmadiyya, African American Muslim movements, and others.[2]

Sunni and Shia Muslims work with similar yet sufficiently different interpretive methodologies in trying to understand what God wants from them as articulated in the Qur'an and through Muhammad's example. It is not as straightforward as one might think to determine what constitutes even the most basic command of God to Muslims or how to fulfill it. For example, the ritual prayer is mentioned numerous times in the Qur'an, but the Qur'an does not actually describe how to do it. The specifics on how to perform the prayer come from Muhammad's example, which is remembered differently by different people. Later legal scholars working with different interpretive methods accepted, rejected, or understood these accounts differently, resulting in distinct movements in the prayer, exactly what to say in them, and even exactly when to perform them. Although Muslims may say that they are following a "timeless" law, nothing could be further from the truth. For all Muslims, no matter their sect, law and even theology are constantly shifting to account for changing times and circumstances.[3]

ENCOUNTERING LGBTQI ISSUES

The Qur'an says little about same-sex relations. For example, there is only one passage that seems to address directly same-sex sexual activity, but it does so only in the context of forbidding adultery and fornication for all people no matter their partner (4:15–16). The earliest commentators of the Qur'an do not seem to have read the story of Lot, for instance, as referring to male-on-male sex. In fact, only in the modern period did the crime of the people of Sodom come to be explicitly associated with what we understand to be homosexuality. In only one case does a commentator refer to male-on-male sex, which comes to be known as *liwat* (in honor of Lot).[4] In another case, the reference is patently benign. What might now be called "queerness" or a "third sex" is acknowledged in the Qur'an when it speaks of the permissibility of male-bodied persons without any desire for women to keep company with them (24:31). The hadith mention men who dress effeminately who even kept company with Muhammad's wives.[5] They may even have had a place specific to them in ritual prayer, standing in between the rows of men and the rows of women.[6]

From a historical perspective, Muslims in early Islamic societies did not have a sense of binary gender or sexuality. They did not consider there to be two genders as we typically speak of today: male and female corresponding to conventionally understood male and female bodies. Or, rather, gender was broken down into two categories: men and not-men. "Men" were cisgender/heterosexual-presenting free males. Not-men were cisgender males who dressed effeminately, cisgender males who were known as "bottoms" (meaning that they were penetrated during anal sex, not penetrators), non-cisgender bodies, female-bodied persons, and the enslaved. Homoerotic desire and homosexual relationships were embedded into the social order of premodern Arab cultures.[7] In premodern Islam, men's desire for male adolescents was celebrated in poetry such as that by the famed Abu Nuwas, who used explicit sexual details in his work, while others spoke merely of longing.[8] Male-on-male sex had its place as long as one was not on the bottom. "Tops" were understood to be simply pursuing sexual satisfaction, whereas "bottoms" were seen as disturbed individuals because they took a "feminine" role in the sex act.[9] Women's same-sex desire was rarely remarked on, because as far as classical scholars were able to imagine, it did not involve penetration and posed little threat to the social order as long as the women held up their role in the family.[10] There was a rich political, literary, and scholarly history of the contributions of "not-men."

But not all same-sex relations were considered acceptable or went unprosecuted. The legal history of what to do with those who have intercourse with someone of the same sex is as complex and varied as the rest of the tradition. In general, legal scholars were most concerned with anal penetration in particular (whether it is a male- or female-bodied person penetrated). Premodern Shia rulings and the Sunni Maliki school of law seem to be the harshest, prescribing execution for penetration. Other Sunni schools took different approaches. For the Shafi'is, it was treated as fornication or adultery, resulting in lashes and a year's banishment from society for the unmarried male or execution for the married male. The Hanafis preferred to leave it to the judge's discretion on a case-by-case basis. Ibn Hazm (d. 1064), a medieval Muslim scholar and philosopher, argued against execution, suggesting there should be no more than ten lashes and a period of imprisonment. Without a thorough study of court rulings on cases such as these, it is difficult to know how these laws might have affected people in daily life. For instance, the burden of proof to convict someone of a capital crime is very high. Thus, those accused of homosexual acts in regions where same-sex acts were punishable by execution might be easily acquitted, but they would nevertheless be made to suffer devastating social shame for themselves and their families. Courts that accepted Ibn Hazm's more lenient views, however, marking same-sex acts as lesser crimes, had a much lower burden of proof, resulting in more convictions.

Reflecting on the extraordinary diversity of Muslim cultures globally, there have always been distinct notions of gender and sexuality in keeping with local needs and expectations. Thus, there have always been distinct ways in which society organizes human bodies around these notions, ways that continue to disrupt prevalent Euro-American assumptions of heteronormative binaries of woman/female and man/male. The *hijra* in South Asia (legally recognized in Pakistan),[11] the *khanith* in the Gulf[12] or *mukhannath* in Medina,[13] *bissu* (among five genders) among the Buginese people of Indonesia,[14] the *waria* in Indonesian culture at large,[15] and the "sworn virgins" in Albania are all examples of non-binary gender and sexuality in Muslim-majority societies.[16] Many Muslims who would be typically characterized as "homosexuals" deny the term as an imposition of binary Western modes of sexual and gender identity, preferring to understand themselves in more culturally traditional terms of spectrum gender and sexual identity. Ironically, Euro-American assumptions about binary gender and sexuality, even assumptions about homosexuality as an innate identity, are considered limiting by some Muslims whose traditional view is more expansive.[17] At the same time, there are many Muslims who do associate themselves with Euro-American norms of gender and sexuality. In those Muslim-majority societies in which Pride marches have been held, one is likely to see a spectrum of Muslim LGBTQI gender and sexuality expressions.[18]

But it should be made perfectly clear that the social organization of these genders and sexes is not without terrifying repercussions in their particular communities, even in supposedly tolerant countries such as Turkey.[19] Executions and forced gender transitions of gay Muslims in Iran are a case in point.[20] But outright persecution, marginalization, and highly qualified acceptance of queer Muslims occur in more complicated contexts than is portrayed in media accounts in both Muslim-majority and non-Muslim regions of the world. For example, the Saud family—those who founded and continue to rule Saudi Arabia—came to rule over Arabia alongside a conservative religious movement now typically known as Wahhabism. These conservative religious scholars have a great deal of popular power; ordinary people will listen to them about what is religiously acceptable or not. If these scholars were to declare the Saud family corrupt or "un-Islamic," the family would have a hard time holding onto their power. As a result, more progressive members of the Saud family can do nothing to prevent human rights abuses. By the same token, because the United States and other countries are so dependent on oil from Arab Gulf states and military bases, they likewise will do little or nothing to demand change in Saudi society. It is not "Islam" that leads to the persecution of LGBTQI Muslims in these regions; persecution is the result of the intersection of certain ways of reading Islam and a complex geopolitical-economic environment.

Contemporary North American attitudes toward homosexuality have been changing. Young conservative Muslim university students who have gay friends have been pressing nationally known religious leaders to respond to their confusion about or acceptance of their gay friends.[21] If these leaders are to remain relevant to their communities, they cannot simply reiterate their old positions. Leaders like

Hamza Yusuf of Zaytuna College, a Muslim liberal arts college in California, have shifted their opinions to claiming that homosexuality is inborn instead of being a "choice," although he and others continue to construe the desire to act on it as akin to the desire to commit a criminal act, which must be suppressed.[22] The youth-oriented organization Taleef Collective is welcoming to queer Muslims.[23] Queer Muslims can attend their meetings with their partners and be open about their identities. This does not mean the leaders accept them as they are, only that they are making a safe space for them to come and worship.[24]

For Muslims globally, but especially in North America, blogs have become a safer space in which difficult conversations, such as homosexuality and Islam, can be explored. Writing a blog under the pen name Orbala, Shehnaz Haqqani shared her experience with young American Muslims struggling to accept and understand their homosexual peers. In this post, she recalls a class discussion (referenced in the opening quotation of this chapter) about a Muslim camping trip in which an openly identified lesbian was removed as a result of the questions that her sexual identity generated. Comments on the blog reveal the confusion and discomfort of young Muslims' experience around queerness. One male commenter expressed that he would be uncomfortable and even scared "sleeping in the same room as a gay man"—unless the gay man, he later notes, is a "'bottom gay,' apparently the type that 'receives only.'" Another male commenter insisted that homosexuality is "unnatural" and not something to be encouraged, but it should also not be discriminated against; he does, however, support gay marriage "if the population wants it."[25]

Intrigued by the responses, Haqqani formally interviewed young Muslims living in and around Austin, Texas, to get a better sense of their views on gender, sexuality, and Islam. Their attitudes markedly differed depending on whether the hypothetical gay person was Muslim or non-Muslim.[26] When she asked her subjects if they would ever befriend a person who identified as homosexual, almost all responded positively, although one individual said he would befriend them only to guide them to heterosexuality. However, when Haqqani specified whether they would befriend Muslims who identified as homosexual, the initial response was almost always some variation of

"A Muslim homosexual? There's no such thing," with some subjects visibly flinching at the question.

Braving the rejection of their peers, queer Muslims who worship in conservative communities have been blogging about their experiences and their self-understanding. Ife Okoye, whose essay appears in the collection *Love InshAllah: The Secret Love Lives of American Muslim Women*,[27] writes openly about coming out in her community and the difficulties she faces.[28] Her posts and the comments she receives support Haqqani's observations demonstrating a real struggle to understand and accept her queerness but also a real concern that she have a place in a community that nevertheless offers her only qualified acceptance. The blog *A Sober Second Look* offers an unflinching and critically sophisticated look at the intersection of LGBTQI identity and the construction and positioning of female bodies and identity in Muslim ritual and social spaces.[29]

TRADITION AND TRANSFORMATION

Examining the ways Islam has dealt with the challenge of gender power dynamics can shed light on how we might progress with LGBTQI integration, especially since the two have always been intertwined. The religious marginalization of LGBTQI Muslims and that of Muslim women are connected, in great part because female-bodied Muslim queers are doubly caught up in heteropatriarchal systems of power.[30] Anyone who does not adequately conform to cisgender maleness is "other." This point is significant because it enables us to make a case regarding the cooperation of Muslim women and LGBTQI Muslims, both of whom are historically marginalized and suppressed categories. Their historical marginalization allows them to unite for a gender-egalitarian cause.

LGBTQI Muslims and straight Muslim women have always had common cause; thus tracking the changes in one community means tracking the changes in both. How bodies are dressed, how they act, where they are placed, and whether or not something is placed in them is of the utmost importance. With respect to the mosque, if one is not dressed "like a man," one's "place" is in between men and women. "Men" are the focal point around whom others—the not-men—are located: women are behind men or to the side; eunuchs, because they are physically male, are behind men but in front of women. One does not stand where one likes, but one is instead given a location that identifies one's social and ritual status exactly.

Despite the gender and sexual fluidity of premodern and, in some cases, contemporary, Muslim societies globally, queers and women typically have been marginalized from centers of religious authority through the control of their bodies. In contemporary North America, debates are carried on about whether homosexual men or any woman may lead the congregational ritual prayer.[31] To lead is to stand ahead of the congregation, and means that one's ritual prayer stands in for all those who follow. Can a homosexual male's or a woman's prayer stand in for a heterosexual man's prayer if they do not share equal status?[32] The answer has been no in almost every case.[33] They are both out of the place of authority. As a result, breaking down the barriers for LGBTQI Muslims has also meant breaking down the barriers for women.

Cisgender heterosexual women have not always seen it that way. Muslim women who might be natural allies in the struggle against dominant male religious authority have not always considered homosexuality and faith to be compatible. Other Muslim women may be allies in private but do not share their thoughts publicly for fear of alienating mainstream Muslims from the cause for women's rights. But there are those who have been openly allied with LGBTQI Muslims, and that number seems to be growing.

LGBTQI Muslim activists and religious leaders, such as Imam Daayiee Abdullah,[34] Muhsin Hendriks,[35] and El-Farouk Khaki, Junaid Jahangir,[36] have generally understood that women's full place in the Muslim community and in religious authority is part and parcel of their own. Even if some gay male activists are unsure about the permissibility of women leading prayer, they understand women's religious authority as essential to change.[37] A male body, even a gay male body, leading prayer is not the obvious break with straight male power that the body of a woman standing before men would be.

Although it may have been unplanned, it is not surprising that the first woman-led prayer in North America was performed by a queer woman at a conference and retreat for LGBTQI Muslims. Al-Fatiha, founded by Faisal Alam in 1998 as an outreach educational and support group for LGBTQI Muslims, has spread across twenty-five countries and has fourteen working chapters in the United States alone.[38] No one knew who would be leading the prayer at the first conference. Alam said that he was not in the room when Ghazala Anwar was chosen by the group. He reported that he came into the room and there she was standing before the crowd to lead the afternoon prayer. In Anwar's account, shared below, one can feel the excitement of the moment and see how deeply the break with male-centered power affects those who have traditionally been understood to be "not-men" in one way or another:

> It was at a time when no other academic or religious leader was willing to be seen near the LGBT community. A room was designated for prayer and when we all gathered there I was asked to lead, spontaneously, and so I did. I remember that many men cried when that happened. The important thing is that this prayer was not staged, or planned, it was spontaneous and an imperative of our faith. It seemed that I was considered an elder and a leader of the community by those around me. The focus and goal was to pray in congregation as an expression of our faith. Many came and thanked me afterwards, some still come up and thank me.[39]

Anwar perceived the need for permanent alternative spaces in which each human being had the right to any place in the room, eventually encouraging El-Farouk Khaki to take the first steps that would lead to the establishment of el-Tawhid Juma Circle, an LGBTQI-open mosque.

The differences in form of the Islamic prayer do not just mark regional or legal differences; they also serve to enforce gender and sexuality norms. Men were commanded by early legal authorities (and still in some schools of law) to take power poses with arms spread out and taking up as much space as possible, whereas women were commanded to restrict their bodily movements and lower their voices. Closing one's body in on itself is a behaviorally submissive pose that has been shown to reduce testosterone levels and raise cortisol.[40] Consider how much more disempowering these gendered distinctions are for genderqueer Muslims who must adopt either "male" or "female" postures in order to pray; in effect, such postures require them to lie about themselves in order to be in God's presence. It is ironic that men take a power pose in prayer given that the goal of prayer is submission to God. Too often, men have remarked that women have the advantage in submitting to God because of the social and personal disempowerment they experience at the hands of men. A disempowering form of the prayer follows the same logic. The conundrum is that it works. In a disempowered state, it is easier to accept the divine command because you are used to giving up your autonomy. You may not experience it negatively given the results. Of course, none of this can be so simply said, since the effects of ritualized behavior are diverse in keeping with a person's intersecting positions of power and authority. For instance, a religious leader's wife may perform a submissive pose and in doing so gain respect and authority in her community as a result.[41] Nevertheless, that form of prayer is rooted in efforts to mark social hierarchies, not in bringing women or the genderqueer closer to God. In other words, just because one is able to transform injustice into personal growth does not mean the injustice is a "good" thing.

For those who do not find spiritual health in these formations of faith and practice, their relationship with God becomes rooted in cognitive and embodied dissonance. Such dissonance affects straight men, too, but women and the genderqueer are most at risk. Because these marginalized groups do not fit as others do, they may experience themselves, their minds, and their bodies as unhealthy, sinful, even perhaps unacceptable to God. They learn that the pain of accepting dissonance is the mark of their struggle to transform themselves into true servants of God.

LOOKING FORWARD

El-Tawhid Juma Circle, an LGBTQI-open mosque in Toronto that can serve as a model community, believes that breaking out of cognitive and embodied dissonance requires cognitive and embodied habituation to what scholar Amina Wadud names the Tawhidic Principle.[42] The space must be one in which human beings can embody divine oneness by recognizing that their relationships with each other are on the horizontal plane and refrain from mediating between any other individual and God on the vertical plane. Wadud has described it as a triangle in which God is at the top, with "self" and "other" at the two points beneath. Each has an individual relationship with God and a relationship of reciprocal community with each other. Wadud argues that to mediate between another and God is nothing other than idolatry because the mediator forces another to accept that satisfying the mediator's expectations is the same as satisfying God.[43]

Several related ground rules guide the establishment and maintenance of el-Tawhid Juma Circle's LGBTQI spaces. They are rooted in the assumption that all human beings, all families, all bodies, and all loves are equal. First, everyone is an imam, a prayer leader. Second, people must be free to stand and sit where they feel comfortable. Third, people must be free to physically express themselves and dress in a way that befits their own relationship with God. Fourth, people must be free to express their experience without correction or silencing.

Everyone has equal access to all possible roles in ritual leadership. Imagine a mosque in which those of all abilities, all gender and sexual expressions, all bodies, all expressions of Islam, and all language abilities are welcome to call out to God by leading the prayer, giving a sermon, making the call to prayer, offering the group supplications, making tea, doing outreach, and sharing in each other's sorrows and joys. Imagine a mosque in which there is no side entrance for anyone (as there has been historically), either literally or metaphorically.[44] This is the vision of the founders and members of el-Tawhid Juma Circle. They say that they pray as they do in Mecca, without segregation of any sort, but it is more than that. Those who have experienced sitting behind and without access to the imam may want to sit and stand in front. Those who have felt they had to hide at the sides or the back because their sexual identity opened them to humiliation or worse at other mosques may want to stand in the center or in the front. Families may want to sit together so children are not separated from their parents, so parents can care for the children together, and so that they may experience community life in prayer together. Men who come to them because they reject the social hierarchy of mosque organization may want to stand in the back to reject the "right" to stand in front.

It seems that from the beginning, LGBTQI Muslim organizations have been inclusive of all intersectional marginalities, whether that be sectarian (no breakdown of Sunni and Shia), interfaith (all seekers of God are welcome), gender and sexual expression, race, class, or ability. The organization of el-Tawhid followed that clarity for the need for total human justice, an outlook that El-Farouk Khaki and Troy Jackson call "human positive." The el-Tawhid community considers it an imperative of their faith to make the ritual prayer together as an expression of faith in a God of all-encompassing unity, openness, justice, and love.

SUGGESTED RESOURCES

Babayan, Kathryn, and Afsaneh Najmabadi, eds. *Islamicate Sexualities: Translations across Temporal Geographies of Desire.* Cambridge, MA: Harvard University Press, 2008.

Habib, Samra. *Female Homosexuality in the Middle East: Histories and Representations.* Routledge Research in Gender and Society. New York: Routledge, 2009.

———, ed. *Islam and Homosexuality.* 2 vols. Santa Barbara, CA: Praeger, 2009.

Jahangir, J. B., and H. Abdul Latif. *Islamic Law and Muslim Same-Sex Unions.* Lanham, MD: Lexington Books, forthcoming.

Kugle, Scott Siraj al-Haqq. *Homosexuality in Islam: Critical Reflection on Gay, Lesbian, and Transgender Muslims.* Oxford: Oneworld, 2010.

———, ed. *Living Out Islam: Voices of Gay, Lesbian, and Transgender Muslims.* New York: New York University Press, 2013.

Judaism

Rabbi Jane Rachel Litman

Whenever love depends on some selfish end, when the end passes away, the love passes away; but if it does not depend on some selfish end, it will never pass away. Which love depended on a selfish end? This was the love of Amnon and Tamar. And which did not depend on a selfish end? This was the love of David and Jonathan.

Pirkei Avot 5:15

LAYING THE GROUNDWORK

Ancient Israelite culture and its religious component were the direct antecedents to Judaism. However, Judaism itself, as distinct from the ancient Israelite religion, emerged in the early centuries before the Common Era, in Israel and possibly Babylonia as a synagogue- and home-based alternative to the sacrificial system and hereditary priesthood of Solomon's Temple described in the Hebrew Bible. The religious leaders of early Judaism were scholars who emphasized the literary skills of writing, storytelling, and legal debate. These scholars were called rabbis (Hebrew: "my teacher") and became leaders by

Rabbi Jane Rachel Litman is the rabbi of Coastside Jewish Community in Half Moon Bay, California, and has served as the rabbi of LGBTQI outreach congregations Sha'ar Zahav and Kol Simcha. She is widely published in the fields of feminism and gay and transgender issues, and is the co-editor of *Lifecycles: Jewish Women on Biblical Themes in Contemporary Life.* Rabbi Litman consults on religious education for alternative families for the Metropolitan Community Church and National Council of Churches. She co-founded the Queer Studies Institute at California State University–Northridge and has been an LGBTQI and AIDS activist at the national level for over twenty-five years.

virtue of ability rather than heredity. One of their accomplishments was adapting much of the ritual performed in the centralized Temple in Jerusalem and relocating it into synagogues and homes in all the villages and cities where Jews resided.

By the time of the final destruction of the Temple in 70 CE, the Jewish Diaspora extended throughout the Persian and Greco-Roman empires. Thereafter, locally based Rabbinic Judaism became the religious way of life of the Jewish people. Although Judaism has continued to change and adapt over the centuries—including some major schisms (such as the emergence of Christianity), and the rise of denominations in the nineteenth century (such as Reform and Orthodox)—it follows in large part the same practice as that of the early Rabbis and their adherents.

As Europe and West Asia divided into Muslim- and Christian-dominated territories, the Jewish community similarly was culturally split into the Ashkenazi (German) Jews of western and central Europe and Sephardi/Mizrachi (Spanish/Eastern) Jews of Byzantium, North Africa, and West Asia, as well as the refugee descendants of the Jews of Islamic Spain. Demographers estimate that at present about three-quarters of Jews worldwide are Ashkenazi and one-quarter Sephardi/Mizrachi. These numbers include tens of thousands (perhaps hundreds of thousands) of Jews who were not born into Jewish families but have converted to Judaism. Jews currently live throughout the world, and there are major Jewish communities in North and South America, Israel, Europe, South Africa, and Australia.

Judaism asserts the existence of one God, Creator of heaven and earth and all that is in them. Jewish theology explicitly refuted both the polytheistic Greco-Roman and the dualistic Zoroastrian belief systems of the surrounding cultures. Thus, unlike the Greco-Roman gods, who are capricious in their use of supernatural power, the Jewish God is supremely concerned with morality. Unlike dualistic Zoroastrianism, which posits the two supreme forces of good and evil in a constant struggle, the Jewish God is unique and undivided, all-powerful and sovereign over everything, including what humans might understand as evil. Judaism teaches that human beings are created in the moral image of God, able to differentiate between good and evil, and have the free choice and responsibility to do so.

The theological trajectory of Judaism is from Creation to Redemption; Judaism is primarily rationalistic and positivist, although there have been significant mystical movements within it. Relatively early in Jewish development, many Jews became deeply attached to their hope for a military leader who would overthrow the Romans and restore national sovereignty to the Jewish people. Eventually this longing became spiritualized and transformed into belief in a Messiah (Hebrew: "anointed one") who would bring Redemption at the end of time. The status of Jews as a minority in other cultures and the ongoing persecution and oppression of Jews—in both the Christian and the Islamic spheres—have served as impetus to significant theological and cultural creativity within Jewish thought, particularly in relation to theodicy (which attempts to explain why a moral, all-powerful God allows evil) and eschatology (what happens at the end of time).

An interesting aspect of Judaism is that actions and behavior supersede belief, and contemporary Jews hold a wide array of beliefs about God, morality, and the end of time, without these beliefs having much impact on their Jewish identity. In many ways, Judaism is the religious expression of the Jewish people or "tribe," and being a "member of the tribe," that is, belonging to the people, is considered more important than any particular belief or set of beliefs.

FOUNDATIONAL NARRATIVES

Jews are often called "the People of the Book," because text plays a major role in Jewish observance and thought. The primary texts of Judaism are the Hebrew Bible and Rabbinic writings such as the Midrash (narrative stories about the Bible) and the Talmud (an extensive legal and narrative compendium compiled around 500 CE). Texts from the medieval period and since the advent of the printing press also shed considerable light on Jewish religious culture but generally are not considered part of the religious canon. Historically, Judaism has understood the Hebrew Bible as the product of divine revelation and inspiration.

The canonization of the Hebrew Bible provided a textual foundation for Jewish life and is often called the Written Torah (Hebrew: "teaching"). The Rabbis added their writings to it, designating them as the Oral Torah. Some parts of the Oral Torah were passed down verbally for possibly hundreds of years. The Rabbis themselves date the Oral Torah back to Moses, but this is not accepted by modern scholarship. In order to address changing circumstances, the Oral Torah contained a process of interpretation of the Written Torah. Interpretation thus replaced revelation as the path to God's wisdom, and the process of legal interpretation is known as halacha (Hebrew: literally "the way"; generally it is used to designate Jewish law).

The halachic process balances flexibility and continuity and gives rabbis a great deal of leeway in interpretation. Throughout Jewish history, communities have had different standards in terms of women's rights, what food is kosher or not, and what prayers are recited, among other subjects. The ongoing nature of halacha means that no denominations of Judaism, even the extremely socially conservative streams, are strict constructionists; all of Judaism exists within an interpretive practice.

In the Hebrew Bible, Genesis opens with the account of Creation. As life is created, ongoing procreation is included in the process (that is, "seed … according to its species"), but sex and gender are specified only with the creation of humankind: "God created humanity in God's own image; created in the image of God, male and female they were created"(Genesis 1:27). Subsequent to this creation of humanity in two binary genders, the Hebrew Bible assumes the existence of only two gender categories and enacts a number of laws pertaining to gender relations, particularly sex and marriage. Gay rights advocates sometimes quote this verse from Genesis, not in relation to the creation of gender, but to underscore that all people, including LGBTQI people, are created in the image of God. This verse is particularly significant to supporters of the "gay by birth" argument.

In addition, the Hebrew Bible regulates the expression of gender in terms of clothing in Deuteronomy 22:5: "Men's effects are not for a woman, and a man shall not wear a woman's garment and all who do this are (ritually) offensive to the Eternal, your God."

The single most quoted text in regard to homosexuality in general and male homosexuality in particular is the cryptic Leviticus 18:22, "Do not lie with a male as in the acts of lying with a woman; it is a (ritual) offense." The odd lack of clarity in terms of the preposition that I have translated "as in"; the use of singular, then plural, then singular in regard to the verb and object; the use of the term "male" (rather than "man") and non-parallel "woman" (rather than

"female"); and the vague meaning of the term I have translated as
"(ritual) offense" make this a very difficult biblical verse to translate
and interpret. Leviticus 20:13 is a similar text.

The charge is directed to a man, which is the norm for biblical
commandments, and seems to discuss a sexual act with a male, possibly anal sex. Most historical Jewish interpreters have seen this as
a ban on male homosexual activities. In the last forty years, a number of scholars and liberal interpreters, often relying on the cryptic nature of the Hebrew phraseology, have suggested that it applies
only to specific pagan cultic acts in ancient Israel: promiscuity, fetish-
ism, coercive sex, or group sex. The very strange Hebrew grammar
actually fits better with some of these explanations. A more creative
modern riff is that homosexual males should not mimic normative
heterosexual gender relations; that is, gay men should be proud of
their sexuality and not pretend to be heterosexual. The verse almost
certainly refers to sexual acts rather than identities/orientations as
we understand them today.

Liberal Jews also point to scriptural narratives such as the story
of Ruth and Naomi, viewing it as a lesbian love story, in which the
two women create a thriving, loving extended family across cultural
boundaries and heal the losses of the past. Similarly, some modern
commentators understand the tale of David and Jonathan as a gay
love story. They explain that David and Jonathan forged a bond of
trust that cut across politics and power. David's elegy for Jonathan,
"How pleasant was your love to me; it surpassed the love of women"
(2 Samuel 1:26), with its explicit gender comparison seems to support this view. Seen in this light, the characters of Naomi, Ruth, and
David are bisexual, Jonathan is gay, and Boaz is a co-parent in a non-
traditional family structure.

The formative period of Judaism (ca. 200 BCE–500 CE) is marked
by both the canonization of the Hebrew Bible and the emergence of
legal and narrative commentaries written by the Rabbis/Sages.

The Rabbis look favorably on the love relationship between David
and Jonathan:

> Whenever love depends on some selfish end, when the
> end passes away, the love passes away; but if it does not
> depend on some selfish end, it will never pass away.
> Which love depended on a selfish end? This was the love

of Amnon and Tamar. And which did not depend on a selfish end? This was the love of David and Jonathan.

—*Pirkei Avot* 5:15

However, the Sages ban same-sex marriage. The Talmud teaches that same-sex marriages are universally forbidden, rather than forbidden merely to Jews (*Chullin* 92a), and the Rabbis reject so-called Egyptian practices in which "a man married a man, a woman married a woman, and a woman married two men" (Sifra, *Acharei Mot* 8:8–9).

Lesbian sexual activity ("women rubbing one on the other") is discussed in the Talmud in relation to whether lesbian sex disqualifies a woman from virginity. The Sages rule that it does not (*Yevamot* 76a). The act of male homosexual anal sex is explicitly discussed and forbidden for both the penetrator and the recipient (*Sanhedrin* 54b).

Unlike the Hebrew Bible, Rabbinic legal texts explore at least four and perhaps as many as six gender categories. The Sages teach that each of the genders has certain kinds of rights and restrictions. The concluding thought on this topic is attributed to Rabbi Yose, who teaches, "An androgyne, he is a case unto herself, and the Sages made no decision whether it is a man or woman" (*Mishnah Bikkurim* 4:5).

The Talmud also tells the story of a miraculous gender transition:

Our Rabbis taught: It once happened that a man's wife died and left behind a nursing child, and the man could not afford to pay a wet nurse. A miracle happened to him and his breasts opened like a woman's breasts and he nursed his son.

Rabbi Yosef said: "Come and see how great this man was, that such a miracle was performed for him!"

Abayye responded to him: "Just the opposite: how terrible was this man, that the order of Creation was changed!"

Rabbi Yehudah said: "Come and see how difficult it is to provide sustenance to a human being, that the order of Creation had to be changed!"

—*Shabbat* 53b

This story can be read as either supporting or condemning gender transition.

The verse in Genesis stating that human beings are created in
God's image, so often quoted by contemporary liberal authorities in
regard to LGBTQI inclusion, is also the basis for an early Rabbinic
midrash (Hebrew: literally, "interpretation," usually a narrative) on
human gender identity:

> Rabbi Samuel bar Nachman said: "At the time that the
> Holy One, Blessed Be He, created the human, God cre-
> ated him as an *androgynos*."
>
> Resh Lakish said that at the time that [Adam] was
> created, he was made with two faces, and [God] sliced
> him and gave him two backs, a female one and a male
> one, as it says: "And He took from his sides" [Genesis
> 2:21, the midrash is playing with the plural form of the
> word "sides"].
>
> —*Leviticus Rabbah* 12:2

The midrash pictures Adam (Hebrew: "human") as both male and
female, each "side" as the frontal half of a man and a woman. Then
God divides the human vertically and places a back half on each
front. In Rabbinic times, this may have been a popular interpretation
of the scriptural dissonance between Genesis 1:27, which portrays the
bi-gender creation of humanity, and Genesis 2:18, which presents the
lone human for whom God must create a companion. Another version of the midrash reads:

> Rabbi Yirmiyah ben Elazar said: "At the hour when the
> Holy One, Blessed Be He, created the first human, it
> was created androgynous. As it is written, 'Male and
> female God created them.'"
>
> Rabbi Samuel bar Nachman said: "When the Holy
> One, Blessed Be He, created the first human, it was cre-
> ated with two front sides, and then God split it, creating
> for it two backs, a back here and a back there."
>
> —*Genesis Rabbah* 8:1

Regarding gender expression, the Talmud comments on the biblical
restrictions on cross-dressing:

> Why does scripture say, "Men's effects are not for a
> woman," etc.? If it were merely to teach that a man

should not dress in a woman's garment, nor a woman in a man's garment, behold it says this is an abomination, but there is no abomination just in that! It must therefore mean that a man should not put on a woman's garment and socialize with women, nor a woman a man's garment and socialize with men.

Rabbi Eliezer ben Jacob says: "How do we know that a woman should not go to war bearing arms? Scripture says, 'Men's effects are not for a woman.'"

Another interpretation of "Neither shall a man wear a woman's garment" is that a man is not to use cosmetics as women do.

—Nazir 59a

Thus, the Sages interpret the biblical verse on cross-dressing as a ban on disguise rather than on wearing gender-variant clothing, which they understand as clearly acceptable. Two minority opinions interpret the verse to indicate that women should not join the army and that men should not wear cosmetics. The relationship between men and cosmetics may have an anti-homosexual subtext. The Talmud elsewhere states:

A man should not go out to the marketplace perfumed. Rabbi Aba, the son of Rabbi Hiyya, said in the name of Rabbi Yohanan, in a place where there is apprehension about "lying with a man."

—Berachot 43b

Perhaps the most significant Jewish religious texts of the Middle Ages are the commentaries to scripture by Rabbi Isaac Shlomo Yitzchaki (Rashi, 1040–1105) and two preeminent legal codes, the *Mishneh Torah* by Moses Maimonides (ca. 1135–1204) and the *Shulchan Aruch* by Joseph Karo (1488–1575).

Rashi elaborates on the issue of clothing, gender, and sexuality by explaining that the prohibition is restricted not only to disguises, but specifically to disguises for the purpose of (hetero)sexual seduction, to obtain greater access and trust across gender lines in a relatively gender-segregated society.

The *Mishneh Torah* forbids both gay male sex acts (*Issurei Bi'ah* 1:14) and lesbian sex acts (*Issurei Bi'ah* 21:8). The *Shulchan Aruch* does not mention either gay male or lesbian sexual acts, although gay male sex acts may fall under the category of "spilling seed," which generally refers to male masturbation.

The *Shulchan Aruch* reiterates the biblical concern with the policing of gender expression and forbids men from dyeing their hair or looking in mirrors on the grounds that these activities are reserved for women (*Yoreh De'ah* 182:6). However, the *Shulchan Aruch* permits cross-dressing on Purim (the Jewish early-spring costume festival) (*Orach Chayim* 696:8). Rabbi Moses Isserles (1520–1572) in his commentary on the *Shulchan Aruch* explains: "On Purim, a man wearing women's clothing or a woman wearing the garments of a man is not prohibited, since they intend to be joyful." Other authorities prohibit cross-dressing even on Purim.

In terms of Jewish cultural, as opposed to liturgical, works, medieval writers produced an extensive collection of Jewish homoerotic love poetry written in both Hebrew and Arabic, some by the most distinguished and respected rabbis of the period. An example:

> *Delightful Spanish fawn,*
> *Creation of mighty God,*
> *Who gave him the power to rule*
> *Every living creature.*
> *His face is the beautiful moon,*
> *Atop a lovely form;*
> *His locks dark royal blue,*
> *Over a brow of pearl;*
> *Like Joseph in face;*
> *His hair like Absalom's;*
> *He is as handsome as David;*
> *And like Uriah, I am murdered.*
>
> —Isaac ibn Mar Saul, ca. tenth century

Jewish mysticism, Kabbalah, and some Jewish messianic movements of the early modern period focused on aspects of gender identity, gender expression, and gender theory, often in a transgressive manner. The adherents of Jacob Frank (1726–1791), in particular, were said to engage in cross-dressing and gender play as part of their anti-nomianism and theological drive to transcend all dichotomies.

ENCOUNTERING LGBTQI ISSUES

Nineteenth-century Europe saw the birth of both Jewish and LGBTQI identities as they are currently understood. Until this time all individual Jews were part of the Jewish collectivity and thus did not have modern personal identities. Sex and, to some extent, gender were viewed as acts or activities, and the focus was on actions rather than the person. After the Enlightenment, individuals were viewed in a different light, as distinct from their communities, and as having a sense of self related to, but not identical with, their actions. Thus, liberal Jews could eat non-kosher food and still consider themselves Jewish, and men could think of themselves as homosexual in inner orientation, an orientation distinct from sex acts.

Ashkenazi Jews such as Magnus Hirschfeld (1868–1935) and Benedict Friedlander (1866–1908) were leaders in the LGBTQI rights movement, and in 1897 Hirschfeld founded the Scientific Humanitarian Committee (SHC), the first support and advocacy group for homosexual and transgender education and rights. Hirschfeld employed the title of Moses Mendlessohn's (1729–1786) famous Jewish essay on the separation of church and state, "The Right to Be Different" (1783), as the mission statement for his committee. Many of the supporters of the SHC were influential Jews, such as Martin Buber. In America, Emma Goldman (1869–1940) advocated for gay rights and was lauded by Hirschfeld. The Hearst newspapers ridiculed Hirschfeld by calling him "the Einstein of sex." The tie between Jews and homosexuality was a constant feature of nineteenth-century anti-Semitic propaganda and continues to this day, as a casual Internet search reveals.

Nineteenth-century literature and pseudoscientific attempts at psychology and biology (some of them produced by such renowned Jews as Marcel Proust and Sigmund Freud) frequently presented all Jews as gender variant in that Jewish men were "feminine," and Jewish women "masculine." Jews and queers shared a joint position as archetypal outsiders. More organized identifiably Jewish groups, such as the religious denominations and emergent Zionist organizations, took no stand on LGBTQI issues. The burgeoning Jewish queer movement of the late nineteenth and early twentieth century was destroyed by Nazism and other forms of anti-Semitism.

In the latter half of the twentieth century, the modern gay rights movement appeared in the United States. Many secular Jews were in its early ranks. The overall Jewish community in America tended to be liberal, at least politically and socially, and was generally supportive of sexual minority rights, seeing them as equivalent to Jewish minority rights.

In 1965 the Federation of Temple Sisterhoods, the national women's organization of Reform Judaism, passed a resolution calling for the decriminalization of homosexual acts between consenting adults. However, the Reform movement as a whole failed to pass a similar resolution at its convention that year but eventually passed a much stronger resolution in 1977, as did the Reform rabbinical organization.

The decision of the women of the Reform movement to engage the issue of the rights and status of LGBTQI people during a period of increasing visibility for LGBTQI people over the last fifty years sets the stage for all the denominations and most of the secular organizations of the Jewish community to articulate a position regarding LGBTQI Jews.

SIGNIFICANT BRANCHES

Reform Judaism is a denomination within the Ashkenazi Jewish community that began in Germany in the early nineteenth century as a response to modernity. Reform Judaism instituted a set of innovations such as music during worship, mixed seating, and vernacular prayer and sermons that made Jewish practice more compatible with modern life. In addition, Reform leaders laid out an ideology that allowed for considerable flexibility in interpreting Jewish texts and norms. Reform Judaism is the largest denomination in North America.

In 1972 Beth Chayim Chadashim, the world's first LGBT outreach synagogue, was founded in Los Angeles by Jews who were inspired by the model of the Metropolitan Community Church. They applied for congregational membership in the Reform movement and were admitted. Jews in other cities followed suit, and now there are over twenty LGBTQI outreach congregations in North America, many affiliated with the Reform movement.

Over the next forty years, the Reform movement adopted a number of increasingly powerful stances and resolutions in support of LGBTQI people. These included over a dozen positions articulated by all the various organizational arms of the movement, including its youth groups, educators, and rabbis. A number of semi-closeted Reform rabbis and their personal friends were key to moving forward much of this political work, and in 1989 the movement began ordaining openly gay and lesbian rabbis. In the year 2003, the movement voted to extend all previous resolutions to include bisexual and transgender people in addition to gay and lesbian people.

In 2000 the seminary of the Reform movement established the Institute for Judaism, Sexual Orientation & Gender Identity to "educate HUC-JIR [Hebrew Union College–Jewish Institute of Religion] students on lesbian, gay, bisexual, and transgender issues to help them challenge and eliminate homophobia and heterosexism; and to learn tools to be able to transform the communities they encounter into ones that are inclusive and welcoming of LGBT Jews." It is the first and only institute of its kind in the Jewish world. There are several dozen LGBTQI Reform rabbis, many serving mainstream congregations. In 2015 Rabbi Denise Eger became the first LGBTQI president of the Reform movement's rabbinical organization.

Soon after the founding of Reform Judaism, some Jewish religious authorities reacted with hostility to its innovations. They founded the Orthodox movement in Germany in the mid-nineteenth century. Orthodox Judaism is not monolithic and has a Modern Orthodox faction, a *Haredi* (Hebrew: "rejectionist") faction, an ultra-Orthodox faction, and a number of Hasidic (Hebrew: "pious") factions that are descended from a populist movement in eighteenth-century Poland. Sephardi/Mizrachi Jews have a different historical path from Ashkenazi Jews, in that there was no Reform movement in their geographical regions. Now most of them live in Israel and tend to identify as Orthodox.

In the last thirty years, the Orthodox movement and its rabbis have, sometimes reluctantly, taken a number of stands regarding male homosexuality, lesbianism, bisexuality, and transgenderism. These have ranged from overt hostility and condemnation to compassionate tolerance based on a medical illness or disability model.

Over 150 Israeli Orthodox rabbis, both Ashkenazi and Sephardi/Mizrachi, have signed a statement intended to promote acceptance of male homosexuals. It forbids anal intercourse but not homosexual orientation per se, rejects heterosexual marriage for gay men, forbids casting discreet gay men out of the community, and allows a gay man to be counted in the religious prayer quorum and to maintain all other religious rights.

A statement by over one hundred North American Modern Orthodox rabbis and lay leaders asserts the religious right of those, male and female, with a homosexual orientation to reject therapeutic approaches they reasonably see as useless or dangerous; opposition to "outing" individuals; full embrace of families of "homosexually active Jews"; and opposition to heterosexual marriage for both gay men and lesbians.[2]

Several American Orthodox rabbis have declared their opposition to secular legal discrimination against LGBTQI people and even support same-sex civil marriage. Two Orthodox rabbis, Steven Greenberg in the United States and Ron Yosef in Israel, have come out as gay. Rabbi Ron Yosef continues to serve an Orthodox Yemenite congregation, challenging the common belief that Mizrachi Jews are more conservative than Ashkenazi Jews on this issue.

Most Orthodox authorities assert there are only two genders and that gender is inherent and fixed. That view is being actively challenged in some congregations in the United States by the parents of several young transwomen. A small minority of Orthodox authorities have accepted the medical view that there is a pathology called gender identity disorder and believe that sexual reassignment surgery (SRS) is valid according to Jewish law, for medical reasons.

The largest Orthodox international rabbinical association has disavowed conversionary or reparative therapy for LGBTQI people, and an Israeli support group sponsored advertisements against conversion therapies for religiously observant Jews. In North America, there are a number of support and advocacy groups for Orthodox families of LGBTQI people, a gay male group, a lesbian group, and a youth group, as well as a number of online groups.

The Conservative denomination also emerged among nineteenth-century Ashkenazi Jews as a response to Reform Judaism, which was viewed as too assimilationist. Outside of North America, the Conservative movement is generally called Masorti (Hebrew: "traditional") and is composed of twelve international communities. The use of the word "Conservative" refers to nineteenth-century European religious issues and does not imply that members are politically or socially conservative. The movement tries to steer a middle ground between Reform (or secular in Israel) and Orthodox Judaism.

Since the 1980s, leaders of the Conservative movement have issued a number of declarations with regard to LGBTQI people, many of them contradictory, ranging from highly restrictive to very inclusive. Overall, the Conservative movement has been supportive of secular equal rights for LGBTQI people, in sympathy with their minority status, making the connection between Jews as a minority and LGBTQI people as a minority.

Over the years, more leaders of the Conservative movement—both religious and lay—have moved in the direction of increasing acceptance and support in the religious realm. In 2006 Conservative Judaism in the United States began accepting lesbian, gay, and bisexual people as candidates for rabbinic ordination. Initially, the Israeli and some European branches of the movement objected, but in 2012 the Israeli seminary also began admitting lesbian, gay, and bisexual students. In 2012 the American Conservative movement affirmed the religious validity of same-sex unions but differentiated them from mixed-gender (heterosexual) marriage. The British arm of the movement reached the same position in 2014. However, despite the formal stance of the movement, many North American Conservative rabbis, and some British and Israeli ones, perform same-sex marriages that are religiously identical to mixed-gender marriages.

In 2003 the Conservative movement affirmed the medical model in regard to transgender people and ruled that SRS (now often called GRS, gender realignment surgery) is religiously binding. There is considerable debate over transgender people who do not have bottom surgery and over genderqueer people. This issue is most hotly debated with regard to a marriage in which a same-gender couple is treated differently than a mixed-gender couple and with regard to conversion, in which there is considerable attention paid to the need for circumcision; there is some confusion over transgender people who have not undergone SRS. At this writing, the Conservative movement is tied to the two-gender model, but that may well change in the next few years.

There are several smaller Jewish denominations based in North America. These are Reconstructionist, Renewal, and Humanist Judaism. All of these groups are highly supportive of LGBTQI people. The

Reconstructionist movement's summer camp is particularly regarded as inclusive and sensitive on this issue. Humanist Jewish organizations and congregations have taken a public stance and are engaged in organizational advocacy against the bullying of LGBTQI youth.

An interesting feature of Judaism is the high percentage of Jews who do not view themselves as religious, particularly in Israel, where Jewish identity is equivalent to national identity, and in the United States, where Jews have bonded socially, communally, and culturally in institutions other than synagogues.

Almost all nonreligious American Jewish communal organizations, such as Jewish Federations, Jewish Community Centers, Jewish Free Loan Associations, Jewish Family and Children's Service centers, and similar groups, are committed to equal secular rights for LGBTQI people and silent on the issue of religious rights, since these are seen as outside their purview. The degree of internal welcome and support is dependent on the greater context in which the organization operates; for example, the Jewish Federation in San Francisco is much more LGBTQI sensitive and affirming than its sibling organization in Des Moines. Jewish institutions organized to fight prejudice, such as the Anti-Defamation League, have been highly supportive of LGBTQI rights.

Large numbers of secular and liberal religious Jews are prominent in the American LGBTQI movement; this may be due to the social liberalism of the American Jewish community in combination with its historical activism.

TRADITION AND TRANSFORMATION

The conquest of Israel by Babylonia, and the consequent exile of the Israelites from their homeland and centralized Temple (which had been destroyed) in 586 BCE, created a crisis of epic proportions. The fact that the Jewish people have maintained a communal identity through twenty-five hundred years of exile and persecution is due to their ability to achieve a creative equilibrium between tradition and innovation.

The transition from a centralized nation-based group identity to a regionalized Diasporic existence rooted in a portable religious culture gave Jews an underlying structural model with which to engage less all-encompassing changes. Similarly, the change from an agricultural and pastoral way of life to an urban existence required successful cultural adaptation.

In addition, the move away from a religious practice based in animal sacrifice in the Temple to personal study, prayer, and right action also provided both flexibility and continuity. As Judaism turned to a textual basis for religious and cultural practice, stories and legal discussions became a process for incorporating change while maintaining core values.

In the nineteenth century, the Reform movement declared that it was not bound by halacha. Yet Reform rabbis consistently work to address modern issues by balancing contemporary values and Jewish tradition using means that are virtually identical to the halachic process, except in that the outcomes are more liberal.

In contemporary North America, it often appears that the Reconstructionist movement is at the forefront of social change, with a lag of five to ten years for the Reform movement, another lag for the Conservative movement, and sometimes, though usually not, even eventual adoption of the change by Modern Orthodox authorities. This was the pattern for gender equality in coming-of-age ceremonies, accepting Jews who have a Jewish father but not a Jewish mother (though the Conservative movement has yet to accept this stance), synagogue membership for intermarried couples, gender-neutral prayer language, LGBTQI ordination, and a number of social issues.

LOOKING FORWARD

Reform, Reconstructionist, Renewal, and Humanist authorities and community members are struggling in various degrees to understand LGBTQI life and respond in an inclusive way. LGBTQI people themselves are in fact not a monolith, and some of these struggles emerge from differing perspectives between gay men and lesbians, between lesbians and transgender women, between queer-identified people and gay men, between bisexual people in mixed-gender marriages and those in same-gender marriages.

Issues of Jewish religious life and law sometimes have unforeseen ties to LGBTQI concerns. The rabbinical association of the Reconstructionist movement recently articulated a position in dealing with Jewish status issues for children who were conceived using donor genetic material. Early in the process, it became clear to some of the movement's rabbis that lesbian culture viewed this issue in a way that was very different from the mainstream heteronormative view. Reaching a consensus that included lesbian (and to some extent gay male and transgender) concerns required a process of education.

Similarly, the Conservative movement is starting to engage the issue of transgender women who haven't had bottom surgery and what that might mean in terms of the movement's requirement of circumcision for converts.

The Reform movement is in the process of fully normalizing LGBTQI people, and for many congregations sexual identity is simply not an issue. The full normalization of LGBTQI people in the movement's leadership is yet to be achieved, but there is good progress. Transgender women and transgender men are generally still fairly often tokenized and exoticized, and perhaps eventually with more congregational and youth education and more transgender people in leadership, this issue will slowly be resolved. The new Reform High Holy Day prayer book has a new "third gender" option for people's ritual Jewish names, to respond to those who do not think of themselves as either a "son" or a "daughter," which is part of the traditional ritual Jewish name.

Since Orthodox Judaism is, by definition, the communal safeguard of continuity and tradition, progress is slow, but it is occurring. The rejection of reparative or conversionary "therapy" is a big step forward in this process.

The uncharted territory of non-binary gender is a challenge. A number of synagogues and other Jewish institutions have taken halting baby steps such as designating gender-inclusive bathrooms; however, most Jewish institutions have yet to even engage the issue. For now, genderqueer may still be the identity "that dare not speak its name."

SUGGESTED RESOURCES

Address, Richard F., Joel L. Kushner, and Geoffrey Mitelman, eds. *Kulanu (All of Us): A Program and Resource Guide for Gay, Lesbian, Bisexual, and Transgender Inclusion.* New York: URJ Press, 2007.

Aviv, Caryn, and David Shneer, eds. *Queer Jews.* New York: Routledge, 2002.

Dzmura, Noach, ed. *Balancing on the Mechitza: Transgender in Jewish Community.* Berkeley: North Atlantic Books, 2010.

Keshet, http://keshetonline.org. An organization working for the full equality and inclusion of lesbian, gay, bisexual, and transgender Jews in Jewish life.

The World Congress of Gay, Lesbian, Bisexual, and Transgender Jews, http://glbtjews.org. Holds conferences and workshops representing the interests of LGBT Jews around the world.

The Lutheran Church

Beth Ann Doerring

Invited to answer the question, "Teacher, which commandment in the law is the greatest?" Jesus answered, "'You shall love the Lord your God with all your heart, and with all your soul, and with all your mind.' This is the greatest and first commandment. And a second is like it, 'You shall love your neighbor as yourself.' On these two commandments hang all the law and the prophets" (Matthew 22:36–40). Christians respond to these commands in the confident hope that by God's grace alone we are set free to worship God and love our neighbor…. How do we understand human sexuality within the context of Jesus' invitation to love God and love our neighbor (Romans 13:9–10; Galatians 5:14)?[1]

—"A Social Statement on Human Sexuality: Gift and Trust"

LAYING THE GROUNDWORK

The Lutheran Church began after Martin Luther of Germany attempted to reform the Roman Catholic Church from within as opposed to starting a new church body. But the patriarchy did not want to be reformed on such matters as indulgences (paying for forgiveness of sins and salvation), education of the people, church finances, hierarchy, and perceived clergy abuses. The pope

---

Beth Ann Doerring is a photographer and writer living in Colorado Springs, Colorado. Previously she was a pastor in the Evangelical Lutheran Church of America in various rural congregations in Texas and Colorado. She has written devotions for Lutheran publications, has had poetry published in various collections, and is currently writing children's books and her life story.

excommunicated Luther and many of his followers as heretics. As a result, the Lutheran Church was born, despite Luther's wish to reform from within—and not to have a church named after him.

Lutherans believe that we are saved by God's grace as a free gift. "For by grace you have been saved through faith ... it is the gift of God—not the result of works" (Ephesians 2:8–9). God has saved us through Jesus Christ's death and resurrection. Our response is to serve and love others as we would Christ. This grace is the major tenet of Lutheranism and is the basis of how we respond to others.

Luther also reformed the liturgy, translated the Bible into the language of the people so they were able to read it for themselves, proclaimed the Bible as the authority for faith and practice as opposed to the pope, married in violation of the Catholic Church's celibacy mandate for priests, and made the religion accessible to all people. Part of our Lutheran heritage is that, like Luther, we step out to be at the forefront of radical change.

The Lutheran denomination has split and joined for hundreds of years and is still doing so. Now the two largest groups are the Evangelical Lutheran Church of America (ELCA) and the Missouri Synod. All other Lutheran denominations are comparable to or more conservative than the Missouri Synod in terms of their doctrine. There are more than fifty Lutheran denominations in North America.

The ELCA's presiding bishop administers the sacraments, preaches, teaches, and oversees all entities in the denomination and is the CEO. The United States is divided into sixty-six geographic groups called "synods," each with its own bishop. The synod consists of member congregations and other institutions such as seminaries, universities, and social ministries. At synod assembly time, voting members from synod congregations gather for business, speakers, teaching, fellowship, and worship. A synod may vote to send a resolution or memorial on a topic to the biennial Churchwide Assembly. The bishops are advocates and visionaries, as well as the leaders of the synod or denomination. Other Lutheran groups have their own organizational structure, which differs from that of the ELCA.

FOUNDATIONAL NARRATIVES

The centrality of the biblical text for Lutherans came from Luther's insistence that scripture, not the pope and his pronouncements, was the authority for faith and practice. His reply to the emperor at the Diet (central assembly or legislature) of Worms about the authority of the pope was as follows:

> Unless I am convicted by scripture and plain reason—I do not accept the authority of popes and councils, for they have contradicted each other—my conscience is captive to the Word of God. I cannot and will not recant anything, for to go against conscience is neither right nor safe. God help me. Amen.[2]

An early text adds that Luther stated, in his now famous proclamation, "Here I stand, I cannot do otherwise."[3]

The seven texts usually interpreted as dealing with homosexuality in the Hebrew Bible and the Christian Scriptures are Genesis 19:1–11; Judges 19:1–29; Leviticus 18:22 and 20:13; Romans 1:26–28; 1 Corinthians 6:9–10; and 1 Timothy 1:9–10. A few of these scriptures, often called the "clobber texts" because of how they have been used against LGBTQI people, will be explored here.

Genesis 19 concerns Lot and his visitors in the town of Sodom, giving rise to the word "sodomite." This text has been used to condemn homosexuality, although the association of the Sodomites' sin and same-sex behavior is only made in later texts and religious commentary.

Judges 19 addresses the Levite and his concubine and was most likely based on the Sodom story in Genesis. Again, this text has been used to condemn homosexuality, particularly male-to-male intercourse. Early commentators read these texts as condemning abusive behavior toward strangers, not homosexuality. In that context, such texts would be more fittingly used to encourage the welcoming of LGBTQI people and anyone else perceived to be strangers.

Leviticus 20:13 reads: "If a man lies with a male as with a woman both of them have committed an abomination; they shall be put to death; their blood is upon them." This text, as well as Leviticus 18:22, is part of the Holiness Code, which exhorts the Israelites, specifically the priests, to be holy. Even within it, there are redundancies, contradictions, and laws that are unclear. Historically, scholars, theologians, and other leaders have picked and chosen which of these laws is more important, valid, or sacred.

The key word "abomination" has taken on a meaning and life of its own through the ages. It has come to mean condemnation of whatever we believe God disfavors. The definition of abomination is "abhorrence for someone or something; loathing; something that elicits great dislike or abhorrence."[4] However, as ELCA pastor Kenneth Thurow points out, abomination is not in fact "God's own very strongly negative judgment."[5] In its historical context, the biblical definition was not necessarily morally grounded, but based rather on that which was forbidden or unclean according to the religious laws of the period.

As Lutherans, we do not believe that our actions bring on God's presence or salvation. Our emphasis on grace negates people's being put to death for sins they have committed. Thus, we may eat shrimp, wear polyester blends, have bodily imperfections, tattoos, and the like—all prohibitions within the Hebrew Bible—and not be condemned to death. We are to be welcomed into the worshipping community. We decide whether laws are relevant, convenient, or taboo in accordance with the rest of scripture, our consciences, cultural context, history, and tradition. This process must be accomplished in keeping with the spirit of the law and its guidance and in accordance with God's love through the Spirit of Christ for all people.

The Christian Scriptures contain lists of vices that are often used to condemn homosexual behavior (including 1 Corinthians 6:9–11; 1 Timothy 1:10; and Galatians 5:10–21), but according to Kenneth Thurow's reading of these texts:

> Paul's focus is on conduct that breaks community, including "enmities, jealousy, anger, quarrels, dissensions, factions...." The point is that the "vice lists" could—and perhaps should—be turned in the opposite direction. Rather than being used against LGBTIQ members, they should be seen as a critique of loveless and judgmental attitudes. The lists stand in the New Testament as evidence of God's passion for inclusion, love, mutual respect, and harmony in the human family and most especially in the church.[6]

On the positive side, there are many more biblical texts that reflect God's love for all people. These scriptures have been used to affirm

LGBTQI equality. The "Bible in a nutshell" text, John 3:16–17, is one of the most important: "For God so loved the world [and note there are *no* exceptions here] that God gave God's only Son, that whoever believes in the Son shall be saved. For God did not come into the world to condemn the world, but that the world should be saved through the Son" (author's paraphrase). This verse, historically used to condemn anyone who does not believe in Jesus, is actually not meant to exclude or condemn. Genesis 1 and 2 support the "no exceptions" concept. It is God who created everything and everyone, and God pronounced all humans, with no exceptions, "good."

Romans 15:7 has also been cited in the inclusion of LGBTQI people within the church: "Welcome one another, therefore, just as Christ has welcomed you, for the glory of God." As Christ has welcomed everyone with no exceptions, despite our sinfulness (and everyone is sinful), and has forgiven us, so are we to do the same for *all* others. The Greek word for "welcome" has the connotation of taking in hand, taking hold of, grasping, receiving, accepting actively, taking up, choosing, suffering, becoming acquainted with, and welcoming.[7]

Other affirming texts with regard to action and belief are Romans 13:8–10 and Galatians 5:13–15. According to Thurow:

> In both passages Paul affirms love as the fulfilling of the law: "Love does no wrong to a neighbor, therefore love is the fulfilling of the law." To be sure, defining what does "wrong to a neighbor" can be a tricky business, but it certainly cannot mean that my neighbor is "wronging me" by any action that bothers or offends me.… It cannot easily be wielded against relationships of love and faithfulness between people who are not heterosexual.[8]

He continues, "In each of those passages the Spirit leads or pushes the church to see past old divisions and proscriptions, and to leave behind some of the 'clean/unclean' categories from their older traditions. Might it be time for us to leave old prejudices behind?"[9]

"Exegesis" and "eisegesis" are terms used to describe how one reads and uses a text. Exegesis employs a critical approach, based on the author's context, in order to carry meaning out of (*ex*) the text. Eisegesis, conversely, reads an interpreter's own meaning into (*eis*) the text. Historically, Lutherans have preferred exegesis to eisegesis.

However, the opposite has been true in relation to texts about homosexuality. Instead of applying a critical approach to the texts in question, viewing them in their historical context, we have read them in light of our current societal or cultural biases. In the last twenty years or so, we have come to that realization and have begun applying an exegetical model to these texts, and we have found that they do not have relevance for our contemporary struggles.

A key phrase that has been hotly debated among Lutherans is the concept of one's "bound conscience." The biblical text from which it emerges is Paul's statement to the Romans (2:15), "They show that what the law requires is written on their hearts, to which their own conscience also bears witness; and their conflicting thoughts will accuse or perhaps excuse them." Martin Luther restated this passage at his heresy trial in defense of his stand against the authority of the pope.

The ELCA's "Human Sexuality" statement used this passage to explain bound conscience in relation to the different views about homosexuality held within the church:

> However, when the question is about morality or church practice, the Pauline and Lutheran witness is less adamant and believes we may be called to respect the bound conscience of the neighbor. That is, if salvation is not at stake in a particular question, Christians are free to give priority to the neighbor's well-being and will protect the conscience of the neighbor, who may well view the same question in such a way as to affect faith itself.[10]

Lutherans are bound by their conscience to respect the opposing view if salvation is not affected. We are free to come to our own conclusions and interpretations but not necessarily hold our opinion against others who differ in opinion or tradition.

ELCA Lutherans can hold differences of opinion with others and still respect them and their views. And then we can pray together. There is not a patriarch who tells us what or whom to believe. We can think things through for ourselves, disagree, and be in relationship. Reconciliation is possible.

According to the "Human Sexuality" statement, there are four opposing views on the basis of conscience-bound belief in the ELCA:

- On the basis of conscience-bound belief, some are convinced that same-gender sexual behavior is sinful, contrary to biblical teaching and their understanding of natural law. They ... call people in same-gender sexual relationships to repentance for that behavior and to a celibate lifestyle.

- On the basis of conscience-bound belief, some are convinced that homosexuality and even lifelong, monogamous homosexual relationships reflect a broken world in which some relationships do not pattern themselves after the creation God had intended.... [They] do not believe that the neighbor or community are best served by publicly recognizing such relationships as traditional marriage.

- On the basis of conscience-bound belief, some are convinced that the scriptural witness does not address the context of sexual orientation and lifelong loving and committed relationships ... [and, therefore,] do not equate these relationships with marriage.

- On the basis of conscience-bound belief, some are convinced that the scriptural witness does not address the context of sexual orientation and committed relationships that we experience today. They believe that the neighbor and community are best served when same-gender relationships are lived out with lifelong and monogamous commitments that are held to the same rigorous standards, sexual ethics, and status as heterosexual marriage.[11]

There have been shifts in biblical interpretation in the Lutheran Church, especially recently. Interpreters have moved from seeing the texts as literal truth to reading them as revealing literary and theological truths that reflect the historical period out of which they emerged. They are still valuable as texts to reflect upon and receive guidance or understanding for our lives. There is a new conviction that the Holy Spirit can open all people's hearts and minds. Through the Holy Spirit people can grow into being welcoming and allowing LGBTQI people to be faithful servants in congregations, to be included at the family dinner table, the altar for Communion, and as pastors.

A distinction is now being made between prescriptive texts and descriptive texts. Traditionally, we have viewed texts such as Genesis 1 and Mark 10:6–9 as being prescriptive for our lives and morals. The prescription for sexuality and marriage is that all couples must comprise one male and one female married to each other for the rest of their lives. From a prescriptive view, these verses model a prototype for all human beings.

A descriptive approach holds that these texts illustrate one way of being among many. Adam and Eve were the first couple, but presenting their relationship in Genesis 1 need not imply that this is the only way to understand human relationships. Relationships can be heterosexual or same-sex, and human beings can engage in sex for purposes other than procreation. Therefore, Adam and Eve represent just *one* possible model of being in relationship.

ENCOUNTERING LGBTQI ISSUES

Thurow suggests that there is a continuum of attitudes toward homosexuality within the Lutheran Church. On the far right of this spectrum, homosexuality is thought to be a "perversity, a chosen immorality that offends against God and seeks to make others into victims or to subvert (pervert?) them into making similar wicked and sinful choices." The next position is "disorder," which he explains as resulting from "negative life experiences, that bad people or events have made the person this way." The third position is that homosexuality is a "flaw," which he describes as an "unchosen, perhaps in some sense unfortunate, factor in one's identity." The far-left position is "diversity," meaning that "God created me this way" as merely "one among many created alternatives."[12] People can move left or right on this continuum at different points in their lives. Many will start at the far right, but perhaps as they get to know LGBTQI people personally, slowly move to the left. Others will stubbornly stay where they are, because "we've never done it that way before!"

The Lutheran Church is beginning to acknowledge the transgender community, although the inclusion of gender-diverse people is considered to be ten to fifteen years behind the acceptance of the LGBTQI community. One area of progress is that the Board of Pensions of the ELCA is studying how best to cover transgender issues as they relate to health insurance. Some in the church are calling transgender rights the "next frontier."

SIGNIFICANT BRANCHES

The ELCA is the largest Lutheran denomination. The Missouri Synod is the second largest and may be distinguished from the ELCA by what it does *not* do or believe. The Missouri Synod does not allow women to be ordained as pastors, practices "closed" Communion for its members only, does not believe homosexuals can be within the will of God, and does not allow people to disagree on doctrine or to have a diversity of belief.

There are many groups working both for and against the issue of homosexuality in the Lutheran Church. One group that mobilized against ordaining homosexuals, same-sex unions or marriages, and any gay or lesbian sexual relationship is the Lutheran Core. Their mission statement is "Mobilizing confessing Lutherans for evangelical renewal." It is an interdenominational Lutheran group that offers a "Common Confession" that churches may adopt. Number six of the seven beliefs in this statement is on "marriage and family":

> We believe and confess that the marriage of male and female is an institution created and blessed by God. From marriage, God forms families to serve as the building blocks of all human civilization and community. We teach and practice that sexual activity belongs exclusively within the biblical boundaries of a faithful marriage between one man and one woman.[13]

Interestingly, their core beliefs say nothing about grace, which is the major tenet of Lutheranism.

One program that works for reconciliation in congregations, synods, colleges, seminaries, and other organizations is Reconciling Works: Lutherans for Full Participation. This is a continuation of Lutherans Concerned/North America. LC/NA began as Lutherans Concerned for Gay People in 1974 and then evolved into Reconciling Works in 2011, changing the name because the reconciling work being done did work! A program within RW is the Reconciling in Christ program, which includes over 550 Lutheran communities that publicly welcome LGBTQI believers. RIC offers a study program or series of educational meetings over six months to five years to create greater insights and understanding on LGBTQI people and other topics. It also lets people know which communities are welcoming to LGBTQI people who are visiting or moving to a new area. An affinity group within Reconciling Works is TransLutherans. They were formed in 2012 with the mission:

> To lift up and support transgendered and gender non-conforming people; to call out to the people of God to welcome us as a part of God's sacred creation; to educate people about transgender and gender non-conforming people and the issues we face; and to advocate for welcome and full inclusion for transgender and gender non-conforming people in the life of the church.[14]

A group that advocates for LGBTQI pastors is ELM, Extraordinary Lutheran Ministries. They formed from the groups Lutheran Lesbian & Gay Ministries (founded in 1990) and the Extraordinary Candidacy Project (founded in 1993) in 2007. Extraordinary Lutheran Ministries "focused its attention on changing church culture by creating immediate ministry opportunities for publicly identified LGBTQI rostered leaders.... They determined that its strength was to change church culture through the prophetic acts of extraordinary ordination and calls issued to publicly identified LGBTQI rostered leaders, relying on authority from the future ELCA policy change anticipated for years."[15] They did this by "providing a candidacy and credentialing process, supporting a collegium of LGBTQI rostered leaders, and designating direct grants to ministry by publicly identified LGBTQI clergy and rostered lay leaders in the Lutheran church."[16] "Proclaim," a professional community for Lutheran pastors, rostered lay leaders, candidates, and seminarians who identify as LGBTQ, "is a living witness of Extraordinary Lutheran Ministries' core belief that ministry by people who publicly and joyfully identify as LGBTQ is one way to change the church and society to become a place more fully inclusive of all people."[17] One of the central issues they face is the gap between the Lutheran leadership's policy of ordaining and allowing LGBTQI people to serve as pastors and the number of congregations actually willing to call them to serve. In 2009 the assembly voted to allow LGBTQI people to serve as pastors as long as they were in a "publicly accountable, lifelong, and monogamous" (PALM) relationship. About 5 percent of the congregations in the ELCA are

Reconciling in Christ members. Not all of these are willing to call an LGBTQI pastor.

Dr. Jay Alanis, director of the Lutheran Seminary Program of the Southwest in Austin, Texas, said of the Hispanic Lutheran culture that historically they have not touched the topic. As it is taboo to talk about sex at all, church members do not talk about homosexuality, but rather look away. However, with online and social media, the younger generation has exposure to LGBTQI people, and "now they are coming out and don't care what anyone thinks."[18] As they do, older Hispanic Lutherans are feeling increasing pressure to come out, despite their own hesitancy to do so.

This seems to also be true of other subcultures (including African Americans, those living in rural areas, and Asian Americans) in which taboos against homosexuality are significant.

TRADITION AND TRANSFORMATION

Because the hierarchy encourages a certain position or the Church-wide Assembly has voted in a particular way does not mean that every congregation immediately or ever follows that ruling. One example is divorce. There has been movement from a lack of acceptance to divorce being viewed as sinful but forgivable, to divorced people being accepted into the general church population, and finally to pastors being able to divorce and remarry if they so choose. Another example is the work that still had to be done even after women were first ordained. It took a good twenty-five years for the number of women in seminary to increase to a point where congregations began to feel that calling a woman was acceptable. Likewise, the LGBTQI population is not being called with any enthusiasm. Congregations are not required to go against their own principles, beliefs, or traditions by calling a woman or someone who is LGBTQI.

For instance, Nicole Garcia, a transgender seminarian, knows that she will most likely be unable to get a regular call to a congregation because she has three strikes against her as a female transgender Latina. She hopes there will be some kind of specialized ministry she will be accepted into. In the meantime, progress is slowly made as various outsider groups or "others" become prevalent and thus acceptable. The first openly transgendered person to be called by a congregation, Asher O'Callaghan, was ordained into ministry in Denver in July 2015.

We who are LGBTQI know that with patience and time, we too will be accepted and welcomed and be free to serve and be members in the ELCA, just as these others have been slowly accepted and welcomed into the norm of Lutheran church life.

LOOKING FORWARD

Unfortunately, I see a negative trend of "been there, done that" within the church. This includes the perception that the ELCA has done the hard work, has settled the battle, and doesn't need to do more. Nicole Garcia, the transgender Latina candidate for ordained ministry in the ELCA mentioned above, said, "People are thinking that what we've done is good enough so there's no more need to spend more money on these issues. People are tired, exhausted even, of the issue and don't want to expend more energy on it."[19]

On a positive note, I also see a very slow trend that as people encounter LGBTQI individuals, especially family members who come out, they tend to become more welcoming, understanding, and accepting. As this happens more and more within congregations, barriers, prejudices, and hatefulness disappear. As the younger generation is more likely to know and be celebratory of LGBTQI people, they may be a key to this important shift over time. Both straight and LGBTQI young adults are choosing to leave non-accepting congregations, as they do not want to be a part of the condemnation, the silence, or the hatefulness. As they grow into adults, however, some of those who had left are slowly returning to these congregations. They are more likely to work toward reducing and eliminating discrimination against LGBTQI people within their churches, creating congregations where the disenfranchised can feel welcomed and accepted.

The church community can deal with tough issues without enmity and with the freedom to believe as our conscience guides us. Reconciliation is possible with patience and ongoing conversation when differing parties can agree on the importance of working through difficult concerns. As the Lutheran Church moves forward on engaging with LGBTQI members and clergy, we need to bear witness to our tradition of being open in discussion and discernment.

SUGGESTED RESOURCES

Evangelical Lutheran Church in America. "A Social Statement on Human Sexuality: Gift and Trust." Adopted at the eleventh biennial Churchwide Assembly, August 19, 2009, Minneapolis, MN. http://download.elca.org/ELCA%20Resource%20Repository /SexualitySS.pdf.

"Human Sexuality." Evangelical Lutheran Church in America. www.elca.org/Faith/Faith-and-Society/Social-Statements/Human -Sexuality.

Reconciling Works: Lutherans for Full Participation, www.reconciling works.org.

Thurow, Kenneth D. *A Place at the Table, Scripture, Sexuality, and Life in the Church.* Bloomington, IN: iUniverse, 2009.

Workin, Joel. *Dear God, I Am Gay—Thank You!* Chicago: Extraordinary Lutheran Ministries, 2015.

The Presbyterian Church

Marvin M. Ellison, PhD, and Sylvia Thorson-Smith, MS

I am someone you know. I am your neighbor, your friend, your child's teacher. I am a mother; I was a wife. I go to your church.... I am a lesbian.... Even though I am "out" to many people in various circles of my life, I have not disclosed who I am at church. Isn't it ironic that of all places, the church is the biggest closet of all, where we need to be the most dishonest and secretive? The Jesus I know from the Bible couldn't possibly want this for gays and lesbians or for the church. I also know that it's increasingly important for me to be truthful about this part of myself with all of the significant people in my life, including my faith community. Can I tell you who I am?[1]

—Name withheld, for now

Marvin M. Ellison, PhD, is Willard S. Bass Professor Emeritus of Christian Ethics at Bangor Theological Seminary at Union Theological Seminary in New York and director of alumni/ae relations at UTS. An ordained Presbyterian minister, he is author of *Erotic Justice: A Liberating Ethic of Sexuality, Same-Sex Marriage? A Christian Ethical Analysis* and most recently of *Making Love Just: Sexual Ethics for Perplexing Times*. With Kelly Brown Douglas, he co-edited *Sexuality and the Sacred: Sources for Theological Reflection*. He sits on the boards of the Religious Institute for Sexual Morality, Justice, and Healing and Maine's Religious Coalition Against Discrimination, which he founded.

Sylvia Thorson-Smith, MS, lives in Tucson, Arizona, and is retired from Grinnell College, where she taught courses in human sexuality, religious studies, and gender/women's studies. She served as staff to the Presbyterian Church (U.S.A.)'s study of pornography and as sexuality educator for Planned Parenthood of Southern Kansas. With Marvin M. Ellison, she co-edited *Body and Soul: Rethinking Sexuality as Justice-Love*. She is also co-editor of *Called Out With: Stories of Solidarity in Support of LGBT Persons* and author of *Reconciling the Broken Silence: The Church in Dialogue on Gay and Lesbian Issues*.

LAYING THE GROUNDWORK

Presbyterians are part of the Reformed branch of Christianity that developed during the Protestant Reformation in the sixteenth century. Reformed Christianity originated in Switzerland under the efforts of Huldrych Zwingli. Like Martin Luther, Zwingli was a Roman Catholic priest. After being called to Switzerland's leading cathedral, he began to break with the Catholic preaching tradition and indicated his commitment to the Bible as the final authority over the church. In 1523 the Zurich city council endorsed Zwingli's preaching and his principle of *sola scriptura* (scripture alone as the primary source of authority). Following disputations over Zwingli's new teachings and practices, Zurich declared itself part of the Reformation and split from the Roman Catholic Church.

John Calvin was born in France and is among the second generation of Protestant Reformers. As a lawyer and trained classicist, he decided by the mid-1530s that he agreed with Reformers against the Roman Catholic Church, and because of hostility against Reformation ideas, he left France. In Basel, Switzerland, he wrote the first edition of his *Institutes of the Christian Religion*, a small catechism, or instruction in theology for beginners. While traveling through Geneva, this respected writer of the *Institutes* was persuaded to stay and help with reform. Theologians came to train with Zwingli and Calvin in Zurich and Geneva, and preachers from Switzerland fanned out across Europe, spreading the Reformed faith.

Presbyterianism is the name given to one of the ecclesiastical bodies that represent the features of Protestantism that John Calvin emphasized. Its history is also rooted in the work of John Knox, a Scotsman who studied with Calvin in Geneva and brought his teachings back to Scotland. The Presbyterian Church primarily traces its ancestry back to England and Scotland.

Presbyterianism is historically a confessional tradition wherein churches express their beliefs in the form of "confessions of faith." In these denominations, theology is not solely an individual matter, and collectively written confessions have some degree of authoritative status. While individuals are encouraged to understand scripture and may challenge current institutional understanding, theology is carried out by the community as a whole. It is this communal understanding of theology that is expressed in confessions.

Presbyterians place great importance upon education and life-long learning. Continuous study of the scriptures, theological writings, and the confessions is encouraged by members and leaders alike. The point of such learning is to enable one to put one's faith into practice. Presbyterians proclaim the gospel of Jesus Christ—the "good news" of life lived in the love of God—and promote a faith that is exhibited in action as well as words, by generosity, hospitality, and the pursuit of social justice and reform.

The belief that good works cannot save you is a cornerstone of Reformed and Presbyterian theology. Salvation and eternal life rest on the forgiveness of sins, which is a completely free and gracious gift from God. Nevertheless, Presbyterians have always had high expectations for moral behavior. The faithful, freed from anxiety about their own salvation, can devote their attention to helping their fellow humans. They do so because the Holy Spirit that brought them to faith continues to work in them to do God's will, and service to fellow humans glorifies God.

Presbyterians have a history of active involvement in American public life, holding leadership roles in political office, public education, the temperance movement, prison reform, and the creation of labor and child welfare laws. Conflict within Presbyterian denominations about moral principles has often focused around interpretation of the Bible. For a long period in American history there was a fair amount of agreement on moral principles found in the Bible, the obvious exception being whether the Bible allowed or forbade slavery.

The twentieth century saw increasing conflict between liberals and conservatives in the Presbyterian Church. Liberals seek to combine religion with science and historical criticism and tend to read the Bible as having an emphasis on social justice issues. Conservatives tend to read the Bible as focusing on individual moral behavior and salvation. As in all Protestant denominations, beliefs about gender and sexuality break down not along denominational lines but along conservative/liberal lines.

Presbyterians began ordaining women as lay leaders in congregations in 1930 and as ministers of Word and Sacrament in 1956. The mid-twentieth-century movement for women's rights in church and society had strong support among most Presbyterians but encountered substantial opposition by conservatives who subscribed to an interpretation of the Bible that assigned women subordinate roles to men. The Presbyterian Church in America (PCA) organized in 1973 in opposition to theological liberalism and conflict over the roles and status of women. The PCA continues to hold traditional positions on gender and does not ordain women as lay leaders or clergy.[2]

One aspect of Presbyterian governance uniquely affects the strides made on LGBTQI ordination. Every Presbyterian church elects elders and deacons and ordains elders to service on the decision-making council, the "session." Since Presbyterians ordain not only clergy but also lay leaders in local congregations, decisions about the suitability of LGBTQI members for ordained leadership is a potential issue for every congregation, not only for those individuals seeking pastoral leadership. The More Light Church Network organized as a movement to refuse compliance with Presbyterian policy that excluded gay and lesbian members from ordination. More Light churches since the 1980s have openly ordained people regardless of their sexual orientation, and several congregations have been charged for not complying with Presbyterian policy. However, no churches were evicted from the denomination as a result of these charges.

FOUNDATIONAL NARRATIVES

As Christians standing within the Protestant Reformed tradition, Presbyterians affirm that the scriptures of the Hebrew Bible and Christian Scriptures serve as the primary and indispensable resource for theological insight and guidance. A position paper adopted by the 123rd General Assembly in 1983 acknowledges the Bible's centrality this way: "That Holy Scripture is the 'rule of faith and life' is a basic principle of the Reformation. This confessional affirmation … is a structural element of all Reformed confessions."[3] At the same time, even though it might be assumed that the Bible serves as a focal point of unity among Presbyterians, the report recognizes a far different reality: scriptural authority is "held and practiced among Presbyterians in a variety of ways."[4]

An earlier study had analyzed how Presbyterians actually use the Bible as the rule of faith and practice and observed several trends among contemporary church members and leaders.[5] Few mainstream Presbyterians were wedded to biblical literalism. Instead, they shifted the locus of authority away from specific texts toward emphasizing broad themes and principles found throughout the entire Bible, considered within their historical and cultural contexts.

In addition, there is a strong consensus that the Bible requires interpretation, and at the same time it is acknowledged that as readers read and interpret scripture, they do so selectively and through their own filters and lenses. There is nothing new about this. In every age Christians have interpreted human experience in light of scripture, and scripture in light of human experience. That dialectic is not always easy to keep in balance, but Christian theology remains dynamic as each generation seeks to interpret the Bible for its own time, while seeking an appropriate equilibrium between experience and tradition. Several pivotal questions then follow. First, who has the authority to interpret biblical texts? Second, what is the principle of selection or the interpretive lens through which scripture is read? Third, what is the relationship between the Bible and non-biblical sources that Presbyterians also typically consult, including church tradition, various disciplines of knowledge (foremost the natural and social sciences along with the humanities), and contemporary experience?

Presbyterian theologian Jack Rogers, whose evangelical credentials grant him legitimacy among conservatives in the denomination, has spoken publicly about his own transformation in thinking about homosexuality and the importance of coming to deep awareness about how the Bible has been misused, time and time again, to legitimate oppression and exclusion. Gaining historical awareness is pivotal to any process of change, especially the recognition that Presbyterians have dramatically altered their theological convictions in the past about other matters, including slavery, divorce and remarriage, and the ordination of women. "On each of these issues," he writes, "at one point the church had near unanimity of opinion and then, over time and painfully, changes its mind to almost the exact opposite view."[6]

Moreover, Rogers has detected a particular pattern at work, at least among the dominant majority, whenever the denomination has begun to wrestle with controversial social issues. First, those who were considered duly authorized to interpret the Bible have been those in power. "White men in the mainstream churches," Rogers points out, "had great power to claim that their experience was normative for all.... They interpreted reality according to their experience of being in a privileged position in society. That gave them the freedom to label others as inferior. Through their complete domination of society, they were able to pass off their biases as 'common sense.'"[7] The privileged and powerful not only controlled how the Bible was read, but also how the social issue was framed and interpreted. "In each case," Rogers continues, "we accepted a pervasive societal prejudice and read it back into Scripture. We took certain Scriptures out of their context and claimed to read them literally, with tragic consequences for those to whom these verses were applied."[8]

What Rogers describes as "a change of mind and heart" might also be termed a conversion experience. Such transformations do not happen automatically nor without personal and intellectual struggle, especially within a denomination that prides itself on theological and biblical literacy. Rogers confesses that when it came to gay men and lesbians in the church, his own social privilege allowed him the luxury of sidestepping the debate insofar as he had never found reason to "really [study] the issue." When he was pressed to do so, "the process was both very serious and painful. I wasn't swayed by the culture or pressured by academic colleagues. I changed my mind initially by going back to the Bible and taking seriously its central message for our lives,"[9] which is a Christ-centered message of inclusion, radical hospitality, and concern especially for those marginalized and often vilified by church and society. Full welcome and inclusion of LGBTQI persons in the life and leadership of the church is theologically warranted, writes the newly converted Rogers, because of a biblically grounded conviction, namely that "the gospel, the good news, is that all people can have a relationship with God through Jesus Christ. We reflect Christ's presence in our lives by showing love for God and each other. Thus, the image of God is not a capacity embodied only in some classes of people but denied to others. To be in God's image is possible for all,"[10] including gay people.

In contrast, traditionalists contend that the theological problem is noncompliance with authority and settled truth, which they argue has not only been the consistent biblical witness but is also reflected in natural law assumptions that most people in the (dominant) culture accept as given. To defend their exclusion of gay men and lesbians, traditionalists cite a list of scriptural texts that they regard as offering biblical "proof" of the immorality of homosexuality: the Sodom and Gomorrah story (Genesis 19) and its parallel in Judges 19, prohibitions in Leviticus (18 and 20), and scattered texts primarily within the Pauline correspondence (Romans, 1 Corinthians, 1 Timothy). Again, as Rogers points out, traditionalists downplay or ignore the point that homosexuality is a minor concern of the Bible, especially in contrast to economic injustice and the plight of the poor and dispossessed. Furthermore, the isolated proof texts that conservatives cite all together "cover a maximum of twelve pages in the Bible. None of these texts is about Jesus, nor do they include any of his words." Moreover, when these texts are cited, they are read apart from linguistic and cultural context and, even more damning, are invoked primarily to bolster a discriminatory agenda at odds with the gospel trajectory, namely in order "to condemn a whole group of people."[11]

If in matters of biblical interpretation the interpretive lens is as important as the text, then during their decades-long conflict over sexuality and denominational leadership, Presbyterians have learned to appreciate that their hermeneutical struggles have been not only about how to read and make sense of scripture, but also about how to read and make sense of human sexuality. Traditionalist views parallel a modernist cultural paradigm about gender and sexuality that assumes that humanity is divided neatly into two and only two genders, that heterosexuality is the natural pathway for normal sexual development, that men and women are "opposites" in social and psychological characteristics and interests, and that heterosexual couples are erotically attracted to each other in order to marry and reproduce children, the natural and distinctive purpose of sexuality. In contrast, progressives operate out of a different cultural paradigm that speaks of sexuality as polymorphous, recognizes the gender binary (male or female) as a social construction and that there are multiple genders and sexual orientations, all of which are "normal" and natural, and understands that eroticism is not only for procreative purposes, but more fundamentally a means of human bonding through the sharing of affection and pleasure.

For progressives, the Bible is authoritative not because it serves as a definitive rulebook or provides a fixed template for normative humanity, but rather because in recording how earlier communities struggled to clarify their identity as people of faith and their moral obligations, the Bible gives witness to how they sometimes succeeded, but oftentimes failed in their effort to live faithfully, even as they engaged in a protracted process of theological and ethical discernment. Biblical scholar Ken Stone observes helpfully that while the Bible may not change, the Bible's readers most certainly do. For example, even though nineteenth-century Presbyterians split over the issue, no contemporary Christian approves of slavery even though slavery is without doubt a biblical practice and even though biblical texts, including specifically Christian textual sources, can be cited "in defense of" enslavement. The biblical texts about slavery have not changed; what has changed is the readers and their operative assumptions.[12] A similar pattern now holds about those biblical texts that some continue to interpret as condemning homosexuality. No matter how those texts are read and interpreted, their progressive interpreters no longer grant them authority. As Jack Rogers writes:

> The best methods of biblical interpretation, from the Reformation on down through today, urge us to reject narrow historical and cultural bias and instead to follow Jesus' example. The purpose of the Bible is not to forever weld us to an ancient culture. The purpose of the Bible is to tell us the story of Jesus' life, death, and resurrection ... [and] see Jesus as the center of the biblical story and interpret each passage in light of his ministry.[13]

ENCOUNTERING LGBTQI ISSUES

Reformers such as Rogers encourage Presbyterians to adopt a more critical reading of biblical texts and of the history of biblical interpretation, including how scriptures have been co-opted to legitimate social injustice. However, the Presbyterian Church has, by and large, not yet adopted a truly liberating, justice-oriented hermeneutic. A Christian liberation theological stance employs a justice lens to interpret texts and grants a privileged place to the marginalized by honoring their theological and moral wisdom gained through their ongoing resistance to injustice and refusal to accept the status quo as normative. Biblical and theological truth is judged not by conformity to inherited norms and patterns, but rather by whether the tradition serves to promote and secure the humanity and dignity of all persons, especially those without power and social status, and whether it allows for both personal and communal well-being and flourishing.

In contrast to liberal reformers, liberation-committed Christians argue that while inclusion is good, transformation is far better. They suspect that the exclusion of racial and ethnic minorities, women, gay people, and others from leadership and a more central place in church life has everything to do with how conventional patterns of power, wealth, and control reinforce the privileges of the few while placing the majority at a disadvantage. Becoming a truly multicultural, multiracial, and multi-gender faith community requires altering the patterns of power along with the foundational assumptions that have undergirded the status quo. They see the sacred at work in the communal persistence of women and LGBTQI persons of all colors to claim their full personhood and in their tenacity to honor their divinely given calling to occupy every leadership role in church and society.

In order to promote the transformation of the church from a heterosexist institution to a genuinely inclusive, welcoming, and hospitable faith community respectful of persons of every gender, race, class, and sexuality, liberationists propose "changing the subject" in two ways. First, it is necessary to change the topic of conversation, moving beyond the misplaced preoccupation with homosexuality and focusing attention instead on the sexualized violence so pervasive in this culture and on race, gender, sexual, and economic oppression. The Christian tradition's sex-negativity and misogyny have been the church's "dirty little secret," undermining the moral integrity and public witness that a liberal Protestant tradition, such as Presbyterianism, has sought to exhibit. Coming of age about sex and sexual difference is a necessary step toward genuine spiritual renewal and revitalization.

Second, changing the subject also requires changing the people who speak and are heard with authority. What is shaking the foundations is a power shift as LGBTQI persons assert their right to be the subjects of their own lives. Fresh insight emerges as queer people refuse to be positioned only as objects of other people's discourse and become self-defining subjects, real persons with whom to relate and engage in constructive dialogue. Non-heterosexual and transgender persons reside in every faith community, so the change agenda is not how to include "outsiders" and bring them inside, but rather how to create together the communal conditions of hospitality, safety, and respect so that people of diverse sexual orientations and gender identities alike can acknowledge and share what they have come to know, often at great risk, about resisting injustice, enhancing human dignity, and revitalizing community.

The pressing problem is that many persons associated with institutionalized Christianity, including many Presbyterians, have been socialized to fear difference and so avoid flesh-and-blood contact with people "not like them," especially when it comes to sexuality. When people lack real-life connection with those harmed by prevailing norms and patterns, they often fail to comprehend the real world and even have trouble discerning injustice in their own lives. Out of touch with their own pain, they often fail to perceive the pain of others.

The way forward—to listen to and learn from those on the margins—is narrow and demanding. Jack Rogers admits as much when he shares that his own transformation was not simply the result of retreating into his study to read the Bible anew, but rather of his connections with the so-called despised other. "I came to know many gay and lesbian people and have had my Christian life enriched by their profound witness to the gospel," Rogers writes, and it was those encounters that encouraged, even pushed him to go "back to the Bible and [take] seriously its central message for our lives."[14] Liberationists agree that respectful listening to marginalized persons is necessary, but underscore how deepening understanding by itself is not sufficient. Solidarity is necessary. Actions and policies are needed that reinforce the dignity of LGBTQI persons and reconstruct community so that no one is excluded and power is redistributed, so that every person has what each person deserves: respect and a fair share of resources to be able to enjoy a dignified and safe life.

TRADITION AND TRANSFORMATION

Presbyterians are far from unique in struggling with social issues that prove, initially at least, far more church dividing than church uniting. In the nineteenth century, Presbyterians in the United States split over slavery and fractured into northern and southern branches. That schism was not finally repaired until 1983, when the two major streams of Presbyterians reunited and formed a new denomination, the Presbyterian Church (U.S.A.). At the close of the twentieth century, the first major social issue that this newly reunited denomination decided to address as a faith community was human sexuality and, more specifically, homosexuality. While some might suggest that this group of Protestant Christians seems especially drawn to theological conflict and internal disruption, others might argue that Presbyterians, along with adherents of almost every other religious tradition, are being prodded by the movement of the Spirit to reexamine their beliefs and practices with respect to human sexuality, sexual difference, and sexual ethics.

One person is particularly remembered for sparking the organized movement for LGBTQI justice in the Presbyterian Church. David Sindt grew up in a Presbyterian family and began to identify as an openly gay man seeking ministry in the early 1970s. At a Presbyterian General Assembly, the annual (now biennial) national gathering of church leaders, David held up a sign asking, "Is anybody else out there gay?" In 1974 he founded the Presbyterian Gay Caucus, which later became Presbyterians for Lesbian and Gay Concerns (PLGC). In 1992 the More Light Churches Network (MLCN) was organized to promote the full inclusion of LGBTQ persons into the life and leadership of the Presbyterian Church. Churches became "More Light" if they were committed to openly opposing Presbyterian anti-ordination policies. PLGC and MLCN merged in 1998, forming More Light Presbyterians (MLP), which is now the primary LGBT advocacy group in the Presbyterian Church (U.S.A.). Presbyterians adopted the term "More Light" from the words of Rev. John Robinson to Pilgrims leaving for the New World in 1620: "God has yet *more light* and truth to break forth from the Word."[15] In a representation of its commitment to inclusivity, MLP welcomed Alex Patchin McNeil, the first openly transgender person to head a mainline Protestant organization, as its executive director in 2013.

More Light Presbyterians has been the group primarily responsible for strategizing and activism on LGBTQI justice. Other groups have formed to advocate for change on the ordination issue. That All May Freely Serve (TAMFS) was organized in 1992 when Rev. Dr. Jane (Janie) Adams Spahr was called to be a minister at the Downtown United Presbyterian Church in Rochester, New York. In a case that went to the Permanent Judicial Commission (supreme court) of the Presbyterian Church (U.S.A.), her call was disallowed for being in conflict with the exclusionary policy of the denomination. In a constructive response to this painful denial, the Downtown Church created the TAMFS mission project and called Reverend Spahr as its "traveling lesbian evangelist" to "visit congregations, pastors and church members throughout the country telling the stories of LGBT Presbyterians, preaching, educating, and challenging exclusive church structures."[16] The Covenant Network of Presbyterians is a broad-based, national group of clergy and lay leaders seeking to support the mission and unity of the Presbyterian Church (U.S.A.) in a time of potentially divisive controversy.[17] It was organized to promote LGBTQ full inclusion and rights of ordination, while preserving the peace and unity of the church. Presbyterian Welcome (now called Parity) was formed in opposition to policies of the Presbyterian Church (U.S.A.) that excluded otherwise qualified candidates for leadership and ministry because of their sexual orientation.[18]

All of these groups work unofficially to affect the life and policies of the Presbyterian Church (U.S.A.), and all of them are outside of the official structures of the church. Groups within the denomination working for social change include the Advisory Committee on Social Witness Policy; the Advocacy Committee for Women's Concerns; and the Presbyterian Health, Education, and Welfare Association. However, none of these groups has an LGBTQI focus, and all of these groups are restrained to some degree from working in opposition to Presbyterian policy on any issue. While the Presbyterian Church (U.S.A.) is widely regarded as a progressive denomination on social justice issues, movement toward inclusion on LGBTQI justice has largely been generated from groups not within the structures of the church. Countless numbers of Presbyterian leaders support change and full inclusion, but they do advocacy work as individuals and not as official members of church entities.

The two predecessor denominations of the Presbyterian Church (U.S.A.), the United Presbyterian Church in the United States of America in 1978 and the Presbyterian Church in the United States in 1980, voted to exclude openly gay candidates from ordination, a restriction that up until that time had been de facto, but never formally legislated. After four decades of internal conflict and intense debate about whether to rescind the formal exclusion of gay men and lesbians from being ordained as congregational leaders (deacons and elders) and as clergy, the reunited Presbyterian Church (U.S.A.) revised its policy in 2010 and now allows, though it does not require, the ordination of non-celibate gay men and lesbians. While the church has long had a practice of accepting non-heterosexual persons as members and more recently has authorized the blessing of same-sex unions (as long as these are not formally recognized as marriages), Presbyterians remain divided over the moral status of homosexuality. Although a more welcoming stance has emerged in recent years, divergent theological opinion remains among clergy and congregants, ranging from outright condemnation to the full acceptance of LGBTQI persons.

In his 1978 study *Embodiment: An Approach to Sexuality and Christian Theology*, Protestant ethicist James B. Nelson, in examining the diversity of theological responses to same-sex love that exists within Christianity, maps out a four-point spectrum to describe divergent views held among mainline Protestants.[19] Historically, the most pervasive attitude in Christendom has no doubt been a rejecting-punitive stance, which has legitimated the persecution of sexual minorities and even violence and killing. A more tolerant but still prohibitive rejecting-nonpunitive stance abhors anti-gay violence but maintains that homosexuality is a moral perversion that should never be condoned by church or state.

In the twentieth century, under the influence of modern science and also because of the emergence of a gay rights movement and the greater visibility of LGBTQI persons, moderates have adopted a more tolerant "qualified acceptance" stance. They recognize that there is a persistent minority of non-heterosexual persons whose sexual orientation differs from the heterosexual majority. They also concede, although often with reluctance, that any radical reorientation of erotic desire is highly unlikely for most people. At the same time, they remain convinced that heterosexuality alone is "divinely willed" and therefore the normative (and normal) pattern for human intimacy.

Even while homosexuality has come to be accepted as a fact of life, traditionalists who occupy a "qualified acceptance" position still judge "the gay lifestyle" negatively as morally questionable because it departs from their understanding of biblical norms and settled tradition. While outright hostility toward homosexual persons has been replaced by tolerance and just as often by pity, Christians are admonished to "love the sinner, hate the sin." At the same time, gay persons are cautioned to remain celibate or, if that option is not manageable, to enter into long-term committed relationships. While these unions may and often do resemble heterosexual marriages, Christians who adopt a qualified acceptance stance are adamant that same-sex unions are not morally equivalent to Christian marriage or compatible with "holy matrimony," which in their judgment remains exclusively heterosexual.

Each of these stances—rejecting-punitive, rejecting-nonpunitive, and qualified acceptance—upholds heteronormativity and identifies the moral problem as the sin of homosexuality. The heterosexual norm is never brought into question. Homosexuality is regarded not only as different but wrong, a sign of willful rebellion against the intended divine plan for human relationality. Whether gayness is considered a deficiency or a moral defect, either way it is seen as a shameful, morally distorted way of being human.

In contrast, a Christian stance of full acceptance begins by acknowledging a diversity of human sexualities, each a benign variation within an acceptable range of sexual orientation and expression. Accordingly, it is entirely possible to affirm theologically that heterosexuality, homosexuality, and bisexuality may each fully embody the love, commitment, and mutual affection that God intends for all persons. Sexual orientation is regarded as morally neutral. What matters ethically is not a person's sexual identity or erotic orientation, but rather that person's moral character and conduct. Persons of differing sexual orientations and identities are entirely capable of living lives of integrity, care, and compassion in intimate association with others. At the same time, while all persons are challenged to claim a self-respecting sexual identity as their divinely willed birthright, they should pursue their religious vocation as advocates and lovers of justice in a principled and ethically responsible manner. The 1991 Presbyterian study "Keeping Body and Soul Together: Sexuality, Spirituality, and Social Justice," which was never officially adopted by the church and in fact was overwhelmingly rejected by the General Assembly, offers this insight:

> Faithfulness to God, therefore, requires seeking justice-love or right-relatedness with self and others. We intentionally connect justice and love in this way, to emphasize that genuine caring for concrete human well-being is never content with a privatized, sentimentalized kind of loving, but rather demonstrates a devotion that enables persons and institutions to flourish in all their rich complexity.... Justice-love knows full well that where there is injustice, love is always diminished.[20]

Many Presbyterians have come to agree with this theological claim about inclusiveness and extending a favorable welcome to LGBTQI persons, but by no means all. On the one hand, after the General Assembly voted in 2010 to permit the ordination of partnered gay men and lesbians, some dissenting Presbyterians formed a new denomination under the name of the Evangelical Covenant Order of Presbyterians. On the other hand, the 2012 General Assembly debated whether to bless same-sex civil marriages in the church and by a very narrow margin failed to adopt the recommended change in policy, but the momentum seems clearly in the direction of enhanced recognition of same-sex persons and their intimate partnerships and families. Even so, sexuality in the early twenty-first century remains a church-dividing issue much as slavery was in the nineteenth century and the status of women in the twentieth.

LOOKING FORWARD

Several trends are becoming more apparent among Presbyterians. First, the momentum continues to build for embracing the freedom to marry for same-sex couples religiously as well as civilly, especially after the 2015 U.S. Supreme Court decision guaranteeing marriage as a constitutional right. For some time, the culture has been out ahead of the church, and the church will either get on board or become more and more culturally marginalized and insignificant. In March 2015 the Presbyterian Church (U.S.A.) legalized same-sex marriage through a vote across the denomination in its regional bodies, the presbyteries. With this vote, the definition of marriage in the Presbyterian Book of Order has been changed from "one man and one woman" to "two people."

Second, while it is nothing new that LGBTQI people have long served the church as clergy and in many other leadership capacities, what is changing is that congregations are becoming interested in calling publicly out, self-affirming LGBTQI persons as their ordained leadership. Here "coming out" means not disclosure of sexual identity, but rather the public affirmation of a community's commitment to justice and inclusive hospitality. Not identity, but ethical integrity is the key matter of personal and collective importance.

Third, there is an emerging, or reemerging, division within Presbyterianism that is similar to a discernible divide between traditionalists and progressives in other religious traditions. Theologian Rosemary Radford Ruether speaks of this split as giving rise to a new ecumenism in which progressives have more affinity with, and more success in collaborating with, progressives from other traditions than they do finding common ground with their conservative counterparts within their own tradition.[21] It seems that the religious landscape is once again shifting, with the outcome still uncertain.

Christian concern should no longer be focused on discouraging, eliminating, or even containing homosexuality, but rather on learning to live more gracefully with sexual difference and working effectively as advocates of sexual justice to dismantle heterosexism, the institutionalized privileging of heterosexuality and the devaluing of all other sexualities. Theologically speaking, sexual difference should be viewed not as a sign of human sinfulness, but as a divine blessing with the potential to enrich communal life for church as well as society.

SUGGESTED RESOURCES

Ellison, Marvin M., and Sylvia Thorson-Smith, eds. *Body and Soul: Rethinking Sexuality as Justice-Love*. Eugene, OR: Wipf & Stock, 2008.

Nelson, James B. *Embodiment: An Approach to Sexuality and Christian Theology*. Minneapolis, MN: Augsburg, 1978.

"Presbyterians and Human Sexuality 1991" (formerly titled "Keeping Body and Soul Together: Sexuality, Spirituality, and Social Justice"). Louisville, KY: Office of the General Assembly, Presbyterian Church (U.S.A.), 1991. www.pcusa.org/site_media/media/uploads/_resolutions/human-sexuality1991.pdf.

Rogers, Jack. *Jesus, the Bible, and Homosexuality: Explode the Myths, Heal the Church.* Rev. ed. Louisville, KY: Westminster John Knox Press, 2009.

Spahr, Jane Adams, Kathryn Poethig, et al., eds. *Called Out: The Voices & Gifts of Lesbian, Gay, Bisexual, and Transgender Presbyterians.* Gaithersburg, MD: Chi Rho Press, 1995.

Protestant Evangelical Traditions

Ryan Bell, DMin

It has taken countless hours of prayer, study, conversation and emotional turmoil to bring me to the place where I am finally ready to call for the full acceptance of Christian gay couples into the Church.[1]

—Tony Campolo

LAYING THE GROUNDWORK

Modern evangelicalism traces its beginnings to the post–World War II era, when a great deal of change was taking place in the American religious landscape. In the aftermath of the Enlightenment and major scientific discoveries—in particular, Darwin's theory of evolution—Christianity became polarized. Liberals embraced these new discoveries and ways of thinking and argued for the primacy of human experience and a this-worldly focus on human social development. Fundamentalists (so named because of a series of books titled *The Fundamentals* that sought to refute liberal theology) saw their role as holding the line against this liberalization. The emerging evangelical leaders—men like Harold Ockenga, Carl F. H. Henry, and Billy Graham—were substantially fundamentalist in their theology and doctrine but sought a less combative approach, preferring

Ryan Bell, DMin, is an international speaker and writer on the subject of religion, atheism, and humanism. He is working on a memoir about his life of faith and ministry and his journey of leaving his faith. He is also the subject of a forthcoming documentary. For nineteen years he was a Seventh-day Adventist pastor but was asked to resign in part because of his advocacy for marriage equality and LGBTQI inclusion in the church.

instead a positive engagement with the culture and a focus on sharing the gospel.[2] It was in this highly politicized context that evangelicals found their voice.

Today, evangelicals can be found in several diverse streams within Christianity, including a variety of Baptist denominations, the Wesleyan and Pentecostal churches, some Anabaptist traditions, and a wide range of nondenominational churches. The recent 2015 Pew Research Center poll indicated that there are roughly sixty-two million evangelicals in America, accounting for a quarter of the total Christian population.[3]

Historian David Bebbington famously names four main qualities that evangelicals share:

- Conversionism: the belief that lives need to be changed
- Activism: the expression of the gospel in effort
- Biblicism: a particular regard for the Bible
- Crucicentrism: a stress on the sacrifice of Christ on the cross[4]

This exploration of evangelicals and LGBTQI issues will deal primarily with biblicism, but all four of these qualities can be seen in the current struggle over the place of LGBTQI people in the church.

FOUNDATIONAL NARRATIVES

For evangelicals, the text of the Bible—the Hebrew Bible and the Christian Scriptures—is paramount for defining morality and ethics. Martin Luther, the father of the Protestant Reformation, declared that the Bible, and the Bible only, was the source of faith and practice for the Christian. This declaration, known as *sola scriptura* (scripture alone), was made in the face of the power of the Roman Catholic Church, which had asserted its authority and the value of its traditions as the primary authority for faith and practice. What *sola scriptura* effectively meant was that each person could read and interpret the Bible for himself or herself rather than depending on the clergy and having its message filtered through the church. In this context, the Protestant Reformation was an anti-church-tradition movement. With the intent to liberate people from the prison of tradition and superstition, the Reformers shifted the locus of authority from the church and its hierarchy to the Bible, understood to be God's infallible, inspired Word.

Modern evangelicals are one of the many offspring of this sixteenth-century reform movement and hew most closely to its teachings about the Bible. Evangelicals of all denominations hold the Bible above every other source of knowledge and authority. While most will admit other sources of knowledge, for nearly all evangelicals the Bible is at the top of the list as the arbiter of all knowledge acquired from other sources.

The Wesleyan quadrilateral is a fine example of how this tradition works with respect to the biblical text. The quadrilateral, a method credited to the late eighteenth-century Methodist revivalist and theologian John Wesley, was coined by twentieth-century theologian Albert C. Outler. He observed that Wesley used four sources in his theological development: scripture, tradition, reason, and experience, often depicted as four quadrants of a square:

Scripture	Tradition
Reason	Experience

But this visual is misleading. Wesley himself stood solidly on the teaching of *sola scriptura*, but he also understood that in order to read and understand the Bible, each person needs some tools. For Wesley, then, tradition, reason, and experience function as a hermeneutical, or interpretive, framework through which scripture is read and understood. The quadrilateral is probably better depicted as a three-legged stool where the seat is scripture and the three legs are tradition, reason, and experience.

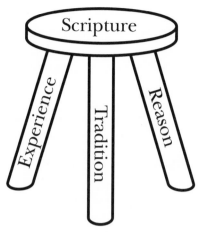

Figure 1. The Wesleyan hermeneutical

The primacy of scripture and the hermeneutical tradition that has emerged around it is fundamental in understanding how evangelical churches consider LGBTQI individuals. Another illustration helps establish the way the primacy of scripture has an impact on the theology and practice of evangelicals.

When science reveals that the earth is approximately 4.5 billion years old and the human species have been walking the earth for roughly two hundred thousand years, the vast majority of evangelicals do not agree. In fact, 42 percent of all Americans polled in a 2014 Gallup survey indicated that they believe that God created humans in their present form within the last ten thousand years. Among those who attend church regularly, that number rises to 69 percent.[5] The reason for this is simple. In the first chapter of Genesis (Genesis 1:1–2:4a), God creates the world in six days. According to evangelical interpretations of Genesis, God spoke and the world came into existence roughly as it is today. In Genesis 6 we read of a worldwide flood not very many generations after Adam and Eve were created by God's hand, and according to evangelical interpreters this flood is responsible for the geological record that we observe today.[6] As a result of their view of scripture, evangelicals are able to deny, or at least work around, the evidence drawn from any number of scientific research projects because they value the text of the Bible above all other sources of knowledge and authority. Their goal is not to follow the scientific evidence wherever it leads, but rather to begin with the text of the Bible in order to create a way for the apparent evidence from science to comport with Bible teachings.

The same hermeneutical approach is taken with respect to sexuality. According to the same Creation account in Genesis, God created a human named Adam. God formed Adam from the dust of the ground and animated Adam with God's breath, which brought God's work of art to life. When Adam realized that all the other animals that God created had opposite-gender partners, Adam asked why he was alone. God, apparently seeing Adam's point, created a woman named Eve from one of Adam's ribs, to be his partner and his helper. From this primal story, theology moves in several directions that become problematic. First, Eve is something of an afterthought and is created from Adam, already indicating subordination. Secondly, and more pertinent to issues of sexuality, the Creation account sets up a pattern of heterosexual partnership as the divine ideal. "God created Adam and Eve, not Adam and Steve" was a quip I grew up hearing quite often.

Beyond the implicit divine order of male-female sexual relationships in Genesis, there are a handful of biblical texts that theologians and lay Christians refer to when it comes to the question of LGBTQI people and their relationships. The first of these texts—and the most strongly worded—appears in the Hebrew Bible book of Leviticus. Notably, Jesus never addresses the subject of homosexuality directly. Paul, on the other hand, echoes the Hebrew Bible's condemnation of same-sex acts.

Canonically, the first such references are found in Leviticus 18 and 20:

> You shall not lie with a male as with a woman; it is an abomination.
>
> —Leviticus 18:22

> If a man lies with a male as with a woman, both of them have committed an abomination; they shall be put to death; their blood is upon them.
>
> —Leviticus 20:13

It is a curious feature of evangelical theology that it has a highly selective relationship with the Hebrew Bible, especially the Pentateuch. Many evangelicals claim that the Hebrew Bible's commandments are done away with because of the life, death, and resurrection of Jesus. In evangelical theology, the Hebrew Bible's rites and rituals, such as the wilderness tabernacle and its ceremonies described in Leviticus, are seen as symbols pointing toward the fulfillment found in Jesus. So, for example, the lamb that is slain and the blood sprinkled on the altar (Leviticus 16) is a symbol of Jesus, the Christ, whose shed blood atones for humanity's sins. In John 1:29, John the Baptist refers to Jesus as "the Lamb of God who takes away the sin of the world." In a similar way, Paul writes that Jesus fulfilled the law. Many evangelicals take this to mean that the Hebrew Bible commands met their end, or their culmination, in Jesus, rendering them obsolete to "New Testament Christians." Still, many evangelicals selectively cite Leviticus 18 and 20 to prohibit same-sex acts.

For example, Leviticus 18:19, just three verses prior to the one quoted above, reads, "You shall not approach a woman to uncover her nakedness while she is in her menstrual uncleanness." One does not hear sermons telling men not to look at their wives naked while they're menstruating, but the command three verses later against male-male sexual relations is applicable to modern sexuality, according to the traditional evangelical interpretation.

The primary text in the Christian Scriptures that evangelicals turn to in their prohibition of same-sex relationships is found in Romans 1 and is attributed to the apostle Paul:

> For this reason God gave them up to degrading passions. Their women exchanged natural intercourse for unnatural, and in the same way also the men, giving up natural intercourse with women, were consumed with passion for one another. Men committed shameless acts with men and received in their own persons the due penalty for their error.

—Romans 1:26-27

It appears that Paul is drawing on his religious tradition to enforce the prohibition of same-sex sexual acts. So while the primary texts prohibiting homosexual sex are in Leviticus, Paul brings the issue into the Christian Scriptures in a fresh way. Were it not for this fact, Christians might be more successful in relegating the proscription of homosexuality to the cultic prohibitions of the ancient Hebrews, but Paul's authority for contemporary evangelicals rivals even that of Jesus.

Those who wish to affirm same-sex loving relationships in the context of Christianity and the infallible inspiration of the Bible have a few interpretive options available to them. Some progressive evangelicals argue that same-sex sexual relationships in the ancient world were nothing like same-sex loving relationships as we know them today. Paul was likely referring to male prostitution and pagan temple rituals. It was also common in the Roman Empire of Paul's day for young male servants to function as sexual partners for their masters. Some theologians attempt to turn a prohibition against homosexual relationships into a social justice case against abusive relationships, and some evidence exists for this interpretation. For others, these interpretations seem strained. The majority of evangelicals interpret the text to mean, in spite of the distance between today's culture and that of the text, that God does not approve of same-sex relationships.

In spite of this fairly consistent evangelical hermeneutical tradition, the evangelical interpretation of these texts (frequently referred to as "clobber texts" by those on the receiving end of their judgment) has changed over time. As more congregations have become aware of the LGBTQI members in their midst, they have had either to enforce the moral code they have received or to return to the theological process with different questions in mind.

As a consequence, more and more room has been made for gay and lesbian individuals in evangelical churches in recent years. Just in the past decade or so the locus of the church's concern has moved from a person's identity as gay or lesbian to same-sex relationships, and especially same-sex acts. While some still believe that sexual identity is a choice, the majority opinion in evangelical churches has moved past this view in light of current scientific research to recognize that a person's sexual orientation is theirs from birth. Homosexuals don't choose their homosexuality any more than heterosexuals choose their heterosexuality. As a result, many churches have resolved to accept gay and lesbian members in their ranks. After all, how could they possibly know the sexual orientation of their members unless they asked everyone?

Thus, the line of unacceptability was moved from gay and lesbian identity itself to same-sex acts. As long as same-sex attracted individuals remain celibate, they can be accepted by God and the church. This is increasingly the position of evangelical churches around the United States. This is sometimes referred to as a "third way" between the supposed extremes of outright rejection of gays and lesbians on the one hand, and full acceptance of their sexuality on the other. This viewpoint often manifests as some version of "love the sinner, hate the sin," in which same-sex relationships and sexual acts are considered sinful. The "third way" approach has enabled churches to welcome LGBTQI individuals to their churches and become accustomed to being in the presence of people who are quite different from themselves, but they then face further questions. Can LGBTQI Christians be church leaders if they are celibate? What if they are not celibate? Can the church learn anything from their LGBTQI members about faith, gender, and sexuality, or is the learning all one directional?

ENCOUNTERING LGBTQI ISSUES

With the recent Supreme Court ruling that same-sex marriage bans are unconstitutional, the pressure is mounting for evangelical churches. Will they change their views and be seen as accommodating themselves to an unbelieving culture, or will they hold their ground and risk being seen by the culture at large as bigoted?

Just in the last year, three churches have gone a step further and said that LGBTQI individuals do not need to be celibate to be accepted into membership and, presumably, leadership, in the church.[7] While this is not unusual for mainline Protestants, it is a radical move for conservative evangelical churches.

The latest congregation to make the move is San Francisco's City Church, led by Pastor Fred Harrell Sr.[8] The congregation is a part of the conservative Reformed Church in America. In a pastoral letter to his congregation, posted on the church website, Pastor Harrell explains that there are three reasons the church took this course:

1. God is bringing LGBTQI people to their church.
2. The current practice of requiring lifelong celibacy from LGBTQI members is causing harm; it does not tend toward human flourishing.
3. The demand for celibacy is inconsistent with the gospel, which prioritizes breaking down barriers.[9]

This evolution is typical of the transition many churches undergo. The more general, affirmative statements of the gospel (e.g., "There is neither Jew nor Gentile, neither slave nor free, nor is there male and female, for you are all one in Christ Jesus"; Galatians 3:28 NIV) are prioritized over the specific teachings about homosexuality or patriarchy (e.g., women should submit to men because they sinned first; see 1 Timothy 2:11–15). Progressive evangelicals understand texts calling for unity in the body of Christ, breaking down barriers of division, and radical inclusivity to overrule specific sexual guidelines, which interpreters believe are limited by culture and context.

In response to the new inclusiveness of churches like City Church in San Francisco, those on the conservative end of the spectrum are pushing back. Writing for the website *First Things*, Robert A. J. Gagnon observes:

> As a church inspired by Tim Keller's Redeemer Presbyterian Church in New York City and founded in the Reformed tradition, City Church is supposed to give preeminence to Scripture. Instead, on the matter of homosexual practice, the Pastor and Elder Board gave preeminence to their judgment regarding what conduces more to human flourishing and, oddly, to a scripturally misguided book written by former Vineyard Pastor Ken Wilson called *A Letter to My Congregation*.[10]

Jennifer LeClaire conflates same-sex loving relationships with adultery, greed, and drunkenness in her article for *Charisma News*:

> But what about listening to the Word of God's stance on practicing homosexuality—or fornication, adultery or greed or drunkenness for that matter? What about dealing honestly with Scripture? Harrell and his board have come to the conclusion that the thrust and focus of the gospel is to break down boundaries of exclusion. He points to "multiple respected evangelical scholars and theologians" who are debating inclusion, and "there is no longer clear consensus on this issue within the evangelical community."[11]

She continues, "I have compassion on LGBT people who are struggling with their identity or feel rejected by society or the church. I agree that the church needs to work harder to help and not hurt LGBT people—and all people. But giving a nod to a sinful lifestyle is not helping—it's hurting."[12]

In the face of a significant cultural shift in America that is sweeping up many evangelical churches in its tide, there are naturally those who wish to hold the line. The "third way" approach is an attempt to "listen to the Word of God" on the issue without rejecting LGBTQI individuals outright.

Standing in this gap are many organizations whose expressed purpose is to help conservative, Bible-believing evangelicals come to terms with issues of gender and sexuality in such a way that "the next generation of LGBT youth will grow up fully loved and embraced by their families, churches, and neighbors; and where Christians worldwide will live up to their calling as instruments of grace and defenders of the outcasts."[13] This is easier said than done.

Organizations like the Gay Christian Network (GCN), led by the charismatic Justin Lee, and the Marin Foundation, led by founder Andrew Marin, are trying to change the narrative as well as the interpretation of the biblical texts without alienating the church in the process.[14] As these leaders struggle to hold the church together around an issue that is threatening to tear it to pieces, the future is far from certain. Justin Lee's own attempt at this takes the form of what he calls side A and side B. Lee argues that God blesses same-sex relationships (side A), but many who identify with his organization disagree. The other side (side B) argues that God loves LGBTQI individuals but that honoring God means remaining celibate. At the end of the day, Lee is attempting to make the case that both sides, A and B, should be able to remain in fellowship in the church.

Too often overlooked in this tug-of-war are the actual LGBTQI individuals themselves. It is one thing for churches to extend acceptance and the hand of fellowship. It is another for the churches to see LGBTQI individuals as valuable members of the body of Christ with something unique to offer. Heteronormative culture has so thoroughly otherized LGBTQI people that churches' best efforts are often aimed at acceptance and tolerance. The examined sexuality that LGBTQI individuals bring to the church is perhaps exactly what the church needs in this time and place.

In that respect, the work that is being done by a fledgling organization called Level Ground is inspiring and hopeful.[15] Level Ground was founded by two young women who graduated with their master's degrees in theology from Fuller Theological Seminary; its mission is to create safe space through film and art for dialogue around faith, gender, and sexuality. Level Ground believes that the telling and hearing of personal stories—often stories of profound pain and suffering—create a different kind of conversation around the controversial issues of gender and sexuality. Because of the way the church has traditionally otherized LGBTQI people, many Christians have never had an authentic conversation with a person of a different sexual orientation or gender identity. The opportunity for face-to-face conversation around honest storytelling holds great promise.

TRADITION AND TRANSFORMATION

Evangelicals, due to their unswerving commitment to as literal an interpretation of the Bible as possible, have been slow to accept major changes as they have occurred in Western society. Each major reform, whether abolition of slavery, suffrage rights for women, the labor movement, and so forth, has developed vis-à-vis the political framework of liberalism. Given evangelicalism's fundamental conservatism, these adaptations have come with great difficulty. Many evangelical denominations are still wrestling with these changes today. On the other hand, once they have been convinced that the Word of God stands on the side of rectifying an injustice, evangelicals are unstoppable.

A fitting example is the case of American chattel slavery. American evangelicals were for it before they were against it. Because the culture of America in the early days of nationhood was overwhelmingly slave owning, there was little concern about the ethics of owning another human being, even for Christians. Even when ethical concerns did arise, they were quickly tamped down with appeals to the Bible and arguments about certain economic collapse should slavery be abolished. Over time, however, the progressive voices grew louder. Many of these progressive Christian voices were members and clergy from the liberal side of the church—Quakers and Unitarians in particular. As the moral voice for change grew louder, the church changed its theology. While the Bible clearly contains passages that can be interpreted as endorsing slavery and even describes how to relate to one's slaves, theologians explained that there was a moral trajectory to the Bible's teaching about slavery. Extrapolated out to the present day, it is difficult for interpreters to argue in favor of the morality of the institution.

Another example is the church's relationship to women. The Bible is unabashedly patriarchal for the simple reason that it was written in a deeply patriarchal time and place. From Genesis 1, where the original sin is blamed unequivocally on Eve, to the writings of the apostle Paul, who explains that women should not exercise authority over a man because Eve sinned first (see 1 Timothy 2:12–15), the Bible thoroughly subordinates women to men.

Many evangelical churches have since abandoned most of their patriarchal practices by once again arguing that Paul's statements are culturally determined, even while they reflect Paul's own theology. There are still, however, dozens of evangelical denominations who will not permit women to be ordained as ministers, including the Lutheran Church–Missouri Synod, Christian and Missionary Alliance, Orthodox Presbyterian Church, and the church of my upbringing, the Seventh-day Adventist Church.

In both of these cases, it was strict commitment to a literal interpretation of the Bible that prevented evangelicals from leading or embracing moral and ethical social reforms as they were happening. Even as evangelical institutions have developed theology that accounts for their changed views on slavery and women, many still claim that the case of same-sex relationships is fundamentally different.

In *Slaves, Women and Homosexuals: Exploring the Hermeneutics of Cultural Analysis*, theologian William J. Webb, former professor of New Testament at Heritage Seminary in Ontario, Canada, makes a very compelling argument for what he calls a redemptive-movement hermeneutic.[16] Biblical instructions regarding slaves, for example, seem reprehensible with respect to our culture today, but in the time those texts were written, Webb argues, they were much more progressive than the cultural norms. In other words, the Bible's instructions about slavery exist along a redemptive trajectory. To be faithful to the text means following that trajectory out to the present day. This is easy to understand and apply in hindsight with reference to women and slaves, and harder to apply with foresight about pressing issues of the day, like LGBTQI people. Indeed, Webb argues in the same book that his redemptive-movement hermeneutic does not apply in the same way to homosexuality.

LOOKING FORWARD

As with other battlefields in the modern culture wars, the trend among evangelicals today regarding LGBTQI individuals and the church is toward polarization. On the one hand, there is clearly a movement toward complete inclusion of LGBTQI individuals in evangelical churches, as indicated by congregations like City Church in San Francisco, GracePointe in Nashville, and EastLake Community Church in Seattle and by parachurch organizations like Level Ground, the Marin Foundation, and the Gay Christian Network. The Reconciling Ministries Network in the United Methodist Church is another sign of movement toward full acceptance and inclusion.

However, there is another movement afoot to counter these efforts. At stake in this conflict, for conservatives, is nothing less than the authority of the Bible and the survival of the church. Underneath this concern is a deep anxiety about pluralism in America. In March 2015 the state of Indiana passed the Religious Freedom Restoration Act, which ostensibly protected the rights of businesses to refuse to violate their religious convictions in the process of conducting their business. Though the proponents of this law denied it, it was clear to most every observer that the law, like the one proposed the previous year in Arizona, was designed to allow businesses to discriminate against same-sex couples. The backlash came quick and strong. Just two business days after Governor Mike Pence signed the bill into law, he signed changes that now stand as the state's first law protecting against discrimination on the grounds of sexual orientation and gender identity.

The casualties in this culture war have been extensive. Thousands of LGBTQI individuals and straight allies no longer identify as Christians as a result of being rejected by their churches. This rejection feels tantamount to rejection by God and has led some to give up their faith altogether. An April 2014 study by Public Religion Research Institute revealed that "among Millennials who no longer identify with their childhood religion, nearly one-third say negative teachings about, or treatment of, gay and lesbian people was either a somewhat important (17 percent) or very important (14 percent) factor in their disaffiliation from religion."[17]

While the general movement in evangelical Christianity appears to be in the direction of full acceptance of LGBTQI individuals by the evangelical churches, the question is whether the change will come fast enough for this branch of Christianity to remain attractive to younger Americans.

SUGGESTED RESOURCES

The Gay Christian Network, www.gaychristian.net. A support organization that includes and seeks to build bridges between Christians supporting same-sex marriage and relationships and those promoting celibacy for Christians with same-sex attractions.

Level Ground, http://onlevelground.org. A community dedicated to using the arts to create safe space for dialogue about faith, gender, and sexuality.

The Marin Foundation, www.themarinfoundation.org. Seeks true reconciliation between LGBTQ and conservative Christians through gatherings, research, and classes on the history of the church and sexuality.

Reconciling Ministries Network, www.rmnetwork.org. Helps churches, campus organizations, and other religious communities, specifically in the United Methodist denomination, through the discernment and growth process in becoming welcoming congregations.

The Roman Catholic Church

Sister Jeannine Gramick, SL

When I meet a gay person ... if they accept the Lord and have goodwill, who am I to judge them? They shouldn't be marginalized. The tendency [to homosexuality] is not the problem ... they're our brothers.[1]

—Pope Francis

LAYING THE GROUNDWORK

The Catholic Church, also called the Roman Catholic Church, has more than 1.2 billion members worldwide. It traces its beginnings to Jesus Christ, a Jew living in Galilee of Palestine more than two thousand years ago. Jesus was a teacher, healer, and prophet whose disciples continued preaching "the Way" after Jesus's earthly death. Followers of the Way, particularly Saint Paul, organized the movement to meet in house churches throughout Palestine and the lands around the Mediterranean Sea. After the first two centuries, followers of the Way grew apart from Judaism and developed their own structure of governance.

Despite persecutions of Christians in the early Roman Empire, the new religion spread. The legalization of Christianity by the emperor Constantine in 313 CE halted persecutions, and by the end of that century Christianity became the state religion. Many Catholics

Sister Jeannine Gramick, SL, is a Roman Catholic nun with the Sisters of Loretto and co-founded, with Father Robert Nugent, New Ways Ministry, a Catholic organization working for justice and reconciliation of LGBT people and the church. Her book *Building Bridges: Gay and Lesbian Reality and the Catholic Church* was the subject of a Vatican investigation. Her ministry with LGBTQI Catholics and her struggle with church authorities is the focus of the film *In Good Conscience: Sister Jeannine Gramick's Journey of Faith.*

today believe that the union of church and state contributed to a certain "loss of soul." The Greek Church in the east was dominated by the eastern emperor, while the Latin Church in the west gained its own political power. Struggles for domination between east and west, often cloaked in different theological language, eventually resulted in a schism in 1054 CE.

Another schism occurred in the sixteenth century when Martin Luther and others called attention to a series of abuses by the Catholic Church, such as the selling of indulgences. Because the pope was not receptive to the ideas of the Reformers, a major fracture, called the Protestant Reformation, occurred. After the rupture, the Roman Church responded by convening the Council of Trent to condemn various beliefs of the challengers. During the period that followed, called the Counter-Reformation, the Roman Church tried to correct many of the abuses that the Reformers had pointed out.

Catholicism spread widely across the globe, though in some geographic areas in Europe Protestantism took hold. In Latin America, Catholicism dominated because of the expansion of the Spanish and Portuguese empires. The Age of Enlightenment challenged Christianity by its appeal to human reason over divine revelation. In the nineteenth century, liberal theologians tried to incorporate the implications of the Enlightenment by more critical approaches to the role of religion in society. A succession of popes resisted all such attempts, condemning the "heresy of modernism." Another schism occurred after the first Vatican Council, when many bishops in attendance rejected the idea of papal infallibility, with some forming the Old Catholic Church.

The most significant event in Catholicism in the twentieth century and, many believe, since the church's first three centuries, was the Second Vatican Council, 1962–65, called by Pope John XXIII. Vatican II, as it is termed, revoked the worldview of the Counter-Reformation and called for the modernization that the Reformers had sought. To the modern observer, many doctrinal differences of the past appear to be simply power struggles, with one party unwilling to acknowledge the sensibility, and thus the authority, of another's argument. The schism of 1054 was put to rest by a Catholic-Orthodox joint declaration that lifted the mutual excommunications that the parties had hurled at each other. The Catholic Church pledged to improve Christian unity and interfaith dialogue. As a result of Vatican II, the church would no longer issue condemnations and disciplinary actions, but instead try to make persuasive presentations of the truth.

The faithful responded in different ways. Some stopped going to church because the changes of Vatican II had not gone far enough. For example, a reaffirmation of the ban on artificial means of birth control caused a mass exodus of Catholics in the United States and western Europe. Others rejected the changes, particularly in the liturgy, and a traditionalist schism followed. The pontificates of Pope John Paul II and Pope Benedict XV tried to roll back the reforms of Vatican II. With the election of Pope Francis in 2013, the atmosphere of fear and rigidity began to lessen, with a return to the open dialogue encouraged by Vatican II.

Regarding governance, the Catholic Church has gone through various phases, from a more democratic form of consulting members to more rigid forms of authoritarianism. In the early Christian community, bishops were overseers of the community. Presbyters were older, respected men who taught and preached and sometimes formed a community council. Deacons ministered to the physical needs of the community. The term "priest" was not used to refer to a Christian leader until the beginning of the second century CE. The term "priest" is still used today to refer to a male ordained to church leadership and service.

The office of pope, the bishop of Rome, evolved because of various cultural factors. The only church in the Western Roman Empire that had apostolic roots was Rome. (Peter and Paul were martyred in Rome.) Rome was the longtime capital of the empire, and it continued to be a prime center of commerce, interactions, and exchange of ideas. For these and other reasons, the bishop of Rome held a place of preeminence among the bishops in the early church. Bishops who could not resolve doctrinal or policy differences often appealed to the bishop of Rome to act as a judge.

For the first thousand years of the Christian era, the bishop of Rome was treated as the first among equals. During the next millennium, as the pope assumed more temporal power, papal primacy deteriorated into rigid and autocratic rule. Vatican II debated this highly centralized ecclesiology, voting to return to a collegial system in which the pope, once again, was seen as the first among equals in the college of bishops. Authority today in Catholicism is vested in the world's bishops, who are all male. Candidates for the office of bishop are recommended in a secret fashion, for the most part, by current bishop and papal nuncios in their respective countries and then appointed by the pope. Laymen and women can make their views known through diocesan councils, but these bodies have no deliberative power. Numerous Catholic groups worldwide are advocating for shared authority through the ordination of women priests, as well as the election of bishops, a common practice in the early church.

FOUNDATIONAL NARRATIVES

When scripture scholars explain the meaning of various portions of the Bible, they interpret passages using either a literal interpretation or a historical-critical one. The literal interpretation accepts that the words in the text mean exactly what they say. In reading the Genesis account of Creation, for example, a literal interpretation maintains that the world was created in seven days.

The historical-critical interpretation of a text takes into account the meaning that the text might have had for the people when it was written and received. This method asserts that the text needs to be understood in its original historical and cultural context, and only then can appropriate applications be made to the present-day situation. The method is called "critical" because it necessitates precise thinking and comprehensive analysis.

The magisterium, biblical scholars, and lay Catholics all apply these two methods to texts that the Catholic Church has traditionally associated with homosexuality. An increasing number of lay Catholics and some Catholic biblical scholars are beginning to apply a historical-critical interpretation to these texts. The magisterium has yet to do this.

Homosexuality is not a major topic of interest in the Bible. The prophets have no words to say about it. The four Gospels contain no condemnations by Jesus on the subject. The scriptural verses, besides the contentious story of Sodom (Genesis 19:1–29), are few. There are only five short passages (Leviticus 18:22; Leviticus 20:13; Romans 1:26–27; 1 Corinthians 6:9; 1 Timothy 1:10).

The most famous biblical passage that has been interpreted to condemn homosexuality is the story of Sodom. When the men of Sodom come to Lot's house and demand to "know" (as in "carnal knowledge") Lot's heavenly visitors, Lot offers to let the men rape his daughters instead of his visitors. The point of this story cannot be sexual ethics. If so, are we to infer that rape of women is morally permissible?

Using the historical-critical method, the vast majority of biblical scholars since the 1950s surmise that Sodom was destroyed because of its inhospitality to strangers. The modern reader may have difficulty in comprehending the mores during Lot's time in which women were considered mere property that could be sacrificed to maintain laws of great obligation. There were no Holiday Inns in these ancient lands, and travelers were dependent on the kindness of townsfolk for shelter and safety. Almost all of the ethical codes of this period held hospitality as a sacred duty. Consequently, most exegetes today infer that the sin of the Sodomites was their willingness to violate the law of hospitality by assaulting or abusing the stranger.

Furthermore, nowhere in the Hebrew or Christian scriptures is Sodom identified with homosexuality. Sodom is used as a sign of wickedness and identified with social sins or lack of charity.[2] For example, the New American Bible translates Ezekiel 16:49, "And look at the guilt of your sister Sodom: she and her daughters were proud, sated with food, complacent in their prosperity, and they gave no help to the poor and needy." Only later did interpreters identify the sin of Sodom as homosexuality.[3]

While the homosexual interpretation of the story of Sodom was made many hundreds of years after the story was written, the passages from Leviticus clearly deal with male homosexual activity, which is called an abomination punishable by death. What is the historical context of these passages? These two passages occur in a section of Leviticus called the Holiness Code, which lists what the Hebrews must do or not do to remain a holy people, set apart from the other cultures surrounding them. Some examples of the practices listed in the Holiness Code were having sex with a menstruating woman and offering child sacrifices to a Canaanite god. Examples of other "abominations" mentioned in the Holiness Code were the eating of crab, clams, oysters, pigs, and certain kinds of birds, all of which were considered unclean.[4] Scholars contend that the Holiness Code was concerned with ritual purity. Homosexual acts made a Hebrew male unclean and associated him with a Canaanite cultic practice. These acts were proscribed because of cultural and religious significance, not ethical or moral significance.

Two texts in the Christian scriptures (1 Corinthians 6:9; 1 Timothy 1:10) contain words that are often translated as "homosexual," but the meanings of the original Greek words are unclear. The third Christian text (Romans 1:26–27) condemns same-sex acts as "unnatural." Homosexual *acts*, not homosexual *people*, are condemned in these texts, and the basis for condemning these acts is the natural law.

Using historical-critical analysis, the interpreter of this text asks, "What did Saint Paul and his contemporaries believe about the nature of human sexuality?" The scripture writers of two thousand years ago had no knowledge that some people are constitutionally attracted to members of their own gender, a fact that emerged only at the end of the nineteenth and beginning of the twentieth centuries. Our knowledge of psychology and of the various facets of the human personality is enormously different today. Current scientific evidence that homosexuality and bisexuality are inborn sexual orientations requires new interpretations of these passages. If this scientific information had been available, perhaps Saint Paul would not have judged homosexual acts as severely or even at all. The writers of the biblical texts do not address adult, loving same-sex relationships as we understand them today.

Those who interpret the "homosexual" texts strictly are not always consistent in their interpretations. For example, the Hebrew scriptures condemn certain sexual activities, such as marital relations during a woman's menstrual period, but strict interpreters often do not forbid this behavior. Similarly, the scriptures recommend practices that strict interpreters no longer accept, such as the death penalty for adulterous persons.

The historical-critical method has helped enormously to put the "homosexual" passages into a proper historical and cultural context. Like many mainline Christian scholars, Catholic biblical scholars have used the historical-critical method for more than one hundred years to interpret the scriptures. However, when it comes to biblical texts on homosexuality, many who reject a literal interpretation of other verses revert to a literal interpretation in this regard, showing that some cultural taboos are difficult to shake.[5]

ENCOUNTERING LGBTQI ISSUES

The magisterial teaching on homosexuality is a logical extension of its teaching on the morality of sexual intercourse and the nature of Christian marriage. It maintains that procreation is part of the very nature of human sexuality and part of the natural law that God ordained for the universe. Because every genital act must result in procreation, contraception and masturbation are also forbidden on these same grounds.

The official Catholic position does not use the Bible as the basis for opposing same-sex acts, as some Christian churches do. In Catholicism, the teaching appeals to the church's tradition about natural law and the purpose of sexuality, incorporating scriptural texts such as the Genesis account of Creation and the heterosexual thrust of the Hebrew and Christian scriptures to support or buttress the argument.

The major architect of the Catholic Church's teaching on sexuality was Saint Augustine, whose attitudes toward sexuality were influenced by the Stoic philosophy he encountered in the late fourth and early fifth centuries. Like the Stoics, Augustine was suspicious of any bodily pleasure, which needed some rational justification to render the pleasure morally good. The obvious justification for sexual pleasure for Augustine was procreation. This logic established the direction of Christian sexual ethics for the next fifteen hundred years.[6]

Sexual desire, Augustine thought, was an evil passion that needed to be ordered rightly and according to reason in order to justify its use in a right and moral way. This could be done only in a heterosexual marriage open to procreation. Any other sexual act was the result of an unnatural or disordered sexual desire. Therefore, anal and oral sex, masturbation, and coitus interruptus were unnatural acts because they did not result in procreation, which was the natural use of the sexual faculty. In this system of moral logic, Saint Thomas Aquinas in the thirteenth century would categorize incest and rape, although immoral, as "natural" acts because they resulted in procreation.

Contemporary theologians recognize that our understanding of natural law continues to change. We no longer believe that women are naturally inferior to men or are "misbegotten males," as Saint Thomas Aquinas and the Christian Church taught in the thirteenth century. Slavery is no longer considered a natural institution. With the knowledge we have gained from the sciences, we now know that a homosexual orientation is natural for at least 10 percent of the human population. Furthermore, homosexual behavior frequently occurs in other mammalian species.

This shift in determining what is natural and what constitutes natural law has brought about a comparable shift among ethicists today in evaluating sexuality in general. "There has been a widespread and general consensus among moralists in moving away from a static, predominantly biological, understanding of natural law to a more dynamic interpretation of it as our participation in God's plan."[7] These theologians have moved from an "act-centered" morality to a "person-centered" morality, where the quality of the relationship determines the ethics, not the gender of the person or the specific act involved.

Unfortunately, the theology of the Vatican has not caught up to the understanding of nature or natural law articulated by contemporary sexual ethicists. While some bishops privately acknowledge that contemporary insights about human nature should affect the church's teaching in many areas, retired bishop Geoffrey Robinson of Sydney, Australia, has publicly called for a reexamination of the traditional teachings on sexuality.[8]

For almost twenty centuries, the magisterium treated homosexuality from the viewpoint of sexual ethics. Only homosexual acts were considered. At the end of the nineteenth century, psychiatrists and psychologists concluded that homosexual acts, in and of themselves, were inadequate or sometimes confusing in assessing whether a person was homosexual. Sexual orientation, not sexual behavior, the scientists said, was the best indicator of a person's homosexuality.

Official Catholic teaching did not refer to a homosexual orientation until the 1980s, when it was judged objectively disordered by the Vatican's Congregation for the Doctrine of the Faith and reiterated in the Catechism of the Catholic Church.[9] The Catechism further asserts that homosexual acts are "intrinsically disordered" and "contrary to the natural law."[10] The sinfulness of any immoral act depends on whether the person has engaged in sufficient reflection and given full consent of their will in performing the act. Here, we can rightly say with Pope Francis, "Who am I to judge?"[11] because only God knows if the person's action is a sin.

Since 1980, the magisterium has recognized that homosexual persons should not be defined merely in terms of "acts" and "orientation." Some church documents speak of dignity, respect, justice, and pastoral care for the homosexual person. One of the most sensitive of these documents is a pamphlet from the U.S. Catholic Bishops, titled *Always Our Children: A Pastoral Message to Parents of Homosexual Children and Suggestions for Pastoral Ministers.* It encourages parents to be supportive when their sons or daughters reveal their sexual orientation. The document ends with the often quoted message to lesbian women and gay men, "In you God's love is revealed."[12]

The pastoral documents declaring the dignity, goodness, and worth of lesbian and gay people as children of God belong to the church's social justice teaching regarding homosexuality. Unfortunately, the social justice teaching does not receive as much attention as the teaching on sexual ethics.

An enormous revolution in beliefs about sexuality has been going on among Catholic theologians since the Second Vatican Council. Most of them do not agree with the traditional moral evaluation of homosexuality. Their disagreement centers on their assessments of orientation and behavior.

For example, some who disagree with the traditional teaching take a moderate stance and maintain that same-sex behavior is morally permissible in the context of a loving, faithful relationship, but they believe that a homosexual orientation is inferior to a heterosexual one. Other moral theologians, who disagree with the traditional teaching, take a more liberal position. They also maintain that same-sex behavior is morally permissible in the context of a loving, faithful relationship, but they teach that a homosexual orientation is not inferior to a heterosexual one. They believe that no orientation is inferior or superior because diversity is a vital part of God's plan for humanity.

What do the Catholic laity, that is, the People of God, believe about homosexuality? A *New York Times/ CBS News* poll conducted in 2013 showed that 62 percent of U.S. Catholics are in favor of legalizing marriage for same-sex couples.[13] Nearly eight in ten Catholics polled said they would be more likely to follow their conscience on "difficult moral questions" than to follow the pope's teachings.[14]

Beyond the issue of same-sex marriage, a 2014 fact sheet from the Public Religion Research Institute reported that Catholic support for the rights of gay and lesbian people was strong. For example, 73 percent of Catholics favored laws to protect gays and lesbians against workplace discrimination, and 61 percent of Catholics favored allowing gay and lesbian couples to adopt children.[15]

There have been some initial polls on Catholic attitudes toward transgender persons. Eighty-nine percent of the U.S. population agrees that transgender people should have the same rights and protections as other persons. This includes overwhelming majorities of all major religious groups, with Catholic agreement of 93 percent surpassing agreement by white evangelical Protestants (83 percent), and by white mainline Protestants (90 percent).[16]

When I became involved in church ministry to lesbian and gay Catholics in 1971, I had never heard any Catholic Church leader speak about homosexuality, much less bisexual, transgender, queer, or intersex issues. Even today there is no discussion of "BTQI" issues by the Catholic hierarchy, and only the beginnings of a dialogue in the theological community and among lay Catholics. The hierarchy generally considers transgender identities to be "against nature." Catholic moral theologians are beginning to take the stance that "no one ought to pass judgment on any configurations of gender."[17]

Among lay Catholics, a respected Catholic psychologist recently examined transgender issues,[18] and a husband-wife team have written about transgender persons from their professional viewpoints as a pastoral theologian and a developmental psychologist.[19] Another pastoral minister wrote about the hardships and joys of beginning the transgender process at a very young age.[20] One religious woman has worked for almost two decades in a pastoral ministry on behalf of transgender persons.[21]

Some churchgoing Catholics are now asking, "What does the 'T' in 'LGBT' mean?" Conversations about transgender persons have occurred in limited venues for the last decade or so. Organizations like New Ways Ministry and DignityUSA are offering workshops, publications, and other resources to provide instruction about sexual and gender diversity, but their efforts have thus far reached only a very small percentage of the U.S. Catholic population. More extensive discussion about bisexual, transgender, queer, or intersex persons is still in the future. The younger generation, especially students at most Catholic colleges and universities, is very much aware and supportive of sexual and gender diversity.

Based on my pastoral experience, I believe that the Catholic response in the United States to homosexuality serves as a barometer to predict attitudinal change toward BTQI in the future. Prior to the 1980s, there was little mention of lesbian and gay people in Catholic publications or Catholic Church documents. In 2014 lesbian and gay couples were being discussed by the church's bishops at an international synod in Rome. I predict that an acceptance of bisexual, transgender, queer, and intersex persons will follow the same trajectory of gradual awareness, tolerance, and finally favorable reception in the next thirty-five years. Education is the key to effect this change.

TRADITION AND TRANSFORMATION

LGBTQI Catholics and their allies are looking for a change of attitude on the part of the Catholic hierarchy. They are also hoping for a change in the magisterium's teaching on sexual ethics, including homosexuality. Others say that the change has already come from the theological community and grassroots Catholics; what is needed is for theologians and lay Catholics to dialogue with church leaders so that an official change can be made as quickly as possible.

This climate change, like the measured melting of polar glaciers, has begun. The U.S. bishops were the first church hierarchy in modern times to address the issue of homosexuality; their documents are substantially more developed and far-reaching in scope and magnitude than others. This is not to say that their documents are particularly sympathetic; however, the topic was put on the church's agenda in the United States before it was done elsewhere, and public discussion is the first step toward institutional change.

In 1973 the U.S. bishops published a pastoral guide to confessors regarding homosexuality. Following the first pastoral guide, a number of U.S. bishops or their state conferences issued statements, letters, or pastoral plans. Numerous U.S. dioceses established lesbian and gay ministries after a controversial letter from the Vatican's Congregation for the Doctrine of the Faith was issued in 1986.

What caused the U.S. bishops to give this attention, and more, to the topic of homosexuality? One answer to these questions can be found in the culture around the bishops. Church authorities must respond to cultural innovations in order to help shape and mold the values of their people in the modern world.

Another factor that impelled the bishops to address homosexuality is the influence of grassroots LGBTQI Catholics and their allies. In those countries where the hierarchy publicly addressed homosexuality, advocacy groups were in place and served to lobby and influence church leadership. In the United States, DignityUSA, founded in 1969, began first as a counseling group, then grew into a support group in Los Angeles, and has been a national organization since 1973. In 1977 Father Robert Nugent and I founded New Ways Ministry, primarily to effect attitudinal change about homosexuality among Catholic leaders and lay Catholics through education and public dialogue. While our immediate religious superiors approved of the work, some high-ranking bishops were able to effect a Vatican censure in 1999. The era of Pope Francis has affected the political position of New Ways Ministry in the Catholic Church. This was evident in 2015 when I led forty-nine LGBTQI pilgrims and their allies to Rome and we were given VIP treatment at a public audience with Pope Francis. Papal ushers seated us within twenty-five yards of Pope Francis's chair.

Fortunate Families provides resources for Catholic families with LGBTQI children, and Call to Action, the largest of the organizations, deals with a multiplicity of church reform issues. In particular, Call to Action is raising concerns about employment discrimination and the firing of church workers because of LGBTQI-related disputes.

If societal culture influenced the church hierarchy to begin to address the pastoral needs of lesbian women and gay men, did the presence of gay men in the clerical culture likewise help the bishops to address these pastoral needs? Did the bishops gain a better understanding of homosexuality and more sympathy for the difficulties of lesbian and gay people after conversations with their gay priests?

The reality is that many bishops are scapegoating gay priests for the current scandal of clerical sexual abuse. In the present climate, gay priests are dealing with a fear that the culture at large may find hard to understand. As if hiding from terrorists, most feel paralyzed to reveal who they really are. Father Bill McNichols, one of the few gay

Catholic priests who is out, said that these psychic closets are wrong and that "the Church of Christ should not be a fearful place."[22]

Gay men who are not priests but feel called to priesthood are also nervous. A 2005 Vatican instruction concerning the admission of gay men to seminaries rejects them from ordination because their sexual orientation is deemed "objectively disordered." Some bishops follow these guidelines while others do not. The coalition Equally Blessed is helping the church to realize that the blame lies in a clerical system that fostered sexual repression instead of psychosexual development and a healthy acceptance of one's sexual identity.

At this point in the church's history, gay priests have not been helpful in moving the discussion of reconsidering the magisterial teaching on homosexuality because of their fear and invisibility. Until recently, many bishops largely wanted to deny there were any gay priests in their dioceses—at least not publicly known as gay. Now that sexual abuse by priests and cover-ups by bishops are out of the closet, some bishops want gay priests out of the priesthood as well.

Until the Second Vatican Council, change was not encouraged in the Catholic Church, but because of Vatican II, the 1960s and '70s was a period of exuberant renewal and change within the church. The liturgy was changed from the Latin language to the vernacular. The church was engaging in ecumenical and interfaith ventures, instead of remaining in a self-imposed ghetto. Parish councils were formed to help the pastor share responsibilities with the laity. In 1975, one year following the irregular ordination of Episcopal women,[23] the first meeting was held in Detroit to discuss the ordination of women to the Roman Catholic priesthood. Many believed this change would happen within a few years.

With the election of Pope John Paul II in 1979 and then of Benedict XVI in 2005, hopes for women's ordination, optional celibacy for priests, acceptance of divorced and remarried people, a lifting of the ban on artificial birth control, support for lesbian and gay persons, and many other reforms were dashed. Almost thirty-five years of repression and fear of voicing a dissenting view ensued. Change, unless it was backward, was stifled, and expectations of change almost evaporated.

Then the election of Pope Francis in 2013 brought excitement and promise back to those who want to see the Catholic Church respected in the modern world. Like the shot heard round the world, "Who am I to judge?" has, without doubt, come to define Pope Francis. These five words represent an unambiguous departure from the harsh language of his predecessors toward LGBTQI persons.

A mere nine months after his election to the papacy, *Time* magazine named him its Person of the Year, in part for his welcome of lesbian and gay people. The *Advocate*, the leading LGBTQI magazine in the United States, chose him as the single most influential person of 2013 for their community, claiming "a significant and unprecedented shift took place this year in how LGBT people are considered by one of the world's largest faith communities."[24] Pope Francis turned into a rock star as he took his place on the cover of *Rolling Stone* magazine alongside other pop icons of American culture.

Pope Francis is the first pope to publicly use the word "gay." He has spoken about freedom and respect for the spiritual life of each person—all in the context of lesbian and gay people. His words affirm the decision that most LGBTQI Catholics have made to follow their conscience regarding sexuality, knowing in their hearts that they are at peace with God. It is particularly reassuring for them to hear such affirmation from the highest authority of their church.

Pope Francis said that the church's "pastoral ministry ... is not obsessed with the disjointed transmission of a multitude of doctrines."[25] Rather, he believes in and promotes "the heart of the Gospel. In this basic core, what shines forth is the beauty of the saving love of God."[26] He does not dwell on issues of sexuality. When he speaks about gay people, he bypasses words like "intrinsically disordered" and "objectively immoral."

Some of his colorful statements seem to be directly aimed at members of the hierarchy who are obsessed with culture wars and the hot-button issues of abortion, gay marriage, and contraception. Even more astonishing are his words about infallibility, a teaching that conservative bishops and cardinals like to invoke and that Pope Francis explained in his first extensive interview: "All the faithful, considered as a whole, are infallible in matters of belief, and the people display this *infallibilitas in credendo*, this infallibility in believing, through a supernatural sense of the faith of all the people walking together."[27] If Catholics take these words to heart, major changes will occur in the Catholic Church. Fear of dissent will be lessened as the faithful come to trust that the Spirit of God will enable the truth to emerge in due time.

LOOKING FORWARD

Certain trends need to be addressed in at least three areas: anti-discrimination laws, pastoral outreach to same-sex couples, and worker justice.

Anti-discrimination laws to protect LGBTQI persons have been passed in large portions of the globe; yet in other geographical areas, such as Uganda, homosexuality is criminalized, often leading to life imprisonment for repeat offenders. Similar persecution is occurring in Nigeria, Zambia, India, Russia, Croatia, and Jamaica, to name but a few nation-states. Catholics and people of faith worldwide are mobilizing to call upon these governments to condemn anti-LGBTQI laws in a campaign called No More Triangle Nations. The campaign, organized by New Ways Ministry and Fellowship Global, encourages people to contact Pope Francis to urge him to speak out against repressive laws. People can tweet at the Pope (@Pontifex), send him an email (av@pccs.va), or write him a letter (His Holiness Pope Francis, Apostolic Palace, Vatican City State, 00120).

A second area of emerging importance is the welfare of same-sex couples and their families, which Pope Francis acknowledged as one of the challenges facing the Catholic Church. He has publicly advocated civil unions, but not gay marriage, for same-sex couples. If the pope is serious about proclaiming Christ to a changing generation, he needs to listen humbly to younger age groups, who overwhelmingly support same-sex marriage. The fact that he placed the topic of same-sex couples on the agenda of the Synods on the Family in 2014 and 2015 and solicited input from the laity is an optimistic sign. Another optimistic sign was his audience with a gay man and his partner during his United States visit in September 2015 (even though the gay man, a former student of Pope Francis, thought the encounter was a personal, not a political, one).

A third trend and an area of great concern in the United States is the matter of worker justice. Since 2008, more than forty church workers have lost their jobs in LGBTQI-related employment disputes. For example, a teacher at a Catholic grade school in Minnesota was fired because she expressed support for marriage equality during a teacher evaluation, and an assistant principal at a Cincinnati Catholic high school was fired because he posted statements in support of marriage equality on his Facebook page. A lesbian woman was fired from an Ohio Catholic high school because her partner was listed in her mother's obituary. A transgender woman was fired from a New York Catholic high school when she transitioned from male to female. Sadly, the number of reported cases of these firings is increasing each year.[28] Catholic students often have been the most vociferous supporters of LGBTQI persons who have lost their jobs because of unjust discrimination. In 2015 the Catholic bishops of Germany changed their employment policies to protect married gay and lesbian employees, as well as divorced and remarried Catholics, from losing their jobs in Catholic establishments. This is a hopeful sign that lesbian and gay Catholics would like to see duplicated in church institutions throughout the world.

As justice seekers continue to address these three areas, the Catholic Church will continue to change. LGBTQI persons and their allies are setting a tone to enable that change to bubble up from below. Mark Segal, a leading gay activist in Philadelphia, rightly observed, "The actual doctrine of the church has not changed, but the message that Pope Francis is sending is more powerful than the doctrines themselves. Francis seems to understand that messages can create instant change, while doctrine can take years."[29] The Catholic community is poised for profound transformation.

SUGGESTED RESOURCES

Call to Action, www.cta-usa.org. A Catholic organization working against prejudice and oppression of all types.

DignityUSA, www.dignityusa.org. A support and advocacy group for LGBTQI Catholics.

Fortunate Families, http://fortunatefamilies.com. Network of Catholic parents of LGBTQI children.

LGBT Catholics: Owning Our Faith (video), www.OwningOurFaith.com. A fourteen-minute interview with LGBTQI Catholics.

New Ways Ministry, www.newwaysministry.org; https://newways ministryblog.wordpress.com. News, commentary, and reflections on LGBTQI issues in the Catholic Church.

Unitarian Universalism

Annette S. Marquis

It didn't seem unusual to me. It seemed normal as apple pie, that I and the two women sitting with me under Channing's portrait were discussing their relationship and their wedding plans.[1]

—Rev. Leslie Westbrook

LAYING THE GROUNDWORK

Unitarianism and Universalism are heretical traditions that have their beginnings in early Christianity. The Greek meaning of *heresy* is "choice." From their earliest roots, Unitarians and Universalists believed in the right to choose what they believed. "Unitarian" refers to the "Oneness of God," a belief that Jesus was sent by God on a divine mission but that he was not God. Universalist belief is centered on the precept that all people will be saved because a loving God would never condemn anyone to eternal damnation. In 325 CE, when the Nicene Creed proclaimed the Trinity as doctrine, Unitarians and Universalists came under intense persecution that lasted for centuries and still exists in some parts of the world today.

It wasn't until the sixteenth century, in Transylvania, that the first Unitarian congregations came into being. King John Sigismund held a debate in 1568, for which he invited Trinitarians to debate those

---

Annette S. Marquis serves the Unitarian Universalist Association (UUA) as the LGBTQ and multicultural programs director. From 2006 to 2012, she was the UUA's district executive for the southeast. She is the author of *Resistance: A Memoir of Civil Disobedience in Maricopa County* and a contributor to *Coming Out in Faith: Voices of LGBTQ Unitarian Universalists.*

who believed in the unity of God. Ferenc (Francis) Dávid was so persuasive in presenting the Unitarian position that many Transylvanians embraced Unitarianism. When a second debate was held a year later, the king not only converted to Unitarianism but also issued an edict allowing religious toleration, a cornerstone of Unitarian Universalism today. As a result, Francis Dávid is considered the founder of Unitarianism, and present-day Romania is home to over two hundred Unitarian congregations, some more than four hundred years old.[2] Many Unitarian Universalists embrace words attributed to Dávid, "We need not think alike to love alike," to form the foundation of their theology.[3]

The first Universalist congregation, a congregation of Universalist Baptists, was organized in 1781 in Philadelphia, Pennsylvania. At the same time, itinerant preachers throughout rural New England and in the middle Atlantic and southern states began to challenge the Calvinist teachings of eternal damnation by proclaiming that salvation was available to all.

The American Unitarian Association, formed in 1825, and the Universalist Church of America, founded in 1793, consolidated as the Unitarian Universalist Association in 1961. This new religion, Unitarian Universalism, is a progressive faith, committed to justice, equity, and compassion, that incorporates the idea that each person is responsible for their own spiritual growth from many sources of truth, which are continuously revealed to us.

The Unitarian Universalist Association (UUA) is an association of congregations, some led by ministers, some by laypeople. Each congregation sends delegates to an annual General Assembly, which elects the UUA board of trustees, the president, and membership on various national committees. Through resolutions and statements of conscience, congregational delegates determine the direction of the UUA, including how it supports efforts of diversity and inclusion.

FOUNDATIONAL NARRATIVES

According to Unitarian theologian James Luther Adams, liberal religion is a living tradition. No one source of truth, no text, no person, no system of beliefs has all the answers to fundamental questions about the meaning of life and our purpose here on earth. Divine wisdom is unfolding every day, and as it is revealed to us, it is our responsibility to use it to build a just and loving community.

Adams identified what he called the five smooth stones of religious liberalism.[4] These five smooth stones form the foundation of Unitarian Universalism:

- Religious liberalism depends on the principle that revelation is continuous.

- All relations between persons ought ideally to rest on mutual, free consent and not on coercion.

- Religious liberalism affirms the moral obligation to direct one's effort toward the establishment of a just and loving community.

- We deny the immaculate conception of virtue and affirm the necessity of social incarnation.

- Liberalism holds that the resources (divine and human) that are available for the achievement of meaningful change justify an attitude of ultimate optimism.

Thomas Starr King, a Unitarian minister who traveled west to California in 1860 and founded the San Francisco Unitarian Society, popularized a quip that sums up the difference between Unitarian and Universalist theology: "The Universalist ... believes that God is too good to damn us forever; and you Unitarians believe that you are too good to be damned."[5] Unitarian Universalism's inclusive theology holds that religious truth is found in all religions and that all people, regardless of sex, color, race, or class (and today defined much more broadly), have inherent worth and dignity.

To Unitarians and Universalists throughout history, Christian scriptures have served as a primary text. Jewish and Christian traditions have much to teach through their stories. However, Unitarian Universalists do not view the Bible as the infallible Word of God but rather as one source of wisdom among many others. Because revelation is continuous, Unitarians and Universalists seek truth from many sources, including:

- Direct experience of that transcending mystery and wonder, affirmed in all cultures, which moves us to a renewal of the spirit and an openness to the forces which create and uphold life;

- Words and deeds of prophetic women and men which challenge us to confront powers and structures of evil with justice, compassion, and the transforming power of love;

- Wisdom from the world's religions which inspires us in our ethical and spiritual life;

- Jewish and Christian teachings which call us to respond to God's love by loving our neighbors as ourselves;

- Humanist teachings which counsel us to heed the guidance of reason and the results of science and warn us against idolatries of the mind and spirit;

- Spiritual teachings of earth-centered traditions which celebrate the sacred circle of life and instruct us to live in harmony with the rhythms of nature.[6]

These sources were adopted through formal votes by the Unitarian Universalist General Assembly as recently as 1985, but the list of sources that compose the Unitarian Universalist "living tradition" developed out of the Transcendentalist movement of the 1820s and '30s. Transcendentalism arose out of Unitarianism, which at the time was the dominant religious movement of Boston. Transcendentalism professed that humans, men and women equally, have knowledge about themselves and the world that transcends that which we can feel, see, hear, and taste. At the same time that some Transcendentalists believed in utopian social reform, others believed that independence and self-reliance were the keys to reaching one's full potential.

In his 1837 speech "The American Scholar," Ralph Waldo Emerson said, "We will walk on our own feet; we will work with our own hands; we will speak our own minds."[7] Emerson believed that people were naturally good, and it is from this belief that Unitarian Universalists formed what is today the first of its seven principles, an affirmation of the inherent worth and dignity of all people.

Today, many Unitarian Universalists have a relationship with Christianity; that is, they grew up in Christian churches, have been inspired by the life of Jesus, but might not practice Christianity in any traditional sense. Generally speaking, for UUs who practice Christianity, God is too big to be contained in one person, one book, one tradition, or one time in history. To UU Christians, Jesus is an inspiration and his teachings are profound; he possesses a divine spark that is born in all of us and can be cultivated throughout our lives.[8]

Any one UU congregation might have members who identify theologically as atheist, agnostic, Buddhist, Christian, Earth-centered, Hindu, Humanist, Jewish, or Muslim. There also might be those who say they are Unitarian Universalists who draw wisdom from many of these teachings. This theological openness to all the world's religions and the dialogue and interaction among them is a source of strength and wisdom for UUs.

It was Emerson's 1838 Divinity School address that moved Unitarian thought farthest along from its adherence to Christian belief in the historical miracles of Jesus to the idea that revelation is continuously unfolding and that God is alive in human souls. Although originally rejected by Unitarian theologians as false teaching, this address opened Unitarianism up to the idea that truth comes from many sources. It is only through understanding Jesus as our equal that we can recognize our own ability to enter into the divine. This revelation, that each of us has a spark of the divine inside of us, made it possible 130 years later for Unitarian Universalism to open the door to LGBTQI people.

A verse in Edwin Markham's 1913 poem "Outwitted" is often quoted by Unitarians as an expression of "the inclusiveness of love against the exclusiveness of faith":

> *He drew a circle that shut me out—*
> *Heretic, rebel, a thing to flout.*
> *But love and I had the wit to win:*
> *We drew a circle and took him in!*[9]

In 1985, the UUA adopted a statement of principles and purposes. Although not a creed or dogma, the Principles and Purposes set forth a set of shared values and shared understandings that enable UUs to talk about and study their faith. They exist as a covenant between member congregations. While the congregation as a whole affirms the covenant, no individual member of the congregation is required to assent to the covenant.

The first principle, which affirms the inherent worth and dignity of every person, and the second, which affirms justice, equity, and compassion in human relations, are most commonly heralded in the UU commitment to LGBTQI welcome and inclusion.[10]

ENCOUNTERING LGBTQI ISSUES

In 2004 Rev. William G. Sinkford, president of the Unitarian Universalist Association, officiated at a wedding at UUA headquarters in Boston. The two women married that day were lead plaintiffs in the case that resulted in Massachusetts becoming the first state to legalize same-sex marriage. Before and since, Unitarian Universalists have been at the forefront of the marriage equality movement, not only in Massachusetts, but in every state across the country.

In the 1980s and '90s, when the word "welcoming" became a code word for accepting lesbian, gay, and bisexual people, the Unitarian Universalist Association launched a Welcoming Congregation Program to help UUs learn how to undo homophobia—and later, bi-phobia and transphobia—in hearts and minds, congregations, and communities. The Welcoming Congregation Program arose as a direct response to the "Report and Recommendations of the Common Vision Planning Committee," published in 1989. The Common Vision Planning Committee was formed after a 1985 recommendation by the UUA board-appointed Task Force on Social Responsibility recommended that the Office of Lesbian and Gay Concerns (OLGC) (an office originally formed in 1973) be eliminated and the functions of that office assumed by the UU gay and lesbian constituency. This recommendation was not well received by the Unitarian Universalists for Lesbian and Gay Concerns (UULGC), a volunteer organization of UUs committed to working on lesbian and gay inclusion.

At the time of this recommendation, the UULGC was advocating for an expansion of the Office of Lesbian and Gay Concerns, arguing that "gay and lesbian people had reached a historic and critical moment in both the denomination and society, and that the Unitarian Universalist Association has a unique role to play in this period of history."[11] UULGC stated "that adoption of the recommendation would result in a seriously inadequate response to gay and lesbian issues."[12]

The reasons for the task force's original recommendation do not appear to be homophobic, as they were not directed specifically at the OLGC. Their recommendations included a redefinition of positions in the Department of Social Responsibility from specialists, such as the director of the OLGC, to generalists who would address many issues. Included in its recommendation was a suggestion that the UULGC employ its own director. With only twenty-five local chapters and very few resources available to it, UULGC wasn't capable of assuming this cost. They claimed their membership was low because "many gay and lesbian UUs remain secretive about their identity because they fear that were they to 'come out' the homophobia and heterosexism that prevail in society—and still in many UU societies[13]—would take too severe a toll in their personal and professional lives."[14]

UUA administration listened to the concerns and appointed the Common Vision Planning Committee to develop recommendations specific to gay, lesbian, and bisexual inclusion and outreach in the UUA.

One of the initial steps taken by the Common Vision Planning Committee was to conduct a survey of UUs about where they stood in regard to gay/lesbian/bisexual inclusion. With the AIDS crisis at its peak, attitudes toward gay, lesbian, and bisexual people were shifting. It is clear, however, from the data gathered in this survey that individual congregations and the national office were still struggling with what gay, lesbian, and bisexual inclusion even looked like. And given that transgender people were not identified in the survey, it is also clear that efforts to welcome transgender and queer people had not begun.

Although some gay, lesbian, and bisexual people felt affirmed by their religious home, 15 percent of gays and 34 percent of lesbians surveyed said that the UUA failed to affirm them, and another 28 percent of gays and lesbians said they experienced only limited acceptance; 41 percent of bisexuals said they felt similarly. Fifty-two percent of lesbians said that the UUA's goals relative to gay, lesbian, and bisexual people were clear but that they were not shared by individual congregations. Thirty-four percent of gay men and 38 percent of bisexuals agreed. This disparity between the affirmation of the national association and the local congregation was a key factor in pointing to the need for a congregationally based education and awareness program.[15]

The heterosexual responses to the survey were evenly split on a number of issues, including the statements "I would have a difficult time voting for an openly gay, lesbian, or bisexual ministerial candidate for my congregation" and "I don't mind having gays, lesbians, and bisexuals in my congregation, if only they would stop discussing it all the time."[16] Responses were also split on whether more could be done to minister to gay, lesbian, and bisexual people.

As part of the survey, a significant number of written comments show the extreme emotional responses among UU congregations during that time. On the positive side, one respondent wrote, "My denomination has gone beyond a paper endorsement of gay rights to a living endorsement in each member's heart of a fellow person's right to an equal quality of life."[17]

The negative comments ranged from the uninformed to the vitriolic. In fact, some views were so hateful that it is doubtful that the people who wrote those comments continue to be members of today's LGBTQI-inclusive UU congregations. One respondent wrote, "Accepting aberrant and abhorrent sexual activity should not be considered the obligation of a religious body any more than accepting a physical abnormality should be the role of medicine.... The sooner we cut loose gays and lesbians as a sovereign group within our church, the better!"[18] Another wrote, "I loathe them regardless. They actively prey upon young people, have multiple sexual partners, and do spread AIDS. Sex is the overriding concern of their tawdry loves, all else is meaningless. Many are hate-filled anti-straight."[19] These two quotes capture only a fraction of the vehemence expressed by those who opposed LGBTQI inclusion. However, even in 1989, in spite of such negative responses, the majority of survey respondents thought their church or minister should offer ceremonies of union to gay, lesbian, or bisexual couples and that gay, lesbian, bisexual people and heterosexual people could benefit from knowing more about each other's lives.

These results point to the challenges of the time and the tremendous efforts that were still needed to move toward full inclusion. It was a time of reevaluation of old prejudices and adoption of new attitudes, which in many cases had not yet fully been embraced.

Today, over 95 percent of Unitarian Universalist congregations with over one hundred members and 65 percent of congregations with one hundred or fewer members have applied for and have been designated Welcoming Congregations by the UUA.[20] This rigorous process requires that congregations vote to become a Welcoming Congregation after they have engaged in education on LGBTQ issues, have revised by-laws and other documents to be inclusive of LGBTQ people, and have reached out to advocate for and support LGBTQ people in the wider community.

Congregations are encouraged to renew their Welcoming Congregation status every five years, a process that is just beginning to gain momentum. Renewing their Welcoming Congregation commitment is especially critical for congregations that became designated Welcoming Congregations in the early to mid-1990s, before transgender and queer were added to the designation of what it means to be a Welcoming Congregation. This is a current area of focus for education and outreach for Welcoming Congregations.

In exploring contemporary responses to LGBTQI issues and members, UUs must explore the role of ministry in Unitarian Universalism. Ministers play, and have played, a vital role in educating Unitarian Universalists and in leading social justice efforts related to LGBTQI equality. The relationship between Unitarian Universalist congregations and LGBTQI ministers has not always been smooth. In order to comprehend it, it is necessary to understand how a person becomes a minister of a UU congregation or serves the community as an ordained UU minister.

Unitarian Universalist congregations have the freedom to invite anyone, or no one, to serve as their ministers. Many UU congregations are lay-led, which means that the members of the congregation work together to meet the spiritual needs of the congregation. Congregations that elect to have a minister can choose someone from their midst or can choose to engage in a more formal process with outside candidates. Ordained ministers might also choose to serve in the community as a staff member of a nonprofit organization, for example, rather than directly as a congregation's minister.

During a congregational search, the ministerial candidate meets with members of the congregation individually, in committees, and for Sunday morning worship. At the end of that time, the congregation votes whether or not to call, or invite, the minister. It is not uncommon for a candidate to refuse a call if they receive less than a 90 percent vote of the congregation, and many, especially ministers of color, would expect a 96 percent vote or higher. This high standard ensures that the minister has the full support of the congregation before beginning to serve.

Unitarian Universalist congregations have called and ordained openly lesbian, gay, bisexual, transgender, and queer ministers to their pulpits for many years. The first openly gay minister was called by a congregation in 1979. Today, many congregations across the country have openly LGBTQI ministers who are fully integrated and accepted into the life of the diverse congregations they serve.

It took some time, however, before congregations were comfortable calling an openly gay or lesbian minister, and even today some congregations struggle with calling LGBTQI ministers. Fears of becoming a "gay church" were expressed so often that, in the 1990s, the UUA's Department of Ministry developed a program called Beyond Categorical Thinking. This program, still offered today free of charge to congregations in search of a new minister, helps congregations explore their fears and concerns about calling a minister from the nondominant culture. Originally developed with a focus on gender, race, sexual orientation, and disability, the program has evolved to include gender identity, ethnicity, mental health, class, age, and size.

In the twenty-first century, congregations are opening their doors more widely to bisexual, transgender, and queer ministers. Since 2000, several congregations have selected openly bisexual, transgender, and queer ministers to serve them. However, for these ministries to be successful, it is necessary for the congregations and UUA leaders to remain mindful of the discrimination these ministers experience in the wider community and, at times, even in their own congregations, and to actively engage in addressing this discrimination.

On a Sunday morning in 2009, a man armed with a shotgun walked into a Unitarian Universalist church in Knoxville, Tennessee, and opened fire. Two people were killed and a number seriously injured. In the manifesto he wrote before the shooting, he claimed that this church's openness to LGBTQI people was one of his motivations for seeking to harm them.

As a result of that event, the UUA began an interfaith public witness campaign called Standing on the Side of Love (SSL), which is focused on harnessing love's power to stop oppression. Since 2010, SSL has supported the work of thousands of activists working in their local communities, their states, and at the federal level, to advocate for rights for LGBTQI people. SSL's recognizable yellow shirts, worn by those who show up at LGBTQI and immigrant justice events around the country, are responsible for SSL activists being dubbed "the love people," a name SSL has fully embraced.

At the 2014 General Assembly, the UUA adopted a revised non-discrimination policy in the UUA Board of Trustee Bylaws that broadened and clarified which groups were included. The new policy redefined "race" as "racialized identity," expanded the category "gender" to include "gender expression, gender identity, and sex," and added "family and relationship structures."

> The Association declares and affirms its special responsibility, and that of its member congregations and organizations, to promote the full participation of persons in all of its and their activities and in the full range of human endeavor without regard to racialized identity, ethnicity, gender expression, gender identity, sex, disability, affectional or sexual orientation, family and relationship structures, age, language, citizenship status, economic status, or national origin and without requiring adherence to any particular interpretation of religion or to any particular religious belief or creed.[21]

This new policy was accompanied by a new statement of inclusion that reads:

> Systems of power, privilege, and oppression have traditionally created barriers for persons and groups with particular identities, ages, abilities, and histories. We pledge to replace such barriers with ever-widening circles of solidarity and mutual respect. We strive to be an association of congregations that truly welcome all persons and commit to structuring congregational and associational life in ways that empower and enhance everyone's participation.[22]

As congregations consider adopting this policy on a local level over the next few years, they will have opportunities to examine how inclusive they are and what they need to do to promote full participation of all people.

Although the UUA and its member congregations have made significant progress in their welcome and inclusion work, their work is not done. A 2014 initiative, the Multicultural Ministries Sharing Project, asked LGBTQI people, among other historically marginalized groups, to share their experiences in UU congregations.[23]

While most respondents reported feeling welcomed and included in their congregations, 28 percent of LGBQ people and 45 percent of transgender people reported experiencing micro-aggressions, such as unintended slights, questions founded on untrue assumptions about identity/experience, unconscious heterosexist language, and subtle alienation.[24]

Other results from the Sharing Project demonstrated that although congregations think they are completely welcoming to LGBTQI people, this is not evident in the lived experience of LGBTQI people. Unless congregations are educating their members about LGBTQI issues on a regular basis, LGBTQI people do not always find a safe home in their faith community.

The UU United Nations Office (UU-UNO), a department of the UUA, is committed to bringing LGBTQI human rights to the forefront of the UN's agenda. However, only a few congregations in the United States have done significant work on understanding and inclusion of people who are intersex. The UUA has not yet added "I" to the acronym it uses to talk about marginalized sexual orientations and gender identities because, except for international advocacy, it has not developed a ministry that explicitly meets the needs of intersex people.

Even in one of the most accepting religious homes for LGBTQI people, growing edges still exist. However, it is rare to find a UU congregation today that is not open to learning how to be ever more inclusive.

Within the UUA, a number of related organizations exist that address the specific needs of one or more historically marginalized groups. These organizations are composed of laypeople, ministers, religious educators, and in some cases congregations, who advocate for and support the needs of identified populations.

One of those organizations, DRUUMM (Diverse & Revolutionary UU Multicultural Ministries), addresses historically marginalized racial or ethnic identities. EqUUal Access promotes equality and access for Unitarian Universalists with disabilities. Both of these organizations are fully supportive of LGBTQI people and welcome them among their memberships.

Three related organizations were formed specifically to promote equality and support LGBTQI people:

- Interweave, a membership organization actively working toward ending oppression based on sexual orientation and gender identity

- Lambda Ministers Guild, an organization for LGBTQI ministers

- TRUUsT, a ministry for transgender UU religious professionals[25]

Unitarian Universalists for Polyamory Awareness's mission is to serve the Unitarian Universalist Association and the community of polyamorous people within and outside the UUA by providing support, promoting education, and encouraging spiritual wholeness regarding polyamory.

Each of these organizations provides a safe place for LGBTQ people to find support and encouragement as they experience discrimination and inequality in the world. In addition, they hold the larger UUA accountable to ensure that LGBTQ people, regardless of race, ethnicity, ability, or family/relationship structure, receive the support they need to live healthy and whole lives as Unitarian Universalists.

TRADITION AND TRANSFORMATION

In 1921 Universalist minister L. B. Fisher wrote, "Universalists are often asked to tell where they stand. The only true answer to give to this question is that we do not stand at all, we move."[26] From the beginning, Unitarians and Universalists have been social reformers, activists, and leaders in social change.

The first Universalist congregation, formed in 1779, in Gloucester, Massachusetts, included a free slave among its charter members. In 1863 Olympia Brown, a Universalist and women's suffragist, regarded as the first woman to graduate from a theological school, was also the first woman of any denomination to be ordained into ministry.[27]

Prominent abolitionist and Unitarian preacher Theodore Parker first described the arc of the universe bending toward justice when he said:

> I do not pretend to understand the moral universe; the arc is a long one, my eye reaches but little ways; I cannot calculate the curve and complete the figure by the experience of sight; I can divine it by conscience. And from what I see I am sure it bends towards justice.[28]

Martin Luther King Jr. quoted Parker over one hundred years later when he declared, "The arc of the moral universe is long, but it bends toward justice."[29]

Unitarians and Universalists worked to end slavery, for women's suffrage, and for civil rights. Two Unitarian Universalists, Rev. James Reeb and Viola Liuzzo, were murdered in 1965, during the Selma voting rights campaign. They, along with hundreds of other UU ministers and laypeople, responded to Martin Luther King Jr.'s call to come to Selma, and they gave up their lives by doing so.

Only five years after the Selma to Montgomery march, the 1970 General Assembly of the Unitarian Universalist Association voted to urge an end to discrimination against homosexuals and to call upon its congregations to end all discrimination in employment practices. It even went so far as to encourage congregations and the UUA itself to expend special effort to find employment for homosexuals "in our midst."

> [This resolution] urges all peoples immediately to bring an end to all discrimination against homosexuals, homosexuality, bisexuals, and bisexuality, with specific immediate attention to the following issues: a person's sexual orientation or practice shall not be a factor in the granting or renewing of federal security clearance, visas, and the granting of citizenship or employment.
>
> Calls upon the UUA (Unitarian Universalist Association) and its member churches, fellowships, and organizations immediately to end all discrimination against homosexuals in employment practices, expending special effort to assist homosexuals to find employment in our midst consistent with their abilities and desires.[30]

Since 1970, the General Assembly has passed over twenty-five resolutions supporting LGBTQ equality. These included creating an Office on Gay Affairs as early as 1973 and supporting ministerial opportunities for gay, lesbian, and bisexual religious leaders as early as 1980. In 1984 the General Assembly affirmed the practice that was already long under of UUA clergy performing services of union between same-gender couples, and requesting that the UUA develop and distribute supporting materials.[31]

As LGBTQI people in the United States secure more and more rights, including the right to serve in the military and the right to marry, the UUA, through its international office, actively promotes rights of LGBTQI people around the world. The 2014 resolution to provide support for the Uganda New Underground Railroad and its ongoing work to support LGBTQI asylum-seekers are examples of such support.

Even with marriage equality sweeping the United States, discrimination against LGBTQI people continues to be widespread. In fact, in 2015 more and more local and state jurisdictions are working to repeal employment, housing, and public accommodation protections as backlash to the rapid advance of marriage equality. Unitarian Universalist congregations and statewide legislative networks are working to preserve these protections and to pass federal legislation to enshrine them.

LOOKING FORWARD

To be relevant as people of faith in the twenty-first century, congregations have to be open to ministering to people whoever they are. Today, people are claiming a host of identities that are impossible to contain in a string of letters. Identity is a very personal matter, and no one can or should be forced into a category because they fit some specific characteristic. Ministry requires listening to people's stories and honoring their experiences.

In the Multicultural Ministries Sharing Project, respondents said over and over again that they want to bring their whole selves with them to their faith community. For example, they don't want to be pushed into one group for bisexuals, another for people of color, and yet another for people with disabilities. Instead, they want to be welcomed into the congregation as a bisexual person of color with disabilities and to trust that people in the congregation understand the unique challenges they face from the world because of who they are. They want to know that people will listen to their unique story and not judge them or exclude them for any of their identities.

The June 2015 marriage equality ruling by the United States Supreme Court does not mean the work to ensure equality for LGBTQI people is done. In fact, marriage equality is not the number one issue among LGBTQI people. Continued violence directed toward LGBTQI people and persecution by families, faith communities, employers, landlords, and government take an emotional toll and foster a system of injustice and economic insecurity. This must change before marriage equality can begin to fulfill its promise. As long as employers and landlords can discriminate against LGBTQI people and families can throw their LGBTQI children out on the streets to fend for themselves, there is no equality. LGBTQI people want to know that their faith community is working toward justice for them. They want to know that they can live in safety. They want to know that their lives are important and that they matter. Only then will LGBTQI people achieve equity and have the freedom to live their lives freely and openly.

Five lessons that Unitarian Universalist's interaction with LGBTQI people or issues teach are:

- All people, regardless of sexual or affectional orientation, gender identity or expression, have inherent worth and dignity.

- Because revelation is continuous, the circles of welcome and inclusion must be ever expanding to bring others in.

- As people come to understand how their various identities affect their experience of the world, we have to be willing to learn from them and accept them as whole persons with unique gifts and needs.

- Practicing faith requires working for justice in the world. The Universalist vision of heaven on earth is only possible if everyone works together for a just and loving community.

- It is the job of faith communities to relieve suffering. In order to do that in the twenty-first century, people of faith must work for economic justice for LGBTQI people.

For forty-five years, Unitarian Universalism has embraced ministry to people outside of society's sexual orientation and gender identity norms. It started in 1969 with a minister who had the courage to come out as a homosexual. Over the years, UUs have grown and deepened their understandings of people's lives and experiences and have challenged each other as individuals and as an association to continue to widen the door. We might still have learning to do, but LGBTQI people can be assured that they are welcome in Unitarian Universalism.

SUGGESTED RESOURCES

Beacon Press, www.beacon.org. The publishing house of the UUA.

Gore, Susan A., and Keith Kron, eds. *Coming Out in Faith: Voices of LGBTQ Unitarian Universalists.* Boston: Skinner House Books, 2011.

Interweave Continental: Unitarian Universalists for Bisexual, Gay, Lesbian and Transgender Concerns, http://interweavecontin ental.ning.com.

Unitarian Universalist Association, www.uua.org.

Unitarian Universalist Association Bookstore, www.uuabookstore.org.

Conclusion

Mychal Copeland, MTS, and D'vorah Rose, BCC

As a Black lesbian feminist comfortable with the many different ingredients of my identity, and a woman committed to racial and sexual freedom from oppression, I find I am constantly being encouraged to pluck out some one aspect of myself and present this as the meaningful whole, eclipsing or denying the other parts of self. But this is a destructive and fragmenting way to live. My fullest concentration of energy is available to me only when I integrate all the parts of who I am, openly, allowing power from particular sources of my living to flow back and forth freely through all my different selves, without the restrictions of externally imposed definition. Only then can I bring myself and my energies as a whole to the service of those struggles which I embrace as part of my living.[1]

—Audre Lorde

Each of us is composed of a complex web of intersecting identities and commitments. Woman, Christian, queer, Muslim, man, straight, lesbian, transgender, Latino, cisgender, friend, parent. These identities often remain neatly in their particular domains, never crossing each other, never informing each other, at times contradicting each other. LGBTQI people often live fragmented lives, bringing only certain aspects of themselves to their jobs, family, school, or church. But, as Lorde writes, eclipsing or denying parts of ourselves is not only internally destructive; it keeps us from accessing our fullest potential. The Hebrew word meaning "peace," at its linguistic root, means "wholeness." Only when we integrate all of these fragments can we truly be at peace. Inviting all who seek spiritual community to bring their disparate identities into one seamless whole will lead us on the path to personal and institutional transformation.

"Radical inclusivity" of LGBTQI people in religion challenges all of us to bring our full selves to our spiritual lives.[2] Both individuals and communities will benefit from that honesty. Our journey across the American religious landscape with those who are struggling in good faith provides us with a unique lens as we work toward healing and transformation. Each chapter gives us hope for a more inclusive future. Without fail, all of our contributors share resources and support groups for LGBTQI people within their religious communities, many of which did not exist until recently. They also reveal where our sacred communities are not at peace with themselves or the larger society as they struggle with LGBTQI inclusion.

The questions remain, "How do we prepare our institutions so that everyone is able to be fully present at the table? What steps can we take to move ourselves steadily toward inclusion for all people?"

This book highlights the diversity among American religious and faith communities. There is obviously no single formula for LGBTQI inclusion, but much can be gleaned from the struggles and celebrations presented by each of our thirteen contributors. Those of us who are working toward LGBTQI inclusion from within can use these chapters as models for further inquiry and action. Where is the locus of discord within our traditions or those of others, and does it lie in the authority of text or with contemporary authorities? In cases where scripture is paramount, are there new interpretations of texts that could be shared across religious or denominational lines? Which attitudes are preached by clergy, and which by families or other spokespeople? Are there differences in opinion between subgroups within our traditions, and do certain factions receive more media attention than others? Where is friction recent, and where is it deeply ingrained? Are there new modalities for change?

Identifying possible partners will be paramount, from both inside and outside of our institutions. Identifying the need for new power structures may bring about strategic partnerships, lifting new voices and even empowering new leaders. Bringing generations with differing cultural contexts and comfort levels with LGBTQI identities into conversation with one another will shed light on the question of LGBTQI inclusion. We can discern whether homophobia or misogyny is at work and where they are linked. When taken together, these questions and areas for growth can inspire the movement of religious leaders and their institutions toward the most expansive position that is possible, while maintaining their integrity. These chapters inspire us to press religious leaders, parents, and coworkers—even amidst their personal struggles—to treat each individual with compassion and as a reflection of the divine.

For those less familiar with particular religious communities, we hope you are inspired to learn more about the groups presented here as well as the numerous others who are not. For many, the task will be discovering the ways in which religions continue to be of relevance for contemporary Americans in an age far different from the times in which these religions were conceived. For all of us, the next step toward acknowledging the complexity of each tradition and the uniqueness of every individual requires us to reject the notion that religion is too sensitive a topic to discuss in public. Rather than hide behind our discomfort or unfamiliarity, let us have the courage and open-mindedness to ask people we encounter in our daily lives about their religious and spiritual lives. Only then can we move past the generalizations and misunderstandings that plague our national conversation about religion, and more specifically about the intersection of religion and LGBTQI issues.

The current landscape surrounding LGBTQI issues in American religion is constantly changing. Please check our website (www .strugglingingoodfaith.com) for additional perspectives and educational resources concerning LGBTQI issues in American religion. News items about the intersection between these two spheres abound and continue to portray a battle between those who fight for LGBTQI equality on one side and religious groups and individuals on the other. For current responses and news stories, follow us on twitter (@struggle_lgbtqi) and Facebook (www.facebook.com /strugglingingoodfaith). We invite you to be part of this ongoing conversation.

We hope *Struggling in Good Faith* and the conversation it engenders lead both individuals and communities to a place of more profound and nuanced understanding about religion, sexuality, and gender.

When researchers study the process of coming out as LGBTQI, they often find that a final stage is one of "integration" or "synthesis," at which point individuals weave together various strands of identity that contribute to who they are into one cohesive whole.[3] Audre Lorde addressed this hope for synthesis when she expressed that "my fullest concentration of energy is available to me only when I integrate all the parts of who I am."[4] Likewise, when religious institutions find ways to integrate the diversity of people who are ready to bring their fullest selves to the table, all of our voices will become clearer. The stone that the builders once rejected can become the cornerstone.[5]

Too many have sought a spiritual community but felt they were not welcome. Let us usher in a new era in which the doors swing open wider than ever before.

Afterword

Ani Zonneveld, founder and president, Muslims for Progressive Values

This is a book that needs to be read by everyone—whether of faith or not, regardless of sexual orientation or gender identity. It is these human stories that highlight how faith ought to be practiced; by illuminating the world with love and light, challenging discrimination, misogyny, and patriarchy in the name of religion with love, compassion, and inclusivity for all peoples.

Across the world, LGBTQI people live in fear of being outed or of mistakenly revealing their true identities. It is an oppressive way of living that only lends to low morale, which can lead to depression and suicidal tendencies. As a grassroots community organizer, I find strangers reaching out to me with their most gut-wrenching stories of torment from family members and their communities. From California to Oman, they call and email me. All I can do is reassure them that God created them as such, encourage them to persevere, and offer our Islamic LGBTQI materials affirming their human dignity.

Often I come across people who believe LGBTQI people are sinners and deserve to be punished, jailed, fined, hanged, or cured. Sometimes LGBTQI people are accused of "choosing this lifestyle." This idea is absurd given that such a "choice" can result in persecution, ostracism, imprisonment, and sometimes death.

As the United Nations takes on its new fifteen-year vision of sustainable development goals, each member state has pledged to do its part, to leave no one behind.[1] It is now up to us, all citizens of the world, to live up to this vision so that LGBTQI people are indeed not left behind.

On a global scale and on an individual level, no matter who you are, each family, village, town, city, and nation is better off when individuals are treated with dignity and respect. It brings out the best in all of us and, collectively, as human beings, we are better off as a result.

Respect and human dignity should be extended to LGBTQI people; after all, LGBTQI people are simply human beings too.

Acknowledgments

I n the spring of 2010, we facilitated a workshop about college students with intersecting identities at the first annual California Institute of Integral Studies conference "Expanding the Circle: Creating an Inclusive Environment in Higher Education for LGBTQ Students and Studies." While preparing for our session, "Getting Past Leviticus and Other Silencing Texts: LGBTQI Students' Struggles with Religious Texts, Dual Identities, and Minority Religious Backgrounds," we looked for resources that would introduce conference participants to the wide variety of American religious traditions and their celebrations and struggles with LGBTQI issues. It did not exist. What we did find was a broad literature from the perspectives of particular religious traditions, a marvelous academic encyclopedia on the subject, and powerful memoirs about life as an LGBTQI person of faith. Yet with so much national attention being paid to the intersection of religion and LGBTQI issues, it seemed implausible that no one had created an easily accessible resource through which professionals, clergy, and lay readers could educate themselves about the various belief systems that were so profoundly influencing personal lives and public policy within contemporary American life.

Of the over fifty people who attended our first session, many were educated about LGBTQI issues but largely unfamiliar with—or even antagonistic toward—religion. As we continued to present and write on this topic with "Expanding the Circle,"[1] we deepened our conversations with workshop attendees and learned that even the strongest LGBTQI allies were frequently unaware that an LGBTQI person would want to be involved with a religious or spiritual community. Many LGBTQI people did not know that there were many communities of faith that are truly open and welcoming. Throughout our work in other multi-faith settings, we found that many religious adherents wanted to know the history, texts, and ideas that have influenced their institutions' attitudes about LGBTQI people. Again and again, we longed for a resource that would educate about LGBTQI issues and religion in a new era. After conceding that the book we wanted to share did not exist, we set out to create it.

We offer deep gratitude to our life partners, Christine Sublett and Kirsti Copeland, who were not only unswervingly supportive but also applied their areas of expertise to our project with love and wisdom. Mychal thanks her sister, Dr. Andrea Vogel, and parents, Ada and Jerry Rosenbaum, for their support, ideas, and enthusiasm.

Emily Wichland and SkyLight Paths have been patient and informative guides on this journey. Many thanks to our contributors, whose dedication to this project and insights have inspired us. For the many conversations, shared ideas, and resources, we thank Noach Dzmura, Rabbi Maurice Harris, Rev. Joanne Sanders, Rabbi Patricia Karlin-Neumann, Ramzi Fawaz, Chris Paige of Transfaithonline .org, Rabbi Danya Ruttenberg, Cristina Spencer, Rabbi Nancy Fuchs-Kreimer, Arinna Weismann, Dr. Marla Brettschneider, Henry Carrigan, Dr. Tamar Kamionkowski, Merle Feld, B'not Esh, Rev. Scotty McLennan, Heather Paul, Daigan Gaither, the team at Transbuddhists.org, and the many contacts throughout North America who helped us locate the thoughtful, knowledgeable people who have become our chapter authors.

Notes

A Brief Overview of LGBTQI Terms

1. http://community.pflag.org/glossary. Consulted in the creation of this glossary, in addition to PFLAG: www.glsen.org/gsa/making-your-club-inclusive-transgender-and-gnc-students, http://keshet.wpengine.netdna-cdn.com/wp-content/uploads/2012/06/Terminology-Sheet.pdf, and http://transbuddhists.org/retreat-guide/about-the-guide, with guidance from Noach Dzmura. Definitions of sexual and gender terminology are changing rapidly and are not universally agreed upon within the LGBTQI community.
2. http://community.pflag.org/glossary.
3. Ibid.
4. The word "they" is used intentionally in this definition and will be used in this book as a gender-neutral, singular personal pronoun instead of writing "he" or "she." Many people employ "they" and "their" in this way because English does not have a singular personal pronoun of indeterminate gender, and using "she" or "he" reifies a gender binary.
5. www.glsen.org/gsa/making-your-club-inclusive-transgender-and-gnc-students.

Introduction

1. Throughout the book we use "LGBTQI," as many struggles of lesbian, gay, bisexual, transgender, queer, and intersex people are bound up together. However, not all issues are shared and not all religious traditions address inclusion for all groups. In these cases we have used "LGB" or "LGBT" to make this distinction clear.
2. Jay Michaelson, *God vs. Gay? The Religious Case for Equality* (Boston: Beacon Press, 2012), xiii.
3. Kenji Yoshino, *Covering: The Hidden Assault on Our Civil Rights* (New York: Random House, 2007), 48.
4. Ibid., 48–49.
5. For more background, see David Kundtz and Bernard Schlager, *Ministry among God's Queer Folk: LGBT Pastoral Care* (Cleveland: Pilgrim Press, 2007).
6. Michelangelo Signorile, *It's Not Over: Getting Beyond Tolerance, Defeating Homophobia, and Winning True Equality* (Boston: Houghton Mifflin Harcourt, 2015), 3.

7. National Coalition of Anti-Violence Programs (NCAVP), *Lesbian, Gay, Bisexual, Transgender, Queer and HIV-Affected Hate Violence in 2012* (New York: NCAVP, 2013), www.avp.org/storage/documents/ncavp_2012_hvreport_final.pdf.

8. "Why the Equality Act?," Human Rights Campaign, www.hrc.org/resources /entry/why-the-equality-act.

9. Ann P. Haas, Philip L. Rodgers, and Jody L. Herman, *Suicide Attempts among Transgender and Gender Non-Conforming Adults: Findings of the National Transgender Discrimination Survey* (Los Angeles, CA: American Foundation for Suicide Prevention and the Williams Institute, January 2014), http:// williamsinstitute.law.ucla.edu/wp-content/uploads/AFSP-Williams-Suicide -Report-Final.pdf.

10. Centers for Disease Control and Prevention, "LGBT Youth," page last modified November 12, 2014, www.cdc.gov/lgbthealth/youth.htm.

11. Haas, *Suicide Attempts among Transgender and Gender Non-Conforming Adults.*

12. Centers for Disease Control and Prevention, "LGBT Youth."

13. "Family Acceptance of Lesbian, Gay, Bisexual and Transgender Youth Protects Against Depression, Substance Abuse, Suicide, Study Suggests," *Science Daily*, December 6, 2010, www.sciencedaily.com/releases/2010/12/101206093701.htm.

14. Beth Kraig, "Exploring Sexual Orientation Issues at Colleges and Universities with Religious Affiliations," in *Working with Lesbian, Gay, Bisexual, and Transgender College Students: A Handbook for Faculty and Administrators*, ed. Ronni L. Sanlo (Westport, CT: Greenwood Press, 1998), 384.

15. Harold G. Koenig, "Religion, Spirituality, and Health: The Research and Clinical Implications," *International Scholarly Research Network Psychiatry*, 2012, doi:10.5402/2012/278730.

16. See Mychal Copeland and D'vorah Rose, "Intersections: A Guide to Working with LGBTQI University Students of Minority Religions or Cultures," in *Expanding the Circle: Creating an Inclusive Environment in Higher Education for LGBTQ Students and Studies*, ed. John C. Hawley (Albany: State University of New York Press, 2015).

17. For more on intersecting minority identities, see Althea Smith, "Cultural Diversity and the Coming-Out Process: Implications for Clinical Practice," in *Ethnic and Cultural Diversity among Lesbians and Gay Men*, ed. Beverly Greene, Psychological Perspectives on Lesbian and Gay Issues 3 (Thousand Oaks, CA: Sage Publications, 1997), 288; and Copeland and Rose, "Intersections."

The Black Church

1. Delman Coates, "A Letter to the National Baptist Fellowship of Concerned Pastors," *Many Voices*, April 9, 2015; Dr. Coates' Response to National Baptist Fellowship of Concerned Pastors.

2. Dwight N. Hopkins, "Slave Theology in the 'Invisible Institution,'" in *Cut Loose Your Stammering Tongue: Black Theology in the Slave Narrative*, 2nd ed., ed. Dwight N. Hopkins and George C. L. Cummings (Louisville, KY: Westminster John Knox Press, 2003), 1, 31.

3. Reggie L. Williams, *Bonhoeffer's Black Jesus: Harlem Renaissance Theology and an Ethic of Resistance* (Waco, TX: Baylor University Press, 2014), 57.

4. Horace L. Griffin, *Their Own Receive Them Not: African American Lesbians and Gays in Black Churches* (Cleveland: Pilgrim Press, 2006), vii.

5. Lawrence N. Jones, "The Black Churches: A New Agenda," *Christian Century*, April 18, 1979, 434, www.religion-online.org/showarticle.asp?title=1219.

6. Griffin, *Their Own Receive Them Not*, 7.

7. Charles Hill, interview with Marcus Moore, "The Kujichagulia Project," January 21, 2015, https://youtu.be/v4WggVorZAc.

8. Mark Sandlin, "Clobbering 'Biblical' Gay Bashing," *The God Article*, October 10, 2011, www.thegodarticle.com/faith/clobbering-biblical-gay-bashing.

9. Jay Emerson Johnson, "Biblical Sexuality and Gender: Renewing Christian Witness to the Gospel" (Berkeley, CA: Pacific School of Religion, Graduate Theological Union, 2011), www.campuspride.org/wp-content/uploads /Biblical-Sexuality-and-Gender-Johnson1.pdf.

10. Griffin, *Their Own Receive Them Not*, 20.

11. Corey Dade, "Blacks, Gays and the Church: A Complex Relationship," NPR, May 22, 2012, www.npr.org/2012/05/22/153282066/blacks-gays-and-the -church-a-complex-relationship.

12. Dwight N. Hopkins, "Toward a Positive Black Male Heterosexuality," *Anglican Theological Review* 90, no. 3 (Summer 2008): 577.

13. Andrew Wilson, interview with Marcus Moore, "The Kujichagulia Project," January 21, 2015, https://youtu.be/v4WggVorZAc.

14. Griffin, *Their Own Receive Them Not*, 6.

15. Ibid., 17.

16. Terrell Jermaine Starr, "Violence Against Black Transgender Women Goes Largely Ignored," *The Root*, January 23, 2015, www.theroot.com/articles /culture/2015/01/violence_against_black_transgender_women_goes_largely _ignored.html.

17. "Addressing Stigma: A Blueprint for Improving HIV/STD Prevention and Care Outcomes for Black & Latino," NASTAD, May 2014, www.nastad.org/sites /default/files/NASTAD-NCSD-Report-Addressing-Stigma-May-2014.pdf.

18. Charles Hill, interview with Marcus Moore, "The Kujichagulia Project."

19. Adelle M. Banks, "Black Lesbian Bishop Yvette Flunder Is 'Using My Energy to Find Peace,'" Religion News Service, March 20, 2015, www.religionnews.com /2015/03/20/black-lesbian-bishop-yvette-flunder-using-energy-find-peace.

20. "'The Black Church,' A Brief History," African American Registry, www .aaregistry.org/historic_events/view/black-church-brief-history.

21. Griffin, *Their Own Receive Them Not*, 122–23.

22. Martin Luther King Jr., "Where Do We Go From Here?," speech presented at the 11th Annual Southern Christian Leadership Conference Convention, Atlanta, GA, August 16, 1967.

23. "Religious Acceptance of Homosexuals on the Rise," *Duke Today*, September 10, 2014, http://today.duke.edu/2014/09/religionstudy.

24. Dennis Cauchon, "Black Churches Conflicted on Obama's Gay Marriage Decision," *U.S.A. Today*, May 13, 2012, http://usatoday30.usatoday.com/news /religion/story/2012-05-13/black-churches-gay-marriage-obama/54941862/1.

25. "The Essence of the Fellowship," The Fellowship, www.radicallyinclusive.com /the-essence-of-the-fellowship.

26. City of Refuge United Church of Christ, http://cityofrefugeucc.org.

27. J. Alfred Smith and Brooks Berndt, *Sounding the Trumpet: How Churches Can Answer God's Call to Justice* (Boiling Springs, NC: A Pair of Docs Publishing, 2013), 32.

28. Ibid., 225.

Buddhism

1. Jeff Wilson, "'All Beings Are Equally Embraced by Amida Buddha': Jodo-Shinshu Buddhism and Same-Sex Marriage in the United States," *Journal of Global Buddhism* 13 (2012): 50.

2. Thich Nhat Hanh, "Dharma Talk" (Plum Village, France, July 20, 1998), www .abuddhistlibrary.com/Buddhism/G%20-%20TNH/TNH/Questions%20 and%20Answers%20July%2020th%201998/Dharma%20Talk%20given%20 by%20Thich%20Nhat%20Hanh%20on%20July%2020.htm.

3. "Mark Epstein Interviews Jeffrey Hopkins," *Tricycle*, Summer 1996, www.tricycle .com/feature/realm-relationship.

4. "Letters to the Editor," *Tricyle*, Fall 1996, www.tricycle.com/letters/letters -editor-22.

5. Helen Tworkov, "Whaddya Mean 'We'?," *Tricycle*, Winter 1996, www.tricycle .com/editors-view/whaddya-meanwe.

6. Some key teachers: Arinna Weisman, Larry Yang, Eric Kolvig, Jeffrey Hopkins. Many dharma centers now promote retreats with LGBTQI teachers, including Insight Meditation Society, Spirit Rock Meditation Center, and San Francisco Zen Center.

7. "Does My Transgender Identity Conflict with the Teachings on No-Self?," *Buddhadharma*, May 14, 2015, www.lionsroar.com/does-my-transgender-identity -conflict-with-the-teachings-on-no-self.

The Church of Jesus Christ of Latter-day Saints (Mormon)

1. John Gustav-Wrathall, "Affirmation Receives a Warm Welcome in Palmyra," Affirmation, May 2015, http://affirmation.org/affirmation-receives-a-warm -welcome-in-palmyra.

2. Restorationism is the belief that Christianity should be restored along the lines of what is known about the apostolic early church, which restorationists see as the search for a more pure and ancient form of the religion.

3. Dispensationalism is belief in a system of historical progression, as revealed in the Bible, consisting of a series of stages in God's self-revelation and plan of salvation.

4. Peggy Fletcher Stack, "Can Mormons Back Same-Sex Marriage and Still Get in the Temple?" *Salt Lake Tribune*, January 17, 2014, www.sltrib.com/sltrib/news /57396344-78/church-lds-marriage-mormons.html.csp.

The Episcopal Church

1. "Rt. Rev Mary Glasspool Preaches at Integrity Eucharist," IntegriTV 2015, June 29, 2015, www.youtube.com/watch?v=zLyekEAsbxo.
2. House of Deputies Committee on the State of the Church, Report to the 78th Convention, p. 14, https://extranet.generalconvention.org/staff/files /download/12702.pdf.
3. "About Us," The Episcopal Church, www.episcopalchurch.org/page /about-us.
4. "Global Anglicanism at a Crossroads," Pew Research Center, June 19, 2008, www.pewforum.org/2008/06/19/global-anglicanism-at-a-crossroads.
5. Unfortunately, I do not have space in this chapter to engage such texts—for example, the writings of Augustine of Hippo, Thomas Aquinas, mystical theologians such as Bernard of Clairvaux or Julian of Norwich, or Anglican theologian Richard Hooker, to name a few of those often classified under the heading of "tradition."
6. For more detail, see Mark D. Jordan, the introduction to *Recruiting Young Love: How Christians Talk about Homosexuality* (Chicago: University of Chicago Press, 2011), especially xvi–xvii. See also Mark D. Jordan, *The Invention of Sodomy in Christian Theology* (Chicago: University of Chicago Press, 1997); and Mark D. Jordan, *Telling Truths in Church: Scandal, Flesh, and Christian Speech* (Boston: Beacon Press, 2004).
7. On "complementarity," see Adrian Thatcher, *God, Sex, and Gender: An Introduction* (Oxford: Wiley-Blackwell, 2011), 41–43, 98–100, 185–89; and James Brownson, *Bible, Gender, Sexuality: Reframing the Church's Debate on Same-Sex Relationships* (Cambridge: Eerdmans, 2013).
8. See, for example, John Bauerschmidt, Zachary Guiliano, Wesley Hill, and Jordan Hylden, "Marriage in Creation and Covenant: A Response to the Task Force on the Study of Marriage," *Anglican Theological Review*, www.anglican theologicalreview.org/static/pdf/conversations/MarriageInCreationAnd Covenant.pdf.
9. See, for example, Oliver O'Donovan, *Transsexualism and Christian Marriage*, Grove Ethics Series 48 (Bramcote, UK: Grove Books, 1982); and Evangelical Alliance Policy Commission, *Transsexuality* (Milton Keynes, UK: Paternoster, 2000).
10. Two major exceptions on the topic of intersex people are the work of theologians Susannah Cornwall and Megan DeFranza. See Cornwall, *Sex and Uncertainty in the Body of Christ: Intersex Conditions and Christian Theology* (London: Routledge, 2010); and DeFranza, *Sex Difference in Christian Theology: Male, Female, and Intersex in the Image of God* (Grand Rapids, MI: Eerdmans, 2015).
11. See especially Dale B. Martin, *Sex and the Single Savior: Gender and Sexuality in Biblical Interpretation* (Louisville: Westminster John Knox Press, 2006), 37–50.

12. See Dale Martin's chapter on this passage in *Sex and the Single Savior.*

13. Jay Emerson Johnson, *Peculiar Faith: Queer Theology for Christian Witness* (New York: Seabury Books, 2014).

14. See, for example, Caroline Hall, *A Thorn in the Flesh: How Gay Sexuality Is Changing the Episcopal Church* (Lanham, MD: Rowman and Littlefield, 2013), 254; and Marilyn McCord Adams, "Hurricane Spirit, Toppling Taboos," in *Our Selves, Our Souls and Bodies: Sexuality and the Household of God*, ed. Charles Hefling (Cambridge, MA: Cowley Publications, 1996), 130.

15. Patrick S. Cheng, *Radical Love: An Introduction to Queer Theology* (New York: Seabury Books, 2011), 2.

16. See, for example, Victoria Kolakowski, "Toward a Christian Ethical Response to Transsexual Persons," *Theology and Sexuality* 6 (1997): 23–29; Justin Edward Tanis, *Trans-gendered: Theology, Ministry and Communities of Faith* (Cleveland, OH: Pilgrim Press, 2003), 69–79; DeFranza, *Sex Difference in Christian Theology*, 68–106.

17. See, for example, Mathew Kuefler, *The Manly Eunuch: Masculinity, Gender Ambiguity, and Christian Ideology in Late Antiquity* (Chicago: University of Chicago Press, 2001).

18. *Book of Common Prayer* (New York: Church Hymnal Corporation, 1979), 423–38. "An Order for Marriage" (435–36) provides a simple, flexible structure for designing one's own service but still requires specific language for the vows.

19. See "Christian Marriage as Vocation," Report of the Task Force on Marriage, 32–44, https://extranet.generalconvention.org/staff/files/download/12485.pdf. See also Tobias Stanislas Haller, *Reasonable and Holy: Engaging Same-Sexuality* (New York: Seabury Books, 2009).

20. Standing Commission on Liturgy and Music, "I Will Bless You and You Will Be a Blessing: Resources for the Witnessing and Blessing of a Lifelong Covenant in a Same-Sex Relationship" (New York: Church Publishing, 2013).

21. These can be found in this supplement from the Standing Commission on Liturgy and Music: https://extranet.generalconvention.org/staff/files/download/13068.pdf.

22. For more information, see Resolution A054, "Adopt Resources and Rites from 'Liturgical Resources I: I Will Bless You and You Will Be a Blessing, Revised and Expanded 2015,'" www.generalconvention.org/gc/2015-resolutions/A054/current_english_text.

23. For a summary of those resolutions related to cisgender gay and lesbian Episcopalians, see Kim Byham, Michael W. Hopkins, and John Clinton Bradley, "Toward a Full and Equal Claim: A Brief History of LGBT Issues in the Episcopal Church" (Rochester, NY: Integrity, 2008), www.integrityusa.org/archive/PrintMaterials/TowardAFullAndEqualClaim2008.pdf.

24. Ibid., 3.

25. See Paul Moore, *Take a Bishop Like Me* (New York: Harper and Row, 1979); Byham, Hopkins, and Bradley, "Toward a Full and Equal Claim," 3.

26. Malcolm Boyd, *Take Off the Masks* (New York: Doubleday, 1978).

27. See Carter Heyward, *Our Passion for Justice: Images of Power, Sexuality, and Liberation* (Cleveland, OH: Pilgrim Press, 1984).

28. See Robert Williams, *Just As I Am: A Practical Guide to Being Out, Proud and Christian* (New York: Harper Perennial, 1992).

29. See Walter C. Righter, *A Pilgrim's Way* (New York: Alfred A. Knopf, 1998); and Will Leckie and Barry Stopfel, *Courage to Love: A Gay Priest Stands Up for His Beliefs* (New York: Doubleday, 1997).

30. On this multiyear effort, see Kevin Ward, *A History of Global Anglicanism* (Cambridge: Cambridge University Press, 2006); and Miranda K. Hassett, *Anglican Communion in Crisis: How Episcopal Dissidents and Their African Allies Are Reshaping Anglicanism* (Princeton, NJ: Princeton University Press, 2007).

31. "Los Angeles Diocese Elects Second Gay Episcopal Bishop, Highlighting an Anglican Split," *New York Times*, December 7, 2009, www.nytimes.com/2009/12/07/us/07episcopal.html.

32. TransEpiscopal, http://blog.transepiscopal.com.

33. For more on these groups, see the Consultation (www.theconsultation.org); Chicago Consultation (www.chicagoconsultation.org); and IntegrityUSA (www.integrityusa.org), which produced the short film *Voices of Witness: Out of the Box* as an educational tool to support transgender people in the Episcopal Church.

34. Karen McVeigh, "Church of England to Consider Transgender Naming Ceremony," *Guardian*, May 21, 2015, www.theguardian.com/society/2015/may/21/proposal-for-transgender-baptism-to-go-before-church-of-england. The Episcopal Church rite is meant to be adaptable to various life circumstances.

35. "Libby Lane: First Female Church of England Bishop Consecrated," *BBC News*, January 26, 2015, www.bbc.com/news/uk-politics-30974547; Caroline Davies, "Church Creates Second Woman Bishop," *Guardian*, March 25, 2015.

36. For more on this history, see Harold T. Lewis, *Yet with a Steady Beat: The African American Struggle for Recognition in the Episcopal Church* (Valley Forge, PA: Trinity Press International, 1996); Gardiner Shattuck, *Episcopalians and Race: Civil War to Civil Rights* (Lexington: University Press of Kentucky, 2003); Fred Vergara, *Mainstreaming Asian Americans in the Episcopal Church* (New York: Episcopal Church Center, 2005).

37. For their feast days, see *Holy Women, Holy Men: Celebrating the Saints* (New York: Church Publishing, 2010).

38. For more on Reverend Oakerhater, see K. B. Kueteman, "He Goes First: The Story of Episcopal Saint David Pendleton Oakerhater," http://digital.library.okstate.edu/Oakerhater/bio.html.

39. See, for example, "House of Bishops Pastoral Letter on Sin of Racism," *Episcopal News Service*, April 21, 1994, 25–31, www.episcopalarchives.org/Afro-Anglican_history/exhibit/pdf/awakening_pastoralletter.pdf.

40. Resolution C019, "Establish Response to Systemic Racial Injustice," www.generalconvention.org/gc/2015-resolutions/C019/current_english_text.

41. Mary Frances Schjonberg, "North Carolina Bishop Michael Curry Elected as 27th Presiding Bishop," Episcopal News Service, June 27, 2015, http://episcopaldigitalnetwork.com/ens/2015/06/27/north-carolina-bishop -michael-curry-elected-as-27th-presiding-bishop.

42. Mary Frances Schjonberg, "North Carolina Bishop Michael Curry elected as 27th Presiding Bishop," Episcopal News Service, June 27, 2015, http://episcopaldigitalnetwork.com/ens/2015/06/27/north-carolina-bishop -michael-curry-elected-as-27th-presiding-bishop; Diana Butler Bass, "Reflecting on Outgoing Presiding Bishop Katharine Jefferts Schori's Tenure as Episcopal Church Brings in New Leader," *Washington Post,* June 27, 2015, www.washingtonpost.com/news/acts-of-faith/wp/2015/06/27/reflecting -on-outgoing-presiding-bishop-katharine-jefferts-schoris-tenure-as-episcopal -church-brings-in-new-leader.

43. For more on the history of women's leadership in the Episcopal Church, see Pamela W. Darling, *New Wine: The Story of Women Transforming Leadership and Power in the Episcopal Church* (Cambridge, MA: Cowley Publications, 1994); and Mary Sudman Donovan, *A Different Call: Women's Ministries in the Episcopal Church, 1850–1920* (Harrisburg, PA: Morehouse, 1986).

44. Bishop James Pike of the Diocese of California had, however, already recognized Rev. Phyllis Edwards as a deacon in 1965.

45. For more on this movement, see Mary Frances Schjonberg, "An Interactive Timeline of the History of Women's Ordination," Episcopal News Service, July 28, 2014, http://episcopaldigitalnetwork.com/ens/2014/07/28/ordination -timeline. See also Darlene O'Dell, *The Story of the Philadelphia Eleven* (New York: Seabury Books, 2014).

46. "Barbara Harris Elected First Woman Bishop," Episcopal News Service, September 29, 1988, www.episcopalarchives.org/cgi-bin/ENS/ENSpress _release.pl?pr_number=88201.

47. Resolution A037, "Continue Work of the Task Force on the Study of Marriage," www.generalconvention.org/gc/2015-resolutions/A037/current_english_text.

First Nations (Native American)

1. Beth Brant, *Writing as Witness: Essay and Talk* (Toronto, ON: Women's Press, 1994), 65.

2. In Canada, Indigenous people include First Nations, Inuit, and Metis peoples. I am a member of a First Nation and, out of respect, will use this term when referring specifically to their experiences.

3. All Indigenous nations in North America come from oral traditions. In some nations, stories, historic events, maps, and other important knowledge were recorded or documented in media such as petroglyphs, petrographs, birch-bark scrolls, wampum belts, or condolence canes, but the primary way to convey knowledge was through oral traditions.

4. Alex Wilson, "How Our Stories Are Told," *Canadian Journal of Native Education* 22, no. 2 (1998): 274–78.

5. The appropriation and commodification of Indigenous ceremonies and spirituality is a particularly sensitive issue for many Indigenous people. Misunderstanding, prohibition, destruction, theft, "mascot-ing," misrepresentation, appropriation, and/or commodification of Indigenous peoples' ceremonies, spirituality, and cultures have been ongoing since colonization began in the Americas. In our communities today, we are able to hold ceremonies and practice traditional spirituality only because we (our ancestors, our families, our friends, our leaders, ourselves) have held close, protected, fought for, recorded, remembered, regathered, reclaimed, and shared our knowledge of those ceremonies and spiritual teachings with each other.

6. I am a two-spirit woman from the Opaskwayak Cree Nation, a reserve that lies approximately five hundred miles north of the border between North Dakota and Canada. In this chapter, I offer my own understanding of knowledge that has been passed to me from my community and through my family, and I draw on my experiences as a community researcher who has worked extensively with Indigenous LGBTQI people. I would like to acknowledge and thank the following people who contributed to this article by transcribing notes, reading drafts, and/or offering discussion: Stan Wilson, Janet Sarson, Roz Dotson, Rebecca Sockbeson Cardinal, and Mychal Copeland. *Kinanaskohmitinawaw.*

Hinduism

1. Rajiv Malik, "Discussions on Dharma," *Hinduism Today*, October-November-December 2004, 30–31.

2. This book uses BCE and CE for consistency. However, in my own writing I use BC and AD rather than BCE and CE because the latter, by removing the word "Christ" yet retaining the date of his supposed birth, disingenuously suggests that this birth is an all-important event common to the world rather than to a particular religion that became dominant and imposed its calendar on the rest of the world.

3. I capitalize "God" and "Goddess" for Hindu divinities because each of them is and has been for centuries worshiped by millions as the absolute embodiment of the divine. Capitalizing only the unseen abstract divinity elevates the God of the Abrahamic religions (into whom the Advaita non-dualist divine gets subsumed) as superior to more complex notions of the divine that foreground femininity and multidimensionality.

4. This account is largely drawn from Ruth Vanita, "Introduction: Ancient Indian Materials," in *Same-Sex Love in India: Readings from Literature and History*, ed. Ruth Vanita and Saleem Kidwai (New York: Palgrave-Macmillan, 2000), 1–30.

5. K. L. Bhishagratna, ed. and trans., *The Sushruta Samhita*, Chaukhamba Sanskrit Series 30 (Varanasi, India: Chaukhamba Sanskrit Series, 1991), 2:36–40.

6. Leonard Zwilling and Michael J. Sweet, "'Like a City Ablaze': The Third Sex and the Creation of Sexuality in Jain Religious Literature," *Journal of the History*

of Sexuality 6, no. 3 (January 1996): 359–84. See also their essay "The First Medicalization: The Taxonomy and Etiology of Queers in Classical Indian Medicine," *Journal of the History of Sexuality* 3, no. 4 (April 1993): 590–607.

7. See Ruth Vanita, *Love's Rite: Same-Sex Marriage in India and the West* (New York: Palgrave-Macmillan, 2005), chap. 6.

8. See Gayatri Reddy, *With Respect to Sex: Negotiating Hijra Identity in South India* (Chicago: University of Chicago, 2005).

9. See Vanita, *Love's Rite*, 39, 305, 307–8.

10. See Ruth Vanita, "Two Gurus on Homosexuality: Sri Sri Ravi Shankar versus Baba Ramdev," *Gaylaxy*, March 18, 2014, www.gaylaxymag.com/articles/ queer-voices/two-gurus-on-homosexuality-sri-sri-ravi-shankar-versus-baba- ramdev.

11. Shakuntala Devi, *The World of Homosexuals* (New Delhi: Vikas, 1977).

12. Ruth Vanita, "Together in Life after Life: Same-Sex Marriage and Hindu Traditions," in *Defending Same-Sex Marriage*, ed. Mark Strasser, vol. 2, *Our Family Values: Same-Sex Marriage and Religion*, ed. Traci C. West (Santa Barbara, CA: Praeger, 2006), 3–18.

13. See Vanita, *Love's Rite*, 315.

14. Rajiv Malik, "Discussions on Dharma," *Hinduism Today*, October-November- December 2004, 30–31.

15. Ibid.

16. Ibid.

17. Sushila Bhawasar, quoted in Chinu Panchal, "'Wedded' Women Cops to Challenge Sack," *Times of India*, February 23, 1988.

Islam

1. Orbala, "'Islamic' Rulings on Muslim Lesbians' Interactions with Other Muslim Women," *Freedom from the Forbidden* (blog), September 16, 2012. http://orbala .blogspot.com/2012/09/muslim-lesbians-interactions-with-other.html.

2. For an accessible introduction to the history of these divisions and their legal, theological, and political consequences, see Omid Safi, *Memories of Muhammad: Why the Prophet Matters* (San Francisco: HarperOne, 2010).

3. For a superb introduction to Islamic legal thinking, see Bernard G. Weiss, *The Spirit of Islamic Law* (Athens, GA: University of Georgia Press, 2006).

4. Aisha Geissinger, "Islam and Same-Sex Sexuality in History: Cultural and Religious Perspectives," in *Muslim LGBT Inclusion Project* (New York: Intersections International, 2011), 32–33. (Note: Much of the content of this section is based on Geissinger's scholarship.) In one interesting section, Geissinger tracks how translators of Ibn Kathir's commentary from Arabic into English even insert the term "homosexuality" into the text when he had not mentioned it.

5. Scott Siraj al-Haqq Kugle, *Living Out Islam: Voices of Gay, Lesbian, and Transgender Muslims* (New York: New York University Press, 2013), 207.

6. Scott Siraj al-Haqq Kugle, *Homosexuality in Islam: Critical Reflection on Gay, Lesbian, and Transgender Muslims* (Oxford: Oneworld, 2010), 252.

7. Samar Habib, *Islam and Homosexuality* (Santa Barbara, CA: Praeger, 2010), 39.

8. Geissinger, "Islam and Same-Sex Sexuality in History," 31.

9. Ibid., 32.

10. Ibid., 33.

11. Adnan Hossain, "Beyond Emasculation: Being Muslim and Becoming *Hijra* in South Asia," *Asian Studies Review* 36, no. 4 (December 2012): 495–513.

12. Angela P. Cheater, *Social Anthropology: An Alternative Introduction* (London: Routledge, 2003), 169.

13. Geissinger, "Islam and Same-Sex Sexuality in History," 29.

14. Sharyn Graham Davies, *Gender Diversity in Indonesia: Sexuality, Islam and Queer Selves* (London: Routledge, 2011).

15. Robert Oostvogels, "The Waria of Indonesia: A Traditional Third Gender Role," in *Third Sex, Third Gender: Beyond Sexual Dimorphism in Culture and History,* ed. Gilbert Herdt (New York: Zone Books, 1996).

16. Roland Littlewood and Antonia Young, "The Third Sex in Albania: An Ethnographic Note," in *Changing Sex and Bending Gender,* ed. Allison Shaw and Shirley Ardener (New York: Berghahn Books, 2005), 74.

17. Momin Rahman, "The Politics of LGBT Muslim Identities," E-International Relations, April 2, 2015, www.e-ir.info/2015/04/02/the-politics-of-lgbt-muslim -identities.

18. Emily Thomas, "7 Stunning Images from What May Be Muslim World's Largest LGBT Celebration," Gay Voices, *Huffington Post,* July 1, 2014, www.huffingtonpost .com/2014/07/01/istanbul-gay-pride-lgbt-festival_n_5545252.html.

19. "5 Muslim Countries Where Gays Are Not Prosecuted by the Law," *Global Voices,* October 28, 2014, http://globalvoicesonline.org/2014/10/28/5-muslim -countries-where-gays-are-not-persecuted-by-the-law.

20. Ali Hamedani, "The Gay People Pushed to Change Their Gender," *BBC News,* November 5, 2014, www.bbc.com/news/magazine-29832690.

21. Peter Skerry, "Problems of the Second Generation: To Be Young, Muslim, and American," *Weekly Standard,* June 14, 2013, www.weeklystandard.com/articles /problems-second-generation_735247.html.

22. Sheikh Hamza Yusuf, "Homosexuality," Islam on Demand, www.youtube.com /watch?v=ueoLkzAGpfg.

23. Taleef Collective, www.taleefcollective.org.

24. Personal accounts of the organization shared with Laury Silvers.

25. Orbala, "'Islamic' Rulings on Muslim Lesbians' Interactions with Other Muslim Women."

26. This informal interview was a part of a project on ethnographic research methods.

27. There are several autobiographical essays written by LGBTQI Muslims in *Love InshAllah: The Secret Love Lives of American Muslim Women,* ed. Nura Maznavi

and Ayesha Mattu (Berkeley, CA: Soft Skull Press, 2012), and its companion volume, *Salaam Love: American Muslim Men on Love, Sex, and Intimacy*, ed. Ayesha Mattu and Nura Maznavi (Boston: Beacon Press, 2014).

28. Ify Okoye, "Yes I Am," August 21, 2012, http://ifyokoye.com/2012/08/21 /yes-i-am.

29. *A Sober Second Look*, https://sobersecondlook.wordpress.com.

30. http://feminismandreligion.com/2013/10/14/prayer-embodied-dissonance.

31. Juliane Hammer, *American Muslim Women, Religious Authority, and Activism: More Than a Prayer* (Austin: University of Texas Press, 2012); Azmat Khan, "Meet America's First Openly Gay Imam," Al-Jazeera America, *Flagship Blog*, December 20, 2013, http://america.aljazeera.com/watch/shows /america-tonight/america-tonight-blog/2013/12/20/meet-america-s -firstopenlygayimam.html.

32. Tellingly, one of the early permissions giving women the unrestricted right to lead the congregational prayer is established on the basis of a free woman having greater status than an enslaved man. Enslaved men are permitted to lead free men. Thus, women being of greater status than enslaved men should be permitted to lead men (Laury Silvers and Ahmed Elewa, "I Am One of the People: A Survey and Analysis of Legal Arguments on Woman-Led Prayer in Islam," *Journal of Law and Religion* 26, no. 1 [2010–2011]: 157).

33. For a discussion of the classical positions on prayer leadership and women, see Marion Holmes Katz, *Prayer in Islamic Thought and Practice* (Cambridge: Cambridge University Press, 2013).

34. Dean Obeidallah, "Meet America's Only Openly Gay Imam," *Daily Beast*, May 21, 2015, www.thedailybeast.com/articles/2015/05/21/and-now-america-an -openly-gay-imam.html; and Khan, "Meet America's First Openly Gay Imam."

35. "About," The Inner Circle, http://theinnercircle.org.za/about.

36. Junaid Jahangir, *Huffington Post*, www.huffingtonpost.ca/junaid-jahangir.

37. Faisal Alam, personal correspondence, February 2015.

38. Ibid.

39. Ghazala Anwar, personal correspondence, February 2015.

40. Amy Cuddy, "Your Body Language Shapes Who You Are," TedGlobal, June 2012, www.ted.com/talks/amy_cuddy_your_body_language_shapes_who _you_are.

41. Saba Mahmood, "Rehearsed Spontaneity and the Conventionality of Ritual: Disciplines of Ṣalat," *American Ethnologist* 28, no. 4 (November 2001): 827–53.

42. Zahra Ayubi, "Owning the Terms of Leadership and Authority: Toward a Gender-Inclusive Framework of American Muslim Religious Authority," in *A Jihad for Justice: Honoring the Work and Life of Amina Wadud*, ed. Kecia Ali, Juliane Hammer, and Laury Silvers (Akron, OH: 48 Hour Books, 2012), 52.

43. Amina Wadud, *Inside the Gender Jihad: Women's Reform in Islam* (Oxford: Oneworld, 2006).

44. Side Entrance, http://sideentrance.tumblr.com.

Judaism

1. "Statement of Principles on the Place of Jews with a Homosexual Orientation in Our Community," Statement of Principles NYA, http://statementof principlesnya.blogspot.com.

The Lutheran Church

1. Evangelical Lutheran Church in America, "A Social Statement on Human Sexuality: Gift and Trust," adopted at the eleventh biennial churchwide assembly, August 19, 2009, Minneapolis, MN.
2. *Luther's Works* 32:112; Weimer edition (*WA*) 7:38; as quoted in "A Social Statement on Human Sexuality."
3. Roland H. Bainton, *Here I Stand: A Life of Martin Luther* (Nashville: Abingdon, 1950), 185.
4. William Morris, ed., *American Heritage Dictionary of the English Language* (New York: Houghton Mifflin, 1978), 4.
5. Kenneth D. Thurow, *A Place at the Table: Scripture, Sexuality, and Life in the Church* (Bloomington, IN: iUniverse, 2009), 62.
6. Thurow, *A Place at the Table*, 56.
7. Walter Bauer, *Greek-English Lexicon of the New Testament and Other Early Christian Literature*, ed. and Rev. Frederick William Danker (Chicago: University of Chicago Press, 1979).
8. Thurow, *A Place at the Table*, 56.
9. Ibid., 55.
10. Evangelical Lutheran Church in America, "A Social Statement on Human Sexuality," 41.
11. Ibid., 19–21.
12. Thurow, *A Place at the Table*, 11, 104, 109.
13. Common Confession, www.lutherancore.org/what-we-believe/the-common -confession.
14. "About TransLutherans," www.reconcilingworks.org/what/translutherans.
15. "ELM History," Extraordinary Lutheran Ministries, www.elm.org/history.
16. Ibid.
17. "Proclaim," Extraordinary Lutheran Ministries, www.elm.org/proclaim.
18. Personal conversation, February 2015.
19. Personal conversation, February 2015.

The Presbyterian Church

1. Sylvia Thorson-Smith, *Reconciling the Broken Silence: The Church in Dialogue on Gay and Lesbian Issues* (Louisville, KY: Congregational Ministry Division, Presbyterian Church U.S.A., 1993), 68.
2. "A Brief History of the Presbyterian Church in America," Presbyterian Church in America, www.pcanet.org/history.

3. "Presbyterian Understanding and Use of Holy Scripture," position statement adopted by the 123rd General Assembly (1983) of the Presbyterian Church in the United States (Louisville, KY: Office of the General Assembly, Presbyterian Church U.S.A., 1985), 1.

4. Ibid.

5. "Biblical Authority and Interpretation: A Resource Document" (New York: Advisory Council on Discipleship and Worship, 1982).

6. Jack Rogers, *Jesus, the Bible, and Homosexuality: Explode the Myths, Heal the Church* (Louisville, KY: Westminster John Knox Press, 2006), 17.

7. Ibid., 35.

8. Ibid., 18.

9. Ibid., 15.

10. Ibid., 88–89.

11. Ibid., 69.

12. Ken Stone, "What the Homosexuality Debates Really Say about the Bible," in *Out of the Shadows into the Light: Christianity and Homosexuality*, ed. Miguel A. De La Torre (St. Louis: Chalice Press, 2009), 19–38.

13. Rogers, *Jesus, the Bible, and Homosexuality*, 109.

14. Ibid., 15.

15. "A History of the More Light Movement at Lincoln Park Presbyterian Church and in the Presbyterian Church (U.S.A.)" (Chicago: Lincoln Park Presbyterian Church), www.mlp.org/wp-content/uploads/2012/05/MLhistory.pdf.

16. "About," That All May Freely Serve, http://tamfs.org/about.

17. "Mission," Covenant Network of Presbyterians, http://covnetpres.org/about/mission.

18. "Mission," Parity, http://parity.nyc/our-mission.

19. James B. Nelson, *Embodiment: An Approach to Sexuality and Christian Theology* (Minneapolis, MN: Augsburg Publishing House, 1978), especially chap. 8, "The Church and Homosexuality," 180–210.

20. "Putting Sex in Perspective: A Framework for Understanding Sexuality," in *Presbyterians and Human Sexuality 1991* (Louisville, KY: Office of the General Assembly, 1991), 7.

21. Rosemary Radford Ruether, *Christianity and the Making of the Modern Family: Ruling Ideologies, Diverse Realities* (Boston: Beacon Press, 2000), 223.

Protestant Evangelical Traditions

1. Tony Campolo, "Tony Campolo: For the Record," June 8, 2015, http://tonycampolo.org/for-the-record-tony-campolo-releases-a-new-statement/#.Vfm9pRFVhHw.

2. See, for example, Carl F. H. Henry, *The Uneasy Conscience of Modern Fundamentalism*, reprint ed. (Grand Rapids, MI: Eerdmans, 2003).

3. "America's Changing Religious Landscape," Pew Research Center, May 12, 2015, www.pewforum.org/2015/05/12/americas-changing-religious-landscape.

4. David W. Bebbington, *Evangelicalism in Modern Britain: A History from the 1730s to the 1980s* (London: Unwin Hyman, 1989), 2–17.

5. Frank Newport, "In U.S., 42% Believe Creationist View of Human Origins," Gallup, June 2, 2014, www.gallup.com/poll/170822/believe-creationist-view-human-origins.aspx.

6. How this account of origins squares with the scientific evidence is the hard work of Christian theologians and scientists. The practical outgrowth of this work ranges from Ken Ham and his organization, Answers in Genesis, to Francis Collins and Biologos. See https://answersingenesis.org and http://biologos.org.

7. The three churches are GracePointe Church in Franklin, TN, EastLake Community Church in Bothell, WA, and City Church in San Francisco, CA.

8. Kimberly Winston, "Prominent San Francisco Evangelical Church Drops Celibacy Requirement for LGBT Members," Religion News Service, March 16, 2015, www.religionnews.com/2015/03/16/san-francisco-evangelicals-drop-celibacy-requirement-lgbt-members.

9. Fred Harrell, "A Letter from the Elder Board," City Church San Francisco, August 27, 2015, www.citychurchsf.org/A-Letter-From-The-Elder-Board.

10. Robert A. J. Gagnon, "Why San Francisco's City Church Is Wrong About Sex," *First Things*, March 17, 2015, www.firstthings.com/web-exclusives/2015/03/why-san-franciscos-biggest-megachurch-is-wrong-about-sex.

11. Jennifer LeClaire, "Evangelical Megachurch Embraces Practicing Gays into Fellowship," *Charisma News*, March 17, 2015, www.charismanews.com/opinion/watchman-on-the-wall/48766-evangelical-megachurch-embraces-practicing-gays-into-fellowship.

12. Ibid.

13. "Our Mission," Gay Christian Network, www.gaychristian.net/mission.php.

14. Gay Christian Network, www.gaychristian.net; Marin Foundation, www.themarinfoundation.org.

15. Level Ground, www.onlevelground.org.   16.   William J. Webb, *Slaves, Women and Homosexuals: Exploring the Hermeneutics of Cultural Analysis* (Downers Grove, IL: InterVarsity Press, 2001).

17. "Survey: A Shifting Landscape: A Decade of Change in American Attitudes about Same-Sex Marriage and LGBT Issues," Public Religion Research Institute, February 26, 2014, http://publicreligion.org/research/2014/02/2014-lgbt-survey/#.VZRJR1weXT0.

The Roman Catholic Church

1. John L. Allen and Hada Messia, "Pope Francis on Gays: 'Who Am I to Judge?,'" *CNN Religion Blog*, July 29, 2013, http://religion.blogs.cnn.com/2013/07/29/pope-francis-on-gays-who-am-i-to-judge.

2. See Deuteronomy 29:23, 32:32; Isaiah 1:9–10, 3:9, 13:19; Jeremiah 23:14, 49:18, 50:40; Lamentations 4:6; Ezekiel 16:46–48; Amos 4:11; Zephaniah 2:9; Matthew 10:15; Luke 17:29; Romans 9:29; 2 Peter 2:6; Jude 7.

3. For background on the development of Sodom interpretations, see Derrick Sherwin Bailey, *Homosexuality and the Western Christian Tradition* (Hamden, CT: Archon Books, 1975), 9–28; John Boswell, *Christianity, Social Tolerance and Homosexuality: Gay People in Western Europe from the Beginning of the Christian Era to the Fourteenth Century* (Chicago: University of Chicago Press, 1980), 92–98; John Boswell, *Same-Sex Unions in Premodern Europe* (New York: Villard Books, 1994), 365–66; Steven Greenberg, *Wrestling with God and Men: Homosexuality in the Jewish Tradition* (Madison: University of Wisconsin Press, 2005).

4. For a listing and explanation of the sixty-seven times that the word "abomination" appears in the Bible (Revised Standard Version), see Linda A. Malcor, "Putting Abominations in Perspective," www.dragonlordsnet.com /abomination.htm.

5. For extensive commentary on each of the "homosexual" passages and how they are interpreted in the light of a historical-critical approach to the Bible, see Daniel Helminiak, *What the Bible Really Says about Homosexuality* (San Francisco: Alamo Square Press, 1994).

6. Margaret A. Farley, *Just Love: A Framework for Christian Sexual Ethics* (New York: Continuum, 2006), 38–45.

7. Anthony Kosnik, William Carroll, Agnes Cunningham, Ronald Modras, and James Schulte, *Human Sexuality: New Directions in American Catholic Thought* (New York: Paulist Press, 1977), 124.

8. Geoffrey Robinson, *Confronting Power and Sex in the Catholic Church: Reclaiming the Spirit of Jesus* (Mulgrave, Victoria: John Garratt Publishing, 2007). See also Geoffrey Robinson, *The 2015 Synod—The Crucial Questions: Divorce and Homosexuality* (Adelaide, South Australia: ATF Press, 2015).

9. *Catechism of the Catholic Church*, 2nd ed. (Washington, DC: United States Catholic Conference, 2000), par. 2358.

10. Ibid., par. 2357.

11. During a press conference on the plane ride back to Rome from World Youth Day celebrations in Brazil, July 2013, reporters asked Pope Francis a question about gay priests. He replied that if a homosexual person is of good will and is in search of God, "Who am I to judge?" Like the shot heard round the world, these five words were repeated in publications around the globe and have come to define the position of Pope Francis toward lesbian and gay persons. See Allen and Messia, "Pope Francis on Gays: 'Who Am I to Judge?'"

12. *Always Our Children: A Pastoral Message to Parents of Homosexual Children and Suggestions for Pastoral Ministers* (Washington, DC: United States Catholic Conference, 1997), www.usccb.org/issues-and-action/human-life-and-dignity /homosexuality/always-our-children.cfm.

13. See "Polling Tracks Growing and Increasingly Diverse Support for the Freedom to Marry," updated June 8, 2015, www.freedomtomarry.org/resources/entry /marriage-polling.

14. Laurie Goodstein and Megan Thee-Brenan, "U.S. Catholics in Poll See a Church Out of Touch," *New York Times*, March 6, 2013, A1, www.nytimes.com /2013/03/06/us/poll-shows-disconnect-between-us-catholics-and-church.html.

15. "Fact Sheet: Gay and Lesbian Issues," Public Religion Research Institute, June 8, 2014, http://publicreligion.org/research/2014/06/lgbt-fact-sheet.

16. "Survey: Strong Majorities of Americans Favor Rights and Legal Protections for Transgender People," Public Religion Research Institute, November 3, 2011, http://publicreligion.org/research/2011/11/american-attitudes-towards -transgender-people.

17. Farley, *Just Love*, 153–56.

18. See "Psychological and Spiritual Explorations of the Transgender Experience," *Bondings 2.0*, https://newwaysministryblog.wordpress.com/2015/01/21 /psychological-and-spiritual-explorations-of-the-transgender-experience.

19. James and Evelyn Whitehead, "Day of Remembrance Honors Transgender Persons Killed for Their Spiritual Journeys," *National Catholic Reporter*, November 19, 2012, http://ncronline.org/news/people/day-remembrance -honors-transgender-persons-killed-their-spiritual-journeys; James and Evelyn Whitehead, "An Epiphany of Transgender Lives Reveals Diversity in Body of CHRIST," *National Catholic Reporter*, January 5, 2013, http://ncronline.org /news/people/epiphany-transgender-lives-reveals-diversity-body-christ.

20. Jeannine Gramick, "Becoming the Person God Wants Us to Be," *National Catholic Reporter*, August 27, 2013, http://ncronline.org/blogs/soul-seeing /becoming-person-god-wants-us-be.

21. Sister Monica, "A Catholic Sister's Ministry in the Transgender Community," Religion, *Huffington Post*, January 15, 2015, www.huffingtonpost.com/sister -monica/a-catholic-sisters-minist_b_6481700.html.

22. Amanda Ripley, "Inside the Church's Closet," *Time*, May 12, 2002, http:// content.time.com/time/magazine/article/0,9171,237034,00.html.

23. The movement for the ordination of women priests in the Episcopal Church gained great energy at the 1970 General Convention. Although not recognized by the Episcopal Church, eleven women were "irregularly" ordained as the first female priests on July 29, 1974, in Philadelphia. Two years later, the General Convention affirmed and authorized the ordination of women to the priesthood.

24. Lucas Grindley, "The *Advocate*'s Person of the Year: Pope Francis," *Advocate*, December 16, 2013, www.advocate.com/year-review/2013/12/16/advocates -person-year-pope-francis.

25. Pope Francis, *Evangelii Gaudium (The Joy of the Gospel)*, Apostolic Exhortation, November 24, 2013, par. 35, http://w2.vatican.va/content/francesco/en /apost_exhortations/documents/papa-francesco_esortazione-ap_20131124 _evangelii-gaudium.html.

26. Ibid., par. 36.

27. Anthony Spadaro, "A Big Heart Open to God: The Exclusive Interview with Pope Francis," *America*, September 30, 2013, www.americamagazine.org/pope -interview.

28. A complete list can be found at "Catholicism, Employment, & LGBT Issues," *Bondings 2.0*, https://newwaysministryblog.wordpress.com/employment.

29. Bob Shine, "Why Pick Pope Francis for Person of the Year?," *Bondings 2.0*, https://newwaysministryblog.wordpress.com/2013/12/13/why-pick-pope -francis-for-person-of-the-year.

Unitarian Universalism

1. Leslie Westbrook, assistant minister at the Arlington Street Church in Boston, recalling when, in 1973, two young women came to her and asked her to perform "a ceremony of love." William Ellery Channing is a forefather of Unitarianism.

2. "Francis Dávid Guilty of Innovation," in *Harvest the Power*, Unitarian Universalist Association Tapestry of Faith Adult Education Program, www.uua .org/re/tapestry/adults/harvest/workshop8/142232.shtml.

3. Although these words are attributed to Francis Dávid, Rev. Dr. Peter Hughes, a retired minister and founding editor of *The Dictionary of Unitarian and Universalist Biography* (http://uudb.org) writes, in an article titled, "Who Really Said That?" on UUWorld.org (www.uuworld.org/articles/uu-rumor-mill -produces-quotes), that these words are probably an adaptation of a quotation from Methodist founder John Wesley, "Though we cannot think alike, may we not love alike?"

4. Adams's five smooth stones are explained in his essay "Guiding Principles for a Free Faith," in *On Being Human Religiously: Selected Essays in Religion and Society*, ed. Max Stackhouse (Boston: Beacon Press, 1976), 12–20.

5. Arliss Ungar, "Homily: Reflections on Thomas Starr King," Starr King School for the Ministry, May 8, 2015, www.sksm.edu/2015/05/08/homily-reflections -on-thomas-starr-king-by-arliss-ungar.

6. *The Principles and Purposes of the Unitarian Universalist Association*, as adopted by the Unitarian Universalist Association General Assembly in 1985 and modified in 1995. Available at www.uuworld.org/articles/the-uuas-principles -purposes-1985.

7. Ralph Waldo Emerson, "The American Scholar," speech given to Phi Beta Kappa in Cambridge, MA, August 31, 1837, www.emersoncentral.com /amscholar.htm.

8. "Christian Unitarian Universalists," Unitarian Universalist Association, www .uua.org/beliefs/who-we-are/people-many-beliefs/christianity.

9. Phillip Hewett, *On Being a Unitarian* (London: Lindsey Press, 1968), 46.

10. For a complete list, see "Our Unitarian Universalist Principles," www.uua.org /beliefs/what-we-believe/principles.

11. Common Vision Planning Committee, "Report and Recommendations to the Board of Trustees," Unitarian Universalist Association, January 1989, www.uua

.org/sites/live-new.uua.org/files/documents/commonvision/1989_report
_to_bot.pdf.

12. Ibid.

13. UU congregations are commonly referred to as churches, congregations, societies, communities, and fellowships.

14. Common Vision Planning Committee, "Report and Recommendations to the Board of Trustees."

15. Ibid., 9.

16. Ibid., 10.

17. Ibid., 15.

18. Ibid., 16.

19. Ibid., 15.

20. Unitarian Universalist Association, Welcoming Congregation statistics, Multicultural Growth and Witness staff group report. www.uua.org /multiculturalism/lgbtq/welcoming/program.

21. Unitarian Universalist Association Board of Trustees Bylaws and Rules as amended through July 1, 2014, rule G-2.3, www.uua.org/sites/live-new.uua .org/files/documents/uua/bylaws.pdf.

22. Unitarian Universalist Association Board of Trustees Bylaws and Rules as amended through July 1, 2014, section C-2.3, www.uua.org/sites/live-new.uua .org/files/documents/uua/bylaws.pdf.

23. See Multicultural Ministries Sharing Project report, June 26, 2014, www.uua .org/sites/live-new.uua.org/files/documents/idbm/mmsp_report.pdf.

24. Ibid.

25. More information can be found through Unitarian Universalist Association Related and Affiliate Organizations, www.uua.org/directory/organizations /truust-transgender-uu-religious-professionals.

26. L. B. Fisher, *A Brief History of the Universalist Church for Young People* (Boston: Universalist Publishing House, 1913).

27. Laurie Carter Noble, "Olympia Brown," in *Dictionary of Unitarian and Universalist Biography*, May 28, 2001, http://uudb.org/articles/olympiabrown.html.

28. Theodore Parker, "Of Justice and the Conscience," in *Ten Sermons of Religion* (Boston: Crosby, Nichols and Company, 1853), 84–85.

29. Martin Luther King Jr., sermon delivered at Temple Israel, Hollywood, CA, February 26, 1965, www.americanrhetoric.com/speeches/mlktempleisrael hollywood.htm.

30. For a complete list of LGBTQ-related resolutions affirmed by the Unitarian Universalist Association, see www.uua.org/lgbtq/history/27682.shtml.

31. Ibid.

Conclusion

1. Audre Lorde, "Age, Race, Class and Sex: Women Redefining Difference," in *Sister Outsider: Essays and Speeches* (Berkeley, CA: Crossing Press, 1984), 114.

2. "What Is Radical Inclusivity?," The Fellowship, www.radicallyinclusive.com /what-is-radical-inclusivity.

3. UNC Safe Zone, "Sexual Identity: The Cass Model—Using Theory to Understand Gay and Lesbian Identity Development," http://multicultural .usf.edu/pdf/safezone/support_identity.pdf, adapted from V. C. Cass, "Homosexual Identity Formation: A Theoretical Model," *Journal of Homosexuality* 4 (1979): 219–35.

4. Lorde, "Age, Race, Class and Sex."

5. Psalm 118:22 reads, "The stone that the builders rejected has become the cornerstone." This verse is highlighted in Ayelet S. Cohen, *Changing Lives, Making History: Congregation Beit Simchat Torah* (New York: Congregation Beit Simchat Torah, 2014), 8.

Afterword

1. Transforming Our World: The 2030 Agenda for Sustainable Development, September 2015, https://sustainabledevelopment.un.org/post2015/ transformingourworld. See also https://sustainabledevelopment.un.org/topics.

Acknowledgments

1. Our chapter, based on our presentations at the annual conference, is titled "Intersections: A Guide to Working with LGBTQI University Students of Minority Religions or Cultures," in *Expanding the Circle: Creating an Inclusive Environment in Higher Education for LGBTQ Students and Studies*, ed. John C. Hawley (Albany: State University of New York Press, 2015).

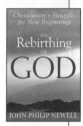
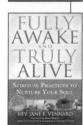

Professional Spiritual & Pastoral Care Resources

Change & Conflict in Your Congregation (Even If You Hate Both)
How to Implement Conscious Choices, Manage Emotions & Build a
Thriving Christian Community *By Rev. Anita L. Bradshaw, PhD* Positive, relational
strategies for navigating change and channeling conflict into a stronger sense of
community. 6 x 9, 176 pp, Quality PB, 978-1-59473-578-3 **$16.99**

Professional Spiritual & Pastoral Care
A Practical Clergy and Chaplain's Handbook
Edited by Rabbi Stephen B. Roberts, MBA, MHL, BCJC
An essential resource integrating the classic foundations of pastoral care with
the latest approaches to spiritual care, specifically in acute care hospitals,
behavioral health facilities, rehabilitation centers and long-term care facilities.
6 x 9, 480 pp, HC, 978-1-59473-312-3 **$50.00**

Spiritual Guidance across Religions
A Sourcebook for Spiritual Directors & Other Professionals Providing Counsel to People of Differing Faith Traditions
Edited by Rev. John R. Mabry, PhD
This comprehensive professional resource offers valuable information for providing spiritual guidance to people from a wide variety of faith traditions. Covers
the world's major faith traditions as well as interfaith, blended and independent
approaches to spirituality. 6 x 9, 400 pp, HC, 978-1-59473-546-2 **$50.00**

College & University Chaplaincy in the 21st Century
A Multifaith Look at the Practice of Ministry on Campuses across America
Edited by Rev. Dr. Lucy Forster-Smith; Foreword by Rev. Janet M. Cooper Nelson
Examines the challenges of the secular context of today's college or university campus.
6 x 9, 368pp, HC, 978-1-59473-516-5 **$40.00**

Disaster Spiritual Care, 2nd Edition
Practical Clergy Responses to Community, Regional and National Tragedy
Edited by Rabbi Stephen B. Roberts, BCJC, and Rev. Willard W. C. Ashley, Sr., DMin, DH
The definitive guidebook for counseling not only the victims of disaster but also
the clergy and caregivers who are called to service in the wake of crisis.
6 x 9, 384 pp (est), HC, 978-1-59473-587-5 **$50.00**

How to Be a Perfect Stranger, 6th Edition
The Essential Religious Etiquette Handbook
Edited by Stuart M. Matlins and Arthur J. Magida
The indispensable guidebook to help the well-meaning guest when visiting other
people's religious ceremonies. Covers: **African American Methodist Churches • Assemblies
of God • Bahá'í Faith • Baptist • Buddhist • Christian Church (Disciples of Christ) • Christian
Science (Church of Christ, Scientist) • Churches of Christ • Episcopalian and Anglican • Hindu
• Islam • Jehovah's Witnesses • Jewish • Lutheran • Mennonite/Amish • Methodist • Mormon
(Church of Jesus Christ of Latter-day Saints) • Native American/First Nations • Orthodox
Churches • Pentecostal Church of God • Presbyterian • Quaker (Religious Society of Friends)
• Reformed Church in America/Canada • Roman Catholic • Seventh-day Adventist • Sikh •
Unitarian Universalist • United Church of Canada • United Church of Christ**
6 x 9, 416 pp, Quality PB, 978-1-59473-593-6 **$19.99**

"The things Miss Manners forgot to tell us about religion."
—*Los Angeles Times*

Caresharing: A Reciprocal Approach to Caregiving and Care Receiving in the
Complexities of Aging, Illness or Disability *By Marty Richards*
6 x 9, 256 pp, Quality PB, 978-1-59473-286-7 **$16.99**; HC, 978-1-59473-247-8 **$24.99**

Learning to Lead: Lessons in Leadership for People of Faith
Edited by Rev. Williard W. C. Ashley Sr., MDiv, DMin, DH
6 x 9, 384 pp, HC, 978-1-59473-432-8 **$40.00**

The Perfect Stranger's Guide to Funerals and Grieving Practices
A Guide to Etiquette in Other People's Religious Ceremonies
Edited by Stuart M. Matlins 6 x 9, 240 pp, Quality PB, 978-1-893361-20-1 **$16.95**

Judaism / Christianity / Islam / Interfaith

Finding Peace through Spiritual Practice
The Interfaith Amigos' Guide to Personal, Social and Environmental Healing
By Pastor Don Mackenzie, Rabbi Ted Falcon and Imam Jamal Rahman
A look at the specific issues in modern pluralistic society and the spiritual practices that can help transcend roadblocks to effective collaboration on the critical issues of today.
6 x 9, 200 pp (est), Quality PB, 978-1-59473-604-9 **$16.99**

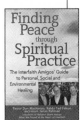

Struggling in Good Faith
LGBTQI Inclusion from 13 American Religious Perspectives
Edited by Mychal Copeland and D'vorah Rose; Foreword by Bishop Gene Robinson
A multifaceted sourcebook telling the story of reconciliation, celebration and struggle for LGBTQI inclusion across the religious landscape in America.
6 x 9, 240 pp, Quality PB, 978-1-59473-602-5 **$19.99**

Practical Interfaith: How to Find Our Common Humanity as We Celebrate Diversity
By Rev. Steven Greenebaum
Explores Interfaith as a faith—and as a positive way to move forward.
6 x 9, 176 pp, Quality PB, 978-1-59473-569-1 **$16.99**

Sacred Laughter of the Sufis: Awakening the Soul with the Mulla's Comic Teaching Stories & Other Islamic Wisdom
By Imam Jamal Rahman
The legendary wisdom stories of the Mulla, Islam's great comic foil, with spiritual insights for seekers of all traditions—or none.
6 x 9, 192 pp, Quality PB, 978-1-59473-547-9 **$16.99**

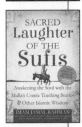

Religion Gone Astray: What We Found at the Heart of Interfaith
By Pastor Don Mackenzie, Rabbi Ted Falcon and Imam Jamal Rahman
Explores that which divides us personally, spiritually and institutionally.
6 x 9, 192 pp, Quality PB, 978-1-59473-317-8 **$18.99**

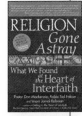

Blessed Relief: What Christians Can Learn from Buddhists about Suffering
By Gordon Peerman 6 x 9, 208 pp, Quality PB, 978-1-59473-252-2 **$16.99**

Christians & Jews—Faith to Faith: Tragic History, Promising Present, Fragile Future *By Rabbi James Rudin*
6 x 9, 288 pp, HC, 978-1-58023-432-0 **$24.99**; Quality PB, 978-1-58023-717-8 **$18.99***

Getting to the Heart of Interfaith: The Eye-Opening, Hope-Filled Friendship of a Pastor, a Rabbi & an Imam *By Pastor Don Mackenzie, Rabbi Ted Falcon and Imam Jamal Rahman*
6 x 9, 192 pp, Quality PB, 978-1-59473-263-8 **$16.99**

The Jewish Approach to God: A Brief Introduction for Christians
By Rabbi Neil Gillman, PhD 5½ x 8½, 192 pp, Quality PB, 978-1-58023-190-9 **$16.95***

The Jewish Approach to Repairing the World (*Tikkun Olam*)
A Brief Introduction for Christians *By Rabbi Elliot N. Dorff, PhD, with Rev. Cory Willson*
5½ x 8½, 256 pp, Quality PB, 978-1-58023-349-1 **$16.99***

The Jewish Connection to Israel, the Promised Land: A Brief Introduction for
Christians *By Rabbi Eugene Korn, PhD* 5½ x 8½, 192 pp, Quality PB, 978-1-58023-318-7 **$14.99***

Jewish Holidays: A Brief Introduction for Christians *By Rabbi Kerry M. Olitzky and
Rabbi Daniel Judson* 5½ x 8½, 176 pp, Quality PB, 978-1-58023-302-6 **$18.99***

Jewish Ritual: A Brief Introduction for Christians *By Rabbi Kerry M. Olitzky
and Rabbi Daniel Judson* 5½ x 8½, 144 pp, Quality PB, 978-1-58023-210-4 **$14.99***

Jewish Spirituality: A Brief Introduction for Christians
By Rabbi Lawrence Kushner 5½ x 8½, 112 pp, Quality PB, 978-1-58023-150-3 **$12.95***

Spiritual Gems of Islam: Insights & Practices from the Qur'an, Hadith, Rumi &
Muslim Teaching Stories to Enlighten the Heart & Mind *By Imam Jamal Rahman*
6 x 9, 256 pp, Quality PB, 978-1-59473-430-4 **$16.99**

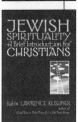

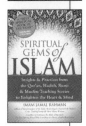

*A book from Jewish Lights, SkyLight Paths' sister imprint

Bible Stories / Folktales

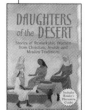

Abraham's Bind & Other Bible Tales of Trickery, Folly, Mercy and Love By Michael J. Caduto
New retellings of episodes in the lives of familiar biblical characters explore relevant life lessons. 6 x 9, 224 pp, HC, 978-1-59473-186-0 **$19.99**

Daughters of the Desert: Stories of Remarkable Women from Christian, Jewish and Muslim Traditions By Claire Rudolf Murphy,
Meghan Nuttall Sayres, Mary Cronk Farrell, Sarah Conover and Betsy Wharton
Breathes new life into the old tales of our female ancestors in faith. Uses traditional scriptural passages as starting points, then with vivid detail fills in historical context and place. Chapters reveal the voices of Sarah, Hagar, Huldah, Esther, Salome, Mary Magdalene, Lydia, Khadija, Fatima and many more. Historical fiction ideal for readers of all ages.
5½ x 8½, 192 pp, Quality PB, 978-1-59473-106-8 **$18.99** Inc. reader's discussion guide

The Triumph of Eve & Other Subversive Bible Tales
By Matt Biers-Ariel These engaging retellings of familiar Bible stories are witty, often hilarious and always profound. They invite you to grapple with questions and issues that are often hidden in the original texts.
5½ x 8½, 192 pp, Quality PB, 978-1-59473-176-1 **$14.99**

Also available: **The Triumph of Eve Teacher's Guide**
8½ x 11, 44 pp, PB, 978-1-59473-152-5 **$8.99**

Religious Etiquette / Reference

How to Be a Perfect Stranger, 6th Edition: The Essential Religious Etiquette Handbook Edited by Stuart M. Matlins and Arthur J. Magida
The indispensable guidebook to help the well-meaning guest when visiting other people's religious ceremonies. A straightforward guide to the rituals and celebrations of the major religions and denominations in the United States and Canada from the perspective of an interested guest of any other faith, based on information obtained from authorities of each religion. Belongs in every living room, library and office. Covers:
African American Methodist Churches • Assemblies of God • Bahá'í Faith • Baptist • Buddhist • Christian Church (Disciples of Christ) • Christian Science (Church of Christ, Scientist) • Churches of Christ • Episcopalian and Anglican • Hindu • Islam • Jehovah's Witnesses • Jewish • Lutheran • Mennonite/Amish • Methodist • Mormon (Church of Jesus Christ of Latter-day Saints) • Native American/First Nations • Orthodox Churches • Pentecostal Church of God • Presbyterian • Quaker (Religious Society of Friends) • Reformed Church in America/Canada • Roman Catholic • Seventh-day Adventist • Sikh • Unitarian Universalist • United Church of Canada • United Church of Christ

"The things Miss Manners forgot to tell us about religion."
—*Los Angeles Times*

"Finally, for those inclined to undertake their own spiritual journeys … tells visitors what to expect." —*New York Times*

6 x 9, 416 pp, Quality PB, 978-1-59473-593-6 **$19.99**

Struggling in Good Faith
LGBTQI Inclusion from 13 American Religious Perspectives
Edited by Mychal Copeland and D'vorah Rose; Foreword by Bishop Gene Robinson
A multifaceted sourcebook telling the story of reconciliation, celebration and struggle for LGBTQI inclusion across the religious landscape in America.
6 x 9, 240 pp, Quality PB, 978-1-59473-602-5 **$19.99**

The Perfect Stranger's Guide to Funerals and Grieving Practices
A Guide to Etiquette in Other People's Religious Ceremonies
Edited by Stuart M. Matlins 6 x 9, 240 pp, Quality PB, 978-1-893361-20-1 **$16.95**

The Perfect Stranger's Guide to Wedding Ceremonies
A Guide to Etiquette in Other People's Religious Ceremonies
Edited by Stuart M. Matlins 6 x 9, 208 pp, Quality PB, 978-1-893361-19-5 **$16.95**

Women's Interest

There's a Woman in the Pulpit: Christian Clergywomen Share Their Hard Days, Holy Moments & the Healing Power of Humor
Edited by Rev. Martha Spong; Foreword by Rev. Carol Howard Merritt
Offers insight into the lives of Christian clergywomen and the rigors that come with commitment to religious life, representing fourteen denominations as well as dozens of seminaries and colleges. 6 x 9, 240 pp, Quality PB, 978-1-59473-588-2 **$18.99**

She Lives! Sophia Wisdom Works in the World
By Rev. Jann Aldredge-Clanton, PhD
Fascinating narratives of clergy and laypeople who are changing the institutional church and society by restoring biblical female divine names and images to Christian theology, worship symbolism and liturgical language.
6 x 9, 320 pp, Quality PB, 978-1-59473-573-8 **$18.99**

Birthing God: Women's Experiences of the Divine
By Lana Dalberg; Foreword by Kathe Schaaf
Powerful narratives of suffering, love and hope that inspire both personal and collective transformation. 6 x 9, 304 pp, Quality PB, 978-1-59473-480-9 **$18.99**

Women, Spirituality and Transformative Leadership
Where Grace Meets Power
Edited by Kathe Schaaf, Kay Lindahl, Kathleen S. Hurty, PhD, and Reverend Guo Cheen
A dynamic conversation on the power of women's spiritual leadership and its emerging patterns of transformation.
6 x 9, 288 pp, Quality PB, 978-1-59473-548-6 **$18.99**; HC, 978-1-59473-313-0 **$24.99**

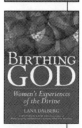

Spiritually Healthy Divorce: Navigating Disruption with Insight & Hope
By Carolyne Call A spiritual map to help you move through the twists and turns of divorce. 6 x 9, 224 pp, Quality PB, 978-1-59473-288-1 **$16.99**

Bread, Body, Spirit: Finding the Sacred in Food
Edited and with Introductions by Alice Peck 6 x 9, 224 pp, Quality PB, 978-1-59473-242-3 **$19.99**

Dance—The Sacred Art: The Joy of Movement as a Spiritual Practice
By Cynthia Winton-Henry 5½ x 8½, 224 pp, Quality PB, 978-1-59473-268-3 **$16.99**

Daughters of the Desert: Stories of Remarkable Women from Christian, Jewish and Muslim Traditions *By Claire Rudolf Murphy, Meghan Nuttall Sayres, Mary Cronk Farrell, Sarah Conover and Betsy Wharton*
5½ x 8½, 192 pp, Illus., Quality PB, 978-1-59473-106-8 **$18.99** Inc. reader's discussion guide

The Divine Feminine in Biblical Wisdom Literature
Selections Annotated & Explained
Translation & Annotation by Rabbi Rami Shapiro; Foreword by Rev. Cynthia Bourgeault, PhD
5½ x 8½, 240 pp, Quality PB, 978-1-59473-109-9 **$18.99**

Divining the Body: Reclaim the Holiness of Your Physical Self
By Jan Phillips 8 x 8, 256 pp, Quality PB, 978-1-59473-080-1 **$18.99**

Honoring Motherhood: Prayers, Ceremonies & Blessings
Edited and with Introductions by Lynn L. Caruso
5 x 7¼, 272 pp, Quality PB, 978-1-58473-384-0 **$9.99**; HC, 978-1-59473-239-3 **$19.99**

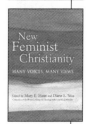

New Feminist Christianity: Many Voices, Many Views
Edited by Mary E. Hunt and Diann L. Neu
6 x 9, 384 pp, Quality PB, 978-1-59473-435-9 **$19.99**; HC, 978-1-59473-285-0 **$24.99**

Next to Godliness: Finding the Sacred in Housekeeping
Edited by Alice Peck 6 x 9, 224 pp, Quality PB, 978-1-59473-214-0 **$19.99**

The Triumph of Eve & Other Subversive Bible Tales
By Matt Biers-Ariel 5½ x 8½, 192 pp, Quality PB, 978-1-59473-176-1 **$14.99**

Woman Spirit Awakening in Nature: Growing into the Fullness of Who You Are
By Nancy Barrett Chickerneo, PhD; Foreword by Eileen Fisher
8 x 8, 224 pp, b/w illus., Quality PB, 978-1-59473-250-8 **$16.99**

Women of Color Pray: Voices of Strength, Faith, Healing, Hope and Courage
Edited and with Introductions by Christal M. Jackson 5 x 7¼, 208 pp, Quality PB, 978-1-59473-077-1 **$15.99**